THE ASSERTIVE CONSUMER

THE
ASSERTIVE
CONSUMER

An everyday
survival guide to
your rights
– at home, work and
in the high street

TOBE ALEKSANDER

Thorsons Publishing Group

First published 1990

Copyright © Tobe Aleksander 1990

This handbook is a guide, written in general terms to be accessible to a wide readership. Please note that the case studies described in this book are only examples and therefore the solutions suggested may not always be appropriate to your individual circumstances. In addition, laws or practices may change. While all reasonable care has been taken in preparing the information contained in this book, neither the author nor the publisher accepts responsibility for any errors it may contain or for any loss, however caused, by reliance on it.

British Library Cataloguing in Publication Data

Aleksander, Tobe
The assertive consumer: an everyday survival guide to your rights — at home, work and in the high street.
1. Great Britain. Consumers. Rights
I. Title
344.10371

ISBN 0 7225 1970 2

Published by Thorsons Publishing Group, Wellingborough, Northamptonshire NN8 2RQ, England

Typeset by Burns & Smith Ltd, Derby.

Printed in Great Britain by William Collins Sons & Co. Ltd, Glasgow

1 3 5 7 9 10 8 6 4 2

Contents

Contents

How to use this book

This book is arranged in four sections:

Section One: The Ground Rules is all about steering clear of trouble. It tells you what to think about and what to look for before you agree to buy something, hire someone or sign a document.

Section One also tells you *how* to deal with problems. It shows you how to make a plan to tackle problems — however large or small; where to look for help and how to approach people.

Finally, Section One takes you through three essential practical skills — letter writing, telephoning and confronting people face to face. Throughout the rest of the book you will find constant references to these pages. Use them to remind yourself how to lay out a letter, get through to an official on the phone or talk effectively to someone.

Whether you have a specific question or you simply want to know how to handle things better in the future, start by reading Section One.

Section Two: The Nuts and Bolts looks at specific everyday issues. It tells you what the laws states or what the normal practice is and guides you step by step through common problem areas.

Section Two is not just about getting out of trouble, but about avoiding it in the first place. So, for example, if you want to borrow money or buy something on credit, have a look at the chapter 'Looking after your money', first. It could save you a lot of bother later on.

The question-and-answer sections look at standard enquiries. You may not find a question that matches your own query exactly, but you should find the same *type* of problem. So, for example, if you bought a dishwasher in a sale and found it didn't work properly and you wanted to know what your rights were and what to do about it, you would find the answer by turning to the chapter on 'Buying goods'. There you will see that the introduction gives you the basic law on goods, there's a specific question on buying goods in a sale and another one on a faulty washing machine, which would give you some ideas about how to deal with a similar bulky item.

Section Three: Useful Tools tells you about the mechanics of taking your case further. It explains how the legal profession works and how to get the most out of working with a lawyer. There's also a chapter on the County court system and how to sue someone using the small claims procedure. Finally, there's a chapter on how to campaign and lobby.

You'll find constant references throughout the book to these pages.

Section Four: Where to Get More Help and Information is there for reference. It gives you details of all the organizations mentioned in the book.

You'll also find the addresses of other organizations which may be helpful in solving particular problems. So if you can't find information about a specific problem, do check this section to see if there's an organization that might be able to provide the answer.

The symbols

You'll find various symbols scattered around the pages. They are intended to point you in the direction of extra useful information or advice given in another part of the book.

(p.00)   Look at the pages given in the brackets.

→
←   This means that you'll find additional information in the preceding or following couple of paragraphs.

✐   Check the 'Practical skills' chapter in Section One for advice on letter writing.

☎   Check the 'Practical skills' chapter in Section One for advice on making telephone calls.

☺   Check the 'Practical skills' chapter in Section One for advice on face-to-face confrontations.

SMALL CAPITALS   You'll find details of the organization in Section Four.

CAB   Citizens' Advice Bureau.

You will also find a section entitled 'What Else?' at the very end of some of the questions. This gives examples of similar cases that can be approached in the same way.

If you live in Scotland or Northern Ireland

You may find certain differences in the law or common practices. The principal differences are outlined at the back of the book but you should always check with a local advice agency or lawyer to find out the current situation.

Prices and limits quoted in this book

Where prices or limits have been quoted you should always check the current amount before taking any action. This is particularly true of County court procedures where the upper limits for small claims is expected to increase.

Acknowledgements

My thanks go to all those who have contributed to this book through their experiences, knowledge and support. Special thanks to: Nicholas Aleksander for his professional expertise and liberal encouragement; Sue Davies and Nik Nicol for their invaluable advice, and to Mick and Peggy Bendeth for their dedication to 'readability'!

Section One

The Ground Rules

Avoiding trouble — Doing your homework

If you take a short time to 'look before you leap' many everyday problems as well as great disasters can be avoided.

Imagine you are a half-hearted swimmer. Would you dive straight into a rock pool without first checking how deep and dangerous it was and whether someone would be there to pull you out if you started drowning? Probably not.

It's exactly the same if you are about to buy an expensive item or employ someone to build your house or mend your leaking tap. Dive straight in and you might live to regret it.

Do your homework first. It will save you a lot of aggravation and possibly a great deal of unnecessary expense later on.

Think before you make a purchase

Decide exactly what you want to buy and why
Before you spend money on a new purchase think about what you want it to do and if it needs to fit in with things you already have.
Think about:

- Where it's going to go — have you got room? Measure the dimensions carefully.
- What's it got to fit in with — do you need a special style or colour?
- Who's going to use it — what kind of wear and tear will it get? Do you need an extra strong fabric or dark colour? Can you wash or clean it?
- Which facilities do you need — how many washing programmes will you use? Do you want a dining room table with extra leaves? Does your food processor need lots of attachments?

15

Make a list of all your requirements

Carry the list around with you and give a copy to anyone else who might be tempted to make the purchase.

Don't rely on guesswork

- Keep a small tape measure in your pocket or handbag.
- Carry a 'swatch' or sample of any colour or fabric you need to match.

Set a limit on how much you will spend

It's very easy to get carried away with excitement and end up spending twice as much as you meant to, especially if you use **credit cards** (p.46).

If you do tend to overspend on an average Saturday in the High Street then take cash. That way you can only spend what's in your pocket!

Avoid impulse buying

If you suddenly see exactly the right shade jumper or a particular sofa you've been after, reduced in a sale, fine, buy it. But avoid simply purchasing something on a whim — the chances are you'll hate it by the time you get home and it'll be a complete waste of money (p.83).

Don't be pressurized into buying

It doesn't matter if the salesman has spent all afternoon extolling the virtues of a particular car, that's what he's paid to do. Don't buy the product just to please him or because you feel guilty about taking up all his time. He may not get his commission but you've got an awful lot more to lose if you go ahead without thinking it through.

Make time to think things over

Ignore all the 'I can't guarantee it'll still be in stock tomorrow, Madam,' type of excuses — especially when they're made at 5.30 in the afternoon!

- Ask to have the goods reserved or put aside for you. Say something like: 'I'm sure you'll understand but I can't make a decision now. I need to talk it over with my husband/wife/daughter. If I decide to take it, I'll come back by 4 pm tomorrow.'

- Ask for a sample of the fabric or colour if you need to match it.
- Ask for written literature so that you can consider all the information at your leisure.

No good retailer or trader would think these requests unreasonable. If they do, consider whether you really want to buy from them.

Find out the facts before you buy

If you are making a major purchase — it could be anything from a dishwasher to a car, a carpet to a holiday — collect all the facts you can about that particular product.

- Read the reports and surveys. Look in newspapers, consumer magazines, *Which?* reports, television and radio programmes. If you want to buy a car, hi-fi or computer, check out the specialist magazines which always keep up to date with the latest products and give full listings of what's available.
- Ask family, friends and colleagues what they bought and why. Find out if they've had any problems. It's always worth bearing in mind how long ago they bought their washing machine, car or whatever because model design, reliability and so on can vary from year to year.
- If you can, obtain written information about the product, either from the shop or directly from the manufacturer.

Look for signs and symbols

Many goods have extra labels attached to them or logos printed on their packaging. These often indicate special care instructions or that the product has reached approved design or safety standards.

- Always check the material and content of anything you buy. For example, is your blouse silk or polyester? What is your new sofa filled with; does it conform to the latest safety standards? Is it fire resistant?
- Read washing and cleaning instructions. Does a wool cardigan need to be dry cleaned or does it have a washable wool symbol indicating you can put it in the machine? A real oak table will have to be cared for differently from one made from a man-made material that looks like oak.
- Look for approved safety symbols like the BEAB (BRITISH ELECTROTECHNICAL APPROVALS BOARD) mark which you will find on or

near the rating plate or attached to the equipment by a swing ticket.

- Similarly watch out for the BSI (British Standards Institute) kitemark which will appear on a wide range of goods complying with BSI standards, from pressure cookers to seat belts and fire alarms.

Check out all your options

Be careful you don't restrict yourself to what could become an expensive or unsuitable choice. Consider a range of manufacturers, models, etc. within your price range.

Shop around

This goes hand in hand with checking out all your options. Once you have decided on the product you want (or perhaps narrowed it down to two or three choices) you want to get the best deal you can. Telephone or visit a number of retail outlets.

Find out:

- The price. Check if it includes VAT.
- Whether they are prepared to do any kind of a deal — part exchange, cash, immediate collection or whatever.
- Any special offers including **interest free credit or other finance packages** (p.51). Be *very* careful that you understand fully exactly what they are offering you.
- About delivery arrangements — is it free?
- Guarantees available.
- Their policy about test drives, trial periods, etc.
- What kind of retail outlet they are. Are they reliable? →

Choose somewhere reliable to buy

If you've searched around and found your new music system at well below the prices you've been quoted elsewhere you might start asking yourself, 'Why?'. Unless there's a good reason such as a department store's end-of-season clearance sale, you might be well advised to steer clear of the bargain basement.

- Generally it's worth paying a little bit more for a product and buying it from a reputable company or shop with a good track record in dealing with customer complaints.
- Chain stores and large department stores are on the whole

reasonably reliable and have a system for dealing with complaints.
- If you go to a small or independent shop buy well-known brands — at least you may have some comeback from the manufacturer (p.76).

Think before you employ an 'expert'

Before you employ a tradesperson
- It's always best to get someone recommended by your family, or a friend or colleague.
- Choose someone suitably qualified. Find out if they are a member of the relevant **trade association** (p.23) or other **professional organization** (p.24). (For a full list refer to the end of the book.)
- Your local Electricity Board showroom will have a list of reliable contractors in your area. Or else look for the NICEIC (NATIONAL INSPECTION COUNCIL FOR ELECTRICAL INSTALLATION CONTRACTING) symbol on advertisements in Yellow Pages or your local paper.
- For someone to deal with a gas problem contact your local gas showroom who will have a list of people registered with CORGI (CONFEDERATION FOR THE REGISTRATION OF GAS INSTALLERS), or again look for the symbol in Yellow Pages or your local paper.
- Find out exactly how much the job will cost; how long it will take to complete; when they intend to start; how many people will be working on it; whether they need anything special, e.g. furniture cleared out of a room; how much mess or noise they think they'll make.
- Get a written **quotation** (p.93) before you finally make up your mind.
- Don't part with any money until the job is completed to *your* satisfaction.
- *Always* get a receipt, particularly if you pay cash.
- Reliable, qualified contractors will have no qualms about working in this way. If they do, consider whether you really want to use them.
- Very often these strangers will be working in your home — if you don't feel happy with them, then don't employ them. If you have no alternative ask a neighbour or friend to stay in the house with you.

For more information about services and contractors see p.92.

Think before you sign

Always read the small print
Don't just read the big banner headlines, read the smallest print in any advertisement or packaging. Buy yourself a magnifying glass — you may well need it!

Before you sign any piece of paper — read it!
- *Never* sign anything without reading it carefully and fully understanding what you are signing.
- If you are unsure ask to take the form away with you and get a friend or a consumer adviser to check it over and explain what you are committing yourself to.
- If your English or eyesight stops you from reading the form yourself, don't rely on the salesperson, however nice they seem, to read it to you — get a friend to do it.
- *Never* sign a blank form even if the trader tells you 'it will save on paperwork' — that's not your problem!
- Always check the 'get out' clauses before you sign. Find out if you can cancel the agreement and by what time you must cancel (p.58).
- Find out what happens if you sign a credit agreement and cannot keep up with any repayments. Will you have to pay a minimum amount even if you return the goods?

Strategies to solve problems

So you've got a problem? How are you going to solve it?

It may be a 'the builders have abandoned me and I've got a leaking roof' type problem; it might be planning a funeral or coping with an Industrial Tribunal. It doesn't matter, the same guidelines apply.

Think first!

Think: What do I want?

You need to be quite clear about what it is you are after. If you're not, you may well find yourself in the middle of a maze wondering why you're not getting anywhere. Even worse is the fact that if *you* don't know what you want, how are you going to communicate your needs to other people? See 'Sound assertive' (p.30).

Your goal could be something quite straightforward — 'I want my money back/the repair done.' Or more complicated — 'I want to get the Industrial Tribunal hearing over with and find a new job.'

Think: How am I going to get what I want?

You need to ask yourself:

- Who can solve my problem?
- What's the best way of approaching them?
- What's likely to be their reaction?
- What's my time limit?
- What shall I do if things don't work out?

Who can solve my problem?

Different problems need different people and organizations to

21

help solve them. You can often start by trying to solve the problem yourself and involve outside people later if you get stuck. However, before you go it alone you will need to check out the facts and your legal position.

Solving it alone

Find out who has the ultimate authority for making a decision about your case. You may in fact find a chain of command. You might decide to start at the bottom and if necessary work your way upwards, as in the example given.

> *Example*
> You buy a piece of luggage from a well-known, high-street store and it falls apart. You are well within your rights to take it back. The chain of command might look like this: Sales Assistant; Deputy Store Manager; Store Manager; Assistant Manager, Customer Relations (Head Office); Manager, Customer Relations (Head Office); Managing Director.
>   It would probably be sensible to go first to the Store Manager and then if necessary to the Customer Relations Manager and finally to the Managing Director.

Getting extra help

This is only a basic guide to the kind of individuals and organizations who may be able to help you solve your problem or take your complaint further. To find out how they can help specific cases refer to the relevant sections of the book. (Details of individual organizations can be found at the back of the book.)

Legal advisers

Solicitors, barristers and other legal specialists may be able to advise you if your problem is very complex and involves a matter of law. They can be expensive (p.241).

A local Law Centre will be staffed by qualified lawyers and their advice is usually free. However, there might not be one in your area.

Free advice agencies

Citizens' Advice Bureaux and local advice centres will give you help on a wide range of issues and won't charge you.

These free advice agencies vary greatly in the service they offer. Many are very experienced and will provide detailed information. They may even act on your behalf. Others are less knowledgeable and will refer you on for specialist advice. So you may have to shop around.

Remember, the person you see won't necessarily be a qualified lawyer.

Trading Standards Departments

Trading Standards Departments or Consumer Advice Departments are run by local authorities to give free general advice on consumer law. Occasionally they will take up individual cases. Your town hall or library will tell you who to contact.

Campaigning organizations

A number of large independent organizations have been set up by the Government to deal with one particular area of the law — for example, the EQUAL OPPORTUNITIES COMMISSION (EOC) which looks at sex discrimination and the COMMISSION FOR RACIAL EQUALITY ((CRE) which is concerned with race discrimination.

They provide very detailed free information and will usually offer advice over the phone. Sometimes they will take up your case on your behalf.

In addition there are numerous groups, charities and other organizations that offer advice, support and counselling on a wide range of subjects. Their ability to help you will depend largely on their resources. The NATIONAL COUNCIL FOR VOLUNTARY ORGANIZATIONS provides information on the different bodies that exist.

Trade associations and consumer organizations

There are numerous trade associations and user organizations covering almost every area of consumerism from dry cleaners to plumbers, mail order to cars.

They are encouraged to produce a Code of Practice telling members the kind of high standards they should maintain. Many asociations have a distinctive logo which members will use on their business paper and other material.

Trade associations can offer an attractive alternative to seeking a solution to your problem through the formal legal system. Associations try and solve problems by way of negotiation and reconciliation which might prove much simpler and cheaper for you.

Most will supply you with a list of their members and free information about their work.

Their ability to help varies enormously. They will usually only help if your complaint is about one of their members. Their powers are also extremely limited. Whilst they can often reprimand the person concerned or even strike them off their list of members they are unlikely to be able to offer you **compensation** (p.246), although some do.

Most of the main services — gas, electricity, telephones, the Post Office, etc. — have separate organizations to deal with enquiries and complaints (p.114-15).

Professional bodies

All the major professions have their own governing bodies who issue a strict code of conduct for their members. Many, such as the Law Society, produce free detailed literature about various aspects of their members' work.

They will only accept complaints about their members. Once again, their powers to give you concrete help can be very limited (p.246).

Ombudsmen

These rather odd-sounding creatures are officials who are empowered to investigate complaints about the way a service is *administered*. There are Ombudsmen for the Health Service, local government and central government as well as for insurance, banking and building societies.

They should be approached only after you have gone through the appropriate 'chain of command' and still had no satisfactory answer.

Most Ombudsmen will supply you with literature telling you about their work and how they can help you.

Ways to communicate

There are three ways you can communicate with someone:

- Write.
- Telephone.
- Face to face.

You will have to think carefully about which would be appropriate to your case.

What are the pros and cons of using each method?

Writing

Pros

- You can think carefully about what you want to say and only put down the right words!
- Complicated information is easier to understand if you can see it in front of you. You could include maps, diagrams, charts, etc.
- You can send supporting documents.
- Some organizations and individuals will only accept complaints or information in writing.
- You can keep an exact copy (possibly for future evidence).
- Easy reference.

Cons

- It can be difficult if you think you don't have good writing skills (p.32).
- Letters take time to write and send.
- You can't get an immediate response or see the other person's reaction.
- Letters don't convey your tone of voice or facial expression — the other person might get the wrong impression.
- They get 'lost in the post'.

Telephoning

Pros

- It's quick.
- You get an immediate response.
- It's good for finding out simple information.
- You may learn something about the other person from their voice or attitude.

Cons

- Problems with the 'system' — bad lines, phone boxes, etc.
- Getting 'lost' in switchboard systems.
- The other person has the power to cut you off (and vice versa).
- You can't guarantee you have the other person's full attention.

- The conversation can seem very disjointed.
- It's expensive.
- Some people will not deal with your enquiry over the phone.

Face to face

Pros

- It's direct and quick.
- You get an immediate response.
- You can judge the situation by the other person's reaction — their voice, facial expression, gestures.
- It may be the most appropriate method, for example, when confronting a family member or colleague.
- You have the opportunity to demonstrate how something happened, or where an article is broken.
- The case is complicated and you need to spend time with someone, for example a solicitor.

Cons

- Some people will not meet you face to face or will require an appointment to be made weeks in advance.
- The person might be very elusive and 'never there'.
- Can be very intimidating.
- You might behave in a way which you did not want, for example lose your temper or cry.
- The environment might be unhelpful, for example, a crowded shop or a building site.
- Possible expensive travelling costs.

Handling reactions

If you are going to be successful in confronting someone you ought to think about how they might react to you or your request.

The other person's reaction might be affected by:

- The time and place you confront them.
- How you confront them.
- Their knowledge of the situation.
- Their knowledge of the law.
- Their ability to communicate.
- What other people have told them about you or your case.

- Other personal factors — their temperament, whether they got out of bed the wrong side!

This means you must do your homework. If you have dealt with the organization or person before you will have some idea of what they can or cannot do and how they usually work. If not, you will need to think carefully.

Avoid being 'lost for words' (see examples given).

Example 1

You need to talk to your boss about an important personal matter. Your boss is always rushing around: she keeps her office door open and the phone never stops ringing. You could:

- Say, 'I know you're extremely busy but I need to speak to you about . . . . Can we make an appointment?'
- Shut the office door as you go in and say, 'I know you usually keep your door open but this matter is personal and I'd prefer not to be overheard.'
- Arrange to meet somewhere other than the office.

Example 2

You bought a radio from a very small retailer and after a week it stopped working. You decide to take it back. What can you do if he refuses to help you?

- He may not be fully aware of his legal obligations and will want to see written evidence. Go to your local advice centre and get a copy of a leaflet about the Sale of Goods Act 1979 (p.70) or take this book along with you.
- Particularly if you are very young/old/female he might say, 'You just don't understand how to work these things. You must have broken it.' Be ready to handle that kind of remark.
- Take someone with you for moral support.

Example 3

You are in dispute with a builder over the amount of money you owe him. You know where he lives but he's a very burly, aggressive character. You could:

- Telephone him — but he might 'never be there'.
- Visit him — are you prepared to deal with the consequences if he becomes aggressive?
- Write to him, recorded delivery.

Time limits

These fall into two categories:

- Time limits and deadlines imposed on you by other organizations, legal procedures, etc.
- Time limits you give yourself.

If you have a problem start to solve it immediately

Even if you don't succeed in getting a solution or a remedy for many months or even years the important thing is to set the wheels in action as soon as you possibly can. If you don't, you may well find that no matter how valid your complaint, it is simply too late to do anything about it.

You also need to make sure that time doesn't run away with you. Always set time limits in your letters and dealings with other people. And always keep them firmly in your own mind. Say to yourself, 'Right, I'll give them two weeks to reply to my letter. If I haven't heard from them by then I'll write again. If I still haven't heard within a further week I'll go and see a solicitor.'

Do be realistic about time limits. If you are writing to someone around Christmas time, remember postal delays, holidays and festivities. If you're dealing with a factory or workshop, bear in mind that they may be shut for a number of weeks in the summer. Do make allowances for holidays, illness and so on, but don't let them become an excuse for not getting an answer!

If things don't work out

Double-check that you've explored all your options. Make sure that you've not only gone upwards as far as you can but that you've also thought about your sideways options! This might mean seeing a different person or talking to another association or agency which has an interest in cases like yours.

- If you haven't already done it, think about seeking the advice of a professional lawyer (p.237) or free advice agencies.
- You could take your case to the courts (p.249) or an Industrial Tribunal (p.202, 229).
- You might start up a campaign (p.266).

Or you might have to face the fact that you've done whatever you can and that it's simply not worth the time, money or effort to continue. Put it down to experience and don't make the same mistake twice.

Putting it all together

Step One
What's the problem?

What's my goal?

Step Two
Who shall I approach first?
(Why them?)

How shall I approach them?
(Are there any risks?)

By when do I expect an answer/something to be done?

What information do I need to carry out Step Two?

Step Three
How far have I got? Am I satisfied?

(If you need to, go on to Step Four.)

Step Four
How shall I approach them?
(What are the risks?)

By when do I want an answer/something done?

What information do I need to carry out Step Four?

How far have I got? Am I satisfied?

Continue step by step until you are satisfied with the result.

Learn the skills

Be assertive

Being assertive is not about crashing your way through life, bossing people around and telling the world how to go about its business. Neither is it about behaving like a quivering mouse in a corner, frightened to open your mouth and letting people walk all over you.

Being assertive means having the confidence to deal with all sorts of people and situations effectively from the belligerent shopkeeper to the bureaucratic ditherer, the demanding parent to the manipulative colleague.

Assertive people learn to confront rather than avoid situations. It may be easier for today not to complain, discuss, challenge and tell people how you really feel, but in the end is it worth all the sleepless nights and soul searching?

Sound assertive
- Decide what you want to say or ask, then:
  (a) say it;
  (b) stick to it and repeat it if necessary.
- Don't be put off by irrelevant comments, for example, 'I can't help you, I wasn't here yesterday.' Ignore them, repeat your request.
- Don't be made submissive by guilt tripping, for example, 'I've another six people to deal with. Is it worth making all this fuss?' Ignore it and repeat your request.
- Don't be led astray by attempts to get you into an argument, for example, 'I can't believe you don't know how to work this. Why did you bother buying it?' Ignore them and repeat your request.
- Do acknowledge what the other person has said: 'I understand

you weren't here yesterday, however . . .'; 'I can see you have other people to deal with, however . . .'.
- Express your own feelings: 'I feel very angry/happy/frustrated/relaxed/hurt/content/let down when . . .'.

Look assertive
- Stand up straight.
- Forget all your nervous habits — hair fiddling, toe wiggling and nose scratching!
- Look at people when you talk to them — friendly (or not so friendly) eye contact is really important.
- Smile when you're happy.
- Don't smile if you're not.
- Avoid trying to have a conversation with someone if you're ten feet apart. This particularly applies to bank managers, senior bosses and their ilk. Go right up to them before you begin speaking.
- Don't let others get the height advantage. If you feel more comfortable saying what you have to say standing up then do it. Don't let people tower over you. If they stand, you stand.

Being angry and assertive
Don't be afraid of expressing anger. It's better to deal with it assertively out in the open than bottle it up and hurt yourself or lash out on innocent people and hurt them.

- Express your feelings←.
- Keep your anger in perspective. Ask yourself, 'How angry am I? How important is this situation?'
- Imagine an 'Anger Ladder':

> going to blow a fuse!
> infuriated
> incensed
> indignant
> cross
> impatient
> displeased

Where are you on the ladder? Is it appropriate to the situation? How far are you prepared to go? If you think that you may have a long way to go to get what you want, don't start in the middle of the ladder.

31

- Think about whether you are 'angry', or if you are really 'hurt' or 'resentful' or 'frustrated'. They are not mutually exclusive.

Writing letters

A good letter brings results. The more business-like your letter the more likely it is to get attention.

Golden rules of letter writing

An effective letter must be:

- Legible.
- Literate.
- Logical.
- Correctly addressed.
- As brief as possible!

What you need

- A word processor or decent typewriter. If you don't possess either of these things then try and find someone who does. Ask a secretary friend to type your letter for you. It's worth the price of a drink or a bunch of flowers.

  If you have to hand-write your letter, then if necessary write in block capital letters. If the receiver of your letter can't read your handwriting or decipher the typing through a sea of correction fluid what's the point of sending it in the first place?
- Good writing paper, preferably A4 size (the size of most file paper). Business letters tend to get written on this type of paper — anything smaller will probably get lost on a cluttered desk or in a file.
- A good quality, long white envelope. Small brown ones look tacky!
- A dictionary. If you can't spell, check the words in a dictionary — don't make them up as you go along!
- A decent pen to sign your name with. It's amazing how many signatures end with an ink-splattered blob or simply fade into oblivion.

Setting out a letter

(A)   Jeremy Penn
6, Biro Lane
Stationers Park
Letterhead
LH7 7HH

(B)   012 345 678 (day)
012 543 876 (after 6 pm)

(C) Ms Thelma Helm
(D) Customer Relations Manager
(E) Horridges Department Store
Knitsbridge
Purley
PU1 KN1

(F)   6th January 2001

(G) Dear Ms Helm

(H) <u>Faulty pair 'Ravisement', gentleman's silk
underpants; pale blue; size, extra large</u>

(I) I am writing to complain about the above garment which I
purchased from your store on December 15th; I enclose a
photocopy of my receipt.

(J)   Having worn the garment once, I washed and dried it according to the manufacturer's instructions. I was then horrified to find that not only had the colour run so that the garment was streaked white and dark blue but that in addition
the stitching had disintegrated at the seams. I enclose the
garment for your inspection.

(K)   Under the Sale of Goods Act 1979 you are obliged to sell
me goods that are of merchantable quality and fit for the purpose. Since my 'Ravisement' silk underpants have fallen
apart after being worn and washed only once, I consider that
you have broken your legal contract with me.

(L)   Would you please forward to me at the above address a
cheque for £77.20, being £75 refund for the faulty garment
plus £2.20 postage for returning the garment to you.

(M)   If I do not receive a cheque from you within fourteen days I will have no alternative but to seek legal advice with a view to taking the matter further.

(N)   Yours sincerely

(O)   *J. Penn*

(P)   JEREMY PENN

(Q)   Encs

(R)   cc Mr Marcus Fade, Managing Director, Horridges.

Notes on setting out a letter

First of all, remember that the exact letter format suggested above will not necessarily be appropriate every time you need to write to someone. Use it as a guide.

To find the appropriate legal information look under the relevant section of the book.

- A — Put your full address at the top of the page and include your postcode.
- B — Give your telephone number both at home and work if you can and if necessary say at what times you can be contacted.
- C — Find out the relevant person's name and check how it's spelt, otherwise just use their title, e.g. 'The Manager'.
- D — If you use their name then put their title down if they have one, e.g. 'Customer Relations Manager'.
- E — Put their full address.
- F — Date all your correspondence. If you need to contact them again you will be able to refer back to your previous letter.
- G — Address the person in one of the following ways:
  - (a) Dr/Mr/Mrs/Ms [surname];
  - (b) first name and surname, particularly when their first name doesn't give you a clue to their sex, e.g. 'Dear Toni Smith';
  - (c) Sir;
  - (d) Madam;
  - (e) Sir or Madam — when you don't know either their name or their sex. Don't assume they must be male or must be female!
- H — Give your letter a one-line title. It's a good way of quickly drawing the person's attention to your case. You could use any of the following:

(a) the reference number they have used for your case or enquiry, e.g. 'Your ref: 1234';

(b) the make, model, colour or size of a product, e.g. 'Singers Radio Cassette Player, Model Number 1234, Red';

(c) the nature of the problem, e.g. 'Disciplinary Hearing' or 'Accident, Crashtown Superstore, 11.06.90'.

- I — In the first paragraph outline the main purpose of your letter. You might begin with one of the following sentences:
  (a) 'I am writing to you about/concerning/regarding/to inform you . . .';
  (b) 'Further to our recent telephone conversation/your letter of [date]/our meeting, I am writing to confirm the details/to explain/concerning/regarding . . .'.

- J — In the second paragraph give specific details of what is wrong with the product or service or what happened in an accident. You may need to use two or three paragraphs if your case is very long or involved.

  Basically start at the beginning of the story and end at the end! Go through the details in chronological order (i.e. the order in which they happened). But be wary of getting so involved in the narrative that you find you have written three pages without stating what is actually wrong. Just mention the highlights of your case.

- K — In paragraph three state any obligations the shop, manager or individual may have as a matter of law or professional conduct and whether you consider they have breached (broken) any of them (see the appropriate sections of this book). Be careful to research your facts thoroughly first. This paragraph may not be relevant to all letters.

- L — Tell the shop, manager or individual what you want them to do about your complaint. You should also set a time limit. Obviously for money-back demands this will be quite specific: 'I look forward to hearing from you/receiving your cheque within seven/fourteen days.'

  Or you might be more open:
  (a) 'I look forward to hearing from you as soon as possible';
  (b) 'I would be most grateful if you would give the matter your urgent attention.'

- M — If necessary spell out what steps you will take if they don't deal with your complaint within the specified time. You only usually need to use this threat if you have already written a number of times and have had no satisfaction. You might include: 'Unless I hear from you/receive a cheque I will have no alternative but to consult my legal adviser with a view to taking the matter further/refer the matter to [a higher authority].'

- N — Signing off causes much confusion. When to use 'Yours sincerely' and when to use 'Yours faithfully'?

  If you started your letter 'Dear Sir/Madam/Sir or Madam, use 'Yours faithfully'. If you started your letter 'Dear Dr/Mr/Mrs/Ms . . .' or 'Dear Toni Smith' use 'Yours sincerely'. It's as simple as that!

- O — Always sign your name as a courtesy.
- P — Type or print your name clearly under your signature.
- Q — 'Encs' means 'enclosures'. If you are sending other material such as photocopies of a receipt or guarantee, witness statement or perhaps the product itself with your letter then write 'Encs'. The person receiving your letter will then know to check what is enclosed.
- R — 'cc' means copied or circulated to. If, for example, you are writing to your boss and you want someone more senior to see the contents of your letter then you might copy the letter to them (perhaps with a covering note). You should always follow 'cc' with the names of the people you are circulating the letter to.

  'cc' can act as a quiet threat if the person to whom you have addressed your original letter thinks that a higher authority is about to find out what is going on!

What else?
- *Always, always* keep a copy of your letter.
- Never send originals of receipts, birth certificates, etc.
- If you want to return the goods to the shop or manufacturer consider sending them recorded or registered delivery.
- Do follow your letters up. You can include a photocopy of your original letter, in the case they may have 'mislaid' it!

Making telephone calls

Before you dial
- Get all the relevant information in front of you.
- Write down what you want to say — along the lines of the letter content (p.34).

- Find somewhere quiet and undisturbed. If you have an important call to make you don't want to be put off by distractions such as small children!
- Choose a sensible time to call. Try to avoid lunchtimes and Friday afternoons. If possible try and find out the best time to telephone. Check whether the person you want to speak to has any regular meetings or times they are out of the office. Remember also that calls made before 1 pm will be very much more expensive for you.
- Avoid using phone boxes. Rather offer to pay a friend for the use of their telephone. If you have to use a phone box, have plenty of change or a phonecard.

Making the call
- Find out the department and/or the name of the person who can help you (you may already have this information). Switchboards and receptionists are particularly useful so use them, don't abuse them!

  'I'd like to speak to someone about my faulty cooker/making a claim/making a complaint . . .. Who should I talk to?'

  If they give you the name of a department, ask for the name of the *head* of that department and ask to speak to him or her.
- If you are asked to hold, find out how long you will have to wait. Sometimes 'holding on' can become a very expensive exercise, so say you'll ring back.
- If you get left 'holding on' for ages without a response from anyone, ring off and call again. Say that you think that they cut you off. Often switchboards are more helpful the second time around.
- If you are told that the person isn't in or available, ask for the name of their secretary. Find out whether someone else with authority is free to speak to you.
- When you get through to the person make sure that they can actually handle your enquiry. Switchboards often put you through to the wrong person.

  'Is that Mr/Ms Smith? I understand that you deal with customer complaints about faulty washing machines. Is that correct?'

  Only launch into your story when they say yes!
- Be pleasant, especially if this is your first call. Don't assume that they will automatically be unhelpful!

'I do hope you can help me . . .'.

- Follow the format suggested in letter writing←. But do remember the other person may not be able to take in everything that you say. They may not have the details of your case in front of them.

- Speak slowly and clearly. Don't gabble. Spell out any difficult names or figures. You may need to say, 'One hundred and fifteen pounds — that's one, one, five pounds,' in case they thought you said, 'One hundred and fifty' — not a difficult mistake to make on a bad line.

- The person may not be able to give you an answer immediately. Take the lead and say, 'I imagine you won't be able to give me an answer right now so please could you get back to me this afternoon?'

  There's no point pushing someone for an immediate answer if they're going to panic and not give you a sensible solution. However, you do want to know the outcome as soon as possible, so be reasonable but firm.

- If they say, 'I'm sorry, I can't help you,' just ask 'Why?' If they are being really unhelpful they won't have a sensible answer so reiterate your original request. You may also want to ask, 'If you can't deal with this problem, then who can?'

  If you get the reply, 'I'm in charge/I don't know/there's no one else here,' etc., be persistent: 'Who's your supervisor?' 'Where do I take my complaint next?' 'I'm prepared to talk to the Managing Director.'

- Be assertive (p.30) throughout the conversation. Listen carefully to the other person and deal with what they say but don't be led astray by it. Stay firmly on course.

- If they have been helpful, it's worth saying, 'Thank you' — you may need their help again!

- Always make sure you know the name of the person you spoke to. If you have been given a tough time on the telephone and ultimately take the matter to a higher authority, it can be helpful if you say, 'I spoke to someone who claimed he was the manager but who wouldn't give his name.' Most organizations can be very embarrassed by that.

Dealing with secretaries

If you want to speak to a senior manager you will probably be confronted with their secretary or personal assistant. These people are vital to you. Be nice to them.

If they are good at their job they will stave off unwanted nuisances (that might mean you) to protect their boss. However, if you can make an ally of them they will be invaluable.

They may even solve your problem for you without you ever needing to speak to the senior manager. Always find out their name.

Follow up
- Make a note of the details of your conversation — the date, who you spoke to, what they said and so on. Do it immediately.
- Confirm the details of your conversation in writing, particularly if the other person agreed to do something.

Practising
If you are really nervous about using the phone gain more confidence by using the phone more often.

- Ring up your local cinema or theatre and ask about what's on and what seats are available.
- Telephone a department store and find out whether they have a particular item in stock.
- Call advertisers who offer free information or brochures — perhaps for holidays. Be careful not to get more than free information!
- If you have two telephones in your home, practise making an important call with a friend or member of your family.
- Telephone a friend and ask them to let you practise making a complaint.

Confronting face to face

Before you confront
- Get all your facts and figures together.
- Write down what you want to say. For a formal complaint follow the letter format (p.33).
- Stand in front of a mirror or grab a friend and rehearse what you are going to say.
- Choose your time and place carefully. Do not go into a shop to complain at the height of rush hour on a Saturday unless you feel particularly brave and/or willing to risk it! In the same way you don't want to confront your neighbour in the middle of a

busy high street or your child when she is half asleep in bed at
night.
- Take someone with you for moral support. Don't take anyone
  who is not assertive, doesn't understand the law or is liable to
  interfere!

Confronting in a shop or organization

- Ask to see the manager/head of department or whoever is appropriate. Don't be fobbed off with someone too junior:
    'I'd like to speak to the manager please.'
    'Perhaps I can help you?' [Young Saturday assistant, eager to
  help but with no authority.]
    'Thank you, but I'd like to speak to the manager. Please will
  you get him for me.'
- Be pleasant. You might not like doing this — the manager probably likes it even less. Smile at them. Don't growl — that may
  come later!
- Explain briefly what it is you've come to see them about, bring
  out the evidence if possible and tell them what you want them to
  do.
- Speak clearly. Don't mumble into a corner. You are more likely
  to win if every other customer can hear you telling the
  shopkeeper that their goods have just fallen apart or failed to be
  delivered.
- Do not shout. Do not lose your temper *under any circumstance*. If
  the manager wants to get hot under the collar, fine. You stay icy
  cool.
- Behave assertively. Don't get side-tracked.
- If you are in a chain store or the department of a large organization and find that you are not getting anywhere ask the manager
  for the address of his or her head office or the name of his or her
  boss. Write it down and then say, 'And your name is?' It can
  work a treat!
- If you find yourself up against a brick wall, think that you are
  about to become violent or burst into tears, then retreat. Say
  something like, 'I can see we are not going to solve this problem
  right now. I'll come back tomorrow/see your manager/write to
  you/contact my solicitors.'
- When you win your case don't gloat. Accept your re-
  fund/replacement or whatever with grace — you may well have
  to deal with exactly the same people in the future.

Confronting family, friends or colleagues

Confronting family, friends or colleagues is often very different from confronting a shop manager. You are not likely to complain about your shoes having fallen apart or that your dishwasher has flooded for the seventh time. That's the easy option — at least you might have the law to back you up!

This type of confrontation is far more vague and usually involves intangible things such as feelings and emotions. It also implies criticism about behaviours and attitudes which is always difficult to handle well.

- *Do* be assertive (p.30).
- *Don't* beat around the bush. Don't spend the whole time talking about everything but the problem. Go straight in: 'I'd like to talk to you about . . .'.

  You might find that you need to say, 'I imagine you won't be very happy about this/you'll be surprised by this but I'd like to discuss . . .'.
- Avoid saying things such as, 'I hope you won't take this personally but . . .', because that's often just what it is!
- Avoid labelling people, 'You're so stupid/clumsy/thoughtless.' Say instead: 'I felt it was thoughtless of you to forget my birthday.' Or: 'It was clumsy of you to knock that Ming vase on to the floor.'
- *Do* be specific about what you think is wrong and give examples: 'I'm very angry about the way your dog keeps digging up my prized flowers. Last Thursday I found him shredding half a dozen of my best pinks all over my lawn.'
- *Do* be specific about what you want done in future: 'Please will you arrange to have your fence mended and keep your dog confined to your garden.'

  In the long run it's much more effective than, 'If I catch your b . . . . . mongrel in my garden again I'll shoot him!'
- *Do* tell people what sort of behaviour you would like to see more of and what you would like to see less of. Make the problem and the solution manageable: 'When you first started here you arrived on time and we got a lot of work done. Recently you haven't been getting in until 10 a.m. which means we are behind schedule. In future will you please arrive at 9 a.m. so we can complete our workload.'
- Avoid ending with, 'I hope you didn't mind me saying all that, I didn't really mean it . . .'. Be positive: 'I'm glad/relieved that

we've had the chance to talk about/get it out in the open . . .'.
- Confrontation can be very stressful. You want to avoid creating a battleground in which neither party can remember what they were originally talking about! Think before you speak and practise by rehearsing thoroughly what you want to say.

Golden rules

Do your homework
- Why do you want your new purchase?
- What do you want it to do?
- Don't buy on impulse. Set a budget.
- Find out the facts.
- Check out all your options.
- Shop around.
- Ask for time to think. Don't feel bad about saying 'No'.
- Look for approval symbols and cleaning instructions.
- Shop somewhere reliable.

Choose a reliable tradesperson
- Ask around for a recommendation.
- Look for professional qualifications or membership of a Trade Association.
- Find out how much. Get a written quotation.
- Find out how they're going to do the work.
- Get a receipt, especially for cash.

If you've got a problem — work out a plan to solve it!
- Who can make the decision.
- Who else can help you.
- Decide whether to write, telephone or meet them face to face.
- Set yourself a time limit.
- Keep your plan up to date.

Learn and practise the skills

Section Two

The Nuts and Bolts

Looking after your money

All about credit

If you want to purchase something there are two ways you can pay for it: cash or credit. Cash means notes or coins, cheques and 'debit' cards. But what about credit?

Whether you take out a mortgage for your new home or a loan for a car, pay for your holiday on your Access or Visa card or sign a hire-purchase agreement for a colour TV, you are using credit.

There are so many types of credit available for the hungry consumer that it's easy to get confused. Credit costs — and sometimes it can cost more than just money.

If you want to buy something you can't afford to pay cash for or you only have limited savings and are considering borrowing to pay for existing debts, be careful you don't fall into a credit trap. Like anything else, do your homework first and find out the true cost of credit before you commit yourself (p.51).

The majority of credit borrowing comes under the Consumer Credit Act 1974 which covers most loans to individuals under £15,000.

Golden rules of borrowing money

- *Do* shop around and compare the real cost of credit (p.51).
- *Do* work out what the whole credit deal will cost you and consider if you can afford it.
- *Don't* sign any agreement until you have fully read and understood it.
- *Do* find out whether you can change your mind and how long you have to change it.
- *Don't* default on the repayments.
- *Do* discuss any difficulties you have making repayments with

the shop or finance company *immediately* you find yourself facing problems.

What kind of credit is available?

Banks

Banks and increasingly building societies offer a wide range of credit facilities, including credit cards→and mortgages→.

Bank overdrafts

You need to get permission from your bank manager to overdraw on your account up to an agreed amount and for a specified period. As you pay money into your account so the loan is repaid.

Interest is payable on the amount by which you are overdrawn and is calculated on a day-to-day basis. For very large overdrafts, perhaps for business projects, the manager may ask you for security, such as your house.

The manager can insist that you repay the loan in full at any time.

Bank loans

There are normally two types of bank loan:

- Ordinary loans which are available to bank customers only, for a particular purpose approved by the manager. A variable rate of interest is charged, usually higher than for overdrafts.
- Personal loans available to customers and non-customers alike. Loans are usually for up to three years although they can be for longer. The interest rate is fixed.

Credit cards

There are three broad types of credit card:

- Bank credit cards.
- Charge cards.
- Store cards which might be credit or charge cards.

Bank credit cards

Although traditionally there have been only two bank credit schemes operating in the UK it is misleading simply to talk about 'Visa cards' or 'Access cards'. They are offered by many different institutions who are not obliged to stick to the same terms, so check them out.

A bank credit card bills you each month, and subject to a minimum payment, you pay off as much or as little as you like.

Usually if you pay in full within twenty-five days no interest is charged. However, if you are just one day late, you may end up paying a full twenty-six days' interest, so be careful. Remember, if you pay your bill over the bank counter it will still take about four days to clear and if you post it you must allow time for delays.

Bank credit cards can also give you some protection against faulty goods. Providing your purchase cost is at least £100 and was paid for with your credit card you may be able to sue (p.250) the card company if you cannot get any satisfaction from the supplier (p.72).

Charge cards
Charge card holders must pay off their account every month. In addition there is a joining fee plus a yearly fee.

Unlike bank credit cards there is no credit limit and you can spend as much as you like as long as you can pay for it when your bill comes in. They are particularly useful for people who travel a lot on business.

Store cards
These come in three varieties:
- Monthly accounts which operate like charge cards except that the card is usually free.
- Option accounts which are similar to bank credit cards but are often more costly.
- Budget accounts where you pay a regular monthly sum and can borrow a multiple of your monthly payment.

If you lose your credit or charge cards
If you lose or have your credit or charge cards stolen report the loss immediately. You normally won't be charged for any purchases which are made on your stolen card *after* you've reported its loss. You may incur a charge of up to £50 for items which are purchased on your stolen card *before* you report its loss.

Extra insurance for credit card holders
Almost all bank credit and charge cards offer card-holders additional travel insurance when the card is used to pay for tickets; the amounts and cover vary considerably.

Hire Purchase (HP)
This is usually offered by shops to enable you to buy goods.
- You pay for the goods in instalments and you only legally own

them when you have paid the last instalment.
- You mustn't sell the goods until they are legally yours.
- Once you've paid one-third of the total amount payable, the owner (usually a finance company) cannot reclaim the goods without a court order.
- Interest is usually at a fixed rate throughout the agreement although it varies from shop to shop.

This can be one of the more expensive means of getting credit.

If you find you cannot keep up with the repayments you can end the agreement by paying at least half of the total amount payable (unless the agreement says otherwise) and, of course, returning the goods.

If you buy a second-hand car always make sure that it is not the subject of an outstanding HP agreement, because although you will normally be protected, you may be liable for the payments. You can, however, check up on this (p.88).

Credit sales from shops
These are offered by individual shops and chain stores and are similar in some ways to Hire Purchase agreements except that the goods belong to you immediately.

You normally pay a deposit and then weekly or monthly instalments over a fairly short period — often six months to a year. Interest is at a fixed rate throughout the agreement but can vary from shop to shop.

Some stores will offer 'interest free credit'. Do still shop around to ensure it's the best deal you can get.

Finance company personal loans
These are normally arranged for you by the shop or dealer from whom you are buying an expensive item, e.g. a car. You can also arrange a deal for yourself.

The minimum amount you can borrow is usually £100, sometimes more. The repayment period is normally up to three years.

If you are offered a credit agreement in a shop and you think you can get a better deal from another finance company or other source, then look around.

Watch out for 'secured' loans. Some companies will ask for your house as 'security' on the loan, similar to mortgage loans. However, if you default on the repayments, they may be a lot less sympathetic than your building society manager. You could find your home being sold at well below the market rate simply so that the finance company can reclaim the money you owe it. Be careful.

Mail order credit

This is offered by the big catalogue companies. Quite often their agents will collect your repayments or you can send them by post. Do make sure that you keep a clear record of any money you send through the post in case a dispute arises.

Sometimes catalogues advertise 'interest free' credit. They can only use this term if all the repayments add up to the original cash price.

Mortgages

Banks and building societies, as well as a growing range of other financial institutions, offer to lend money on a mortgage to buy property.

The bank or building society will usually offer to lend money according to your income. Repayments can last up to thirty years or more depending on your age.

Interest rates will most likely vary during the term of your mortgage, perhaps as much as 6 per cent.

Your home will be used as security, so if you default on the repayments, the institution concerned may proceed to repossess your house.

There are three basic types of mortgage available:

- **Repayment mortgages** where your monthly payment goes to pay off both the capital you have borrowed and the interest that has accrued on it. To begin with your money will be going largely to pay off the interest. Since you get tax relief on this, you can get a low start repayment mortgage which means that you can start off making smaller monthly payments. Most institutions insist that you take out an additional life insurance policy so that the repayment is covered if you die.
- **Endowment mortgages** where part of your monthly repayment pays the interest on the money you've borrowed and the rest is paid to an insurance company for the premium on an endowment policy. The policy is designed to pay off the mortgage at the end of the term and in some cases give you an extra lump sum. There is built-in life assurance so that the loan is automatically repaid if any of the borrowers die.

- **Pension mortgages** are similar to endowment mortgages in that you make a monthly interest payment on your mortgage plus a premium payment to an approved pension scheme. On your retirement you will get a cash sum to pay off the remainder of the mortgage plus a small pension for the rest of your life. Most lenders will insist that you take out additional life insurance.

Obviously, you should always seek advice from an *independent* financial adviser to see what would be most advantageous for you. For more information on mortgages and home buying see p.145.

Moneylenders

Anyone who stops you in the street or calls uninvited at your home offering you a loan is committing a criminal offence.

Most moneylenders need a licence — check with your local Trading Standards Department (p.23).

Moneylenders often make loans where no one else will, but they tend to be extremely expensive. They can also be less than scrupulous in recovering any unpaid debts.

If they ask you for any of your benefit books as security — hang on to them! It's illegal to demand them.

Pawnbrokers

The pawnbroker sign — three balls — is becoming a familiar sight once again in the high street. Many of the new establishments have lost their rather seedy image and are really smart.

If you pawn anything the pawnbroker must give you a receipt in the proper form, headed 'Notice to Debtor'. Read this carefully because it tells you exactly what your rights are in getting your pawned articles back.

The receipt will tell you how to get your articles back and when the pawnbroker is entitled to sell it.

If you cannot repay the full amount by the agreed date, you will have to pay regular interest to prevent your articles from being sold.

Trading checks and vouchers

These are more common in some parts of the country than in others. Although it can be a convenient way of borrowing, it is usually quite expensive.

Checks and vouchers are issued by specialist companies and can be exchanged for goods in selected shops.

An agent calls at your home and issues you with a 'check' or a voucher depending on the amount. You repay in weekly instalments over a fixed period, including a charge for credit outstanding.

Credit unions

These operate like a club. Members make regular savings to form a central fund. Out of this they can get low-cost loans to buy goods or pay for bills.

Hiring goods

Hiring makes sense for expensive items that you're not likely to use often, if indeed ever again, like a cement mixer or floor sander.

Before you agree to hire anything for a long period of time consider whether you can keep up the repayments and whether it might not be cheaper in the long run to buy the goods outright.

Find out the minimum length of the hire agreement and decide if you're prepared to commit yourself to it.

Find out whether free maintenance or repair is included in the deal. This might be a real plus factor in hiring items like TVs and video recorders.

Calculating the cost of credit

Before you consider shopping around for credit you *must* understand *APR* — **Annual Percentage Rate of Charge**.

Almost all credit deals will include an extra charge or 'interest'. Interest can be either fixed or variable. If it's variable (this means it could go up or down depending on the state of the financial

---

Example
If you bought a sofa on credit through a department store the sums might look like this:

Cash price of sofa	£200	
Credit deal	£25	per month over twelve months
Total price of sofa on credit	£300	
Amount of interest payable	£100	

---

markets) you take a bit of a gamble because you might be paying a lot more (or a lot less) in the long term.

However, since the arrangements for repaying credit, the length of the loans and perhaps the inclusion of deposits can vary so greatly, it would be almost impossible for the consumer to compare the relative merits of a number of credit deals.

Would you know at a glance whether you were better off taking up the department store's credit offer or borrowing £200 from the bank at 20 per cent simple interest over two years? (In fact you would be better with the bank loan as it would only cost you £80 over two years.)

The APR is a standard way of quoting the total cost for credit because interest can be calculated in so many different ways. APR means you can compare the real cost of the different types of credit on offer without having to do a whole lot of complicated sums. The APR represents the total cost of borrowing the money, calculated as a yearly percentage. Always look for the APR.

If you're offered credit make sure that you get a quote for the APR in writing.

Need to borrow money? — Working out the cost of credit

'My wife and I want to have a new kitchen but they are so expensive. We have some savings but certainly not enough to cover the cost of the kitchen. We've had a number of quotes in from kitchen fitting companies and one of them offered to let us pay in instalments over eighteen months. We quite like the kitchen units but we preferred the designs of another smaller company who couldn't offer any kind of deal. Even if we pay for the kitchen we'll still have to find someone to do the decorating, tiling and so on. How should we go about finding the necessary finance?'

Step one: Work out how much you want to spend

Before you begin shopping around for the best credit deal you will need to work out the maximum you are prepared to spend on installing your new kitchen. Do the sums first and then be prepared to cut the suit to fit the cloth.

- Work out exactly how much installing a kitchen will cost. Include everything — units, structural work, electrical, plumbing, fitting, appliances, lights, tiling, flooring, decorating. Don't leave anything out. Add another 5 per cent for contingencies.

- Decide whether you are prepared to spend this amount of money.
- Consider where you can make savings if necessary. Perhaps a cheaper type of unit, keeping existing appliances or doing less structural work. Be very clear about what you *have* to do, for example rewiring for safety reasons.

Step two: Decide how much cash you will put up

You have some savings. How much are you prepared to put into the new kitchen?
   Consider:

- Is it worth forfeiting any interest your savings may be gaining? On the whole, interest rates on money borrowed are much higher than interest rates on money invested. For example, if you had £5000 in a building society earning interest at 8 per cent it would not make much sense to leave it there and borrow £5000 at 20 per cent interest. You would pay out more in interest on the money borrowed than you would gain on the money invested.
- Do you have to make special arrangements to withdraw the money?

Step three: Work out how much you need to borrow

Subtract from the total cost of the kitchen the amount of cash you have decided to put in and you'll have left the amount you need to borrow.
   You may find that this is more than you are able or prepared to borrow. This is where your list of possible savings will be useful ←. But you must be realistic about the minimum amount of money that needs to be spent in order to install any new kitchen.

Step four: Find out your options

Now you have calculated the amount of money you need to borrow you can shop around for the best offer.
   Whoever you go to you must establish:

- The rate of interest or APR charged. ←
- Whether the interest rate is fixed or variable. If it's the latter, consider whether you could afford an increased rate.
- Any deposit payable — this may be true for the kitchen company.

- The period of the loan.
- Whether or not you will have to offer any security for the loan.

You must also work out:
- The total cost of the loan.
- Your weekly or monthly repayments.

Who can you go to?
- The kitchen fitting company. Think about whether they will require a cash deposit. Take this into consideration together with all the extras that you will have to pay someone else to do like the tiling and decorating. Will you have enough cash from your savings?
- The bank or building society. Ask about an overdraft or loan. You might also find out if you could take out a second mortgage or increase your existing one.
- A finance company. Ask around to find someone reputable.

Step five: Decide how you are going to borrow the money

By this point you should have perhaps half a dozen options in front of you.

Write them all down on paper. Include:

- The name of the lender.
- The type of scheme — loan, mortgage.
- Amount they've agreed to lend.
- Period of loan.
- Interest rates — APR.
- Total cost of the loan.
- Monthly repayments.
- Any security.

You will now have to weigh up who gives you the best financial deal (i.e. the total cost of the loan, the period of the loan and the monthly repayments).

You need to decide first whether you can afford to keep up with the payments for the length of the loan and second if you are prepared to spend that much on your kitchen.

You then need to consider the risks involved. Will you have to agree to give your house as security? Is there a chance you might have problems with the repayments? What will happen if you default?

If you're worried about your job security or ill health or you simply want peace of mind you can always think about taking out insurance against being unable to repay the loan. In fact some lenders insist on this, particularly for large loans.

You also need to consider which you think is the most reputable place to borrow money from.

You may at this point need to revise your budget and your plans before you can come to a final decision.

Step six: What next?
Once you've made up your mind, remember to read through any agreements very carefully before you sign them. Make sure you have a copy of any documents.

If you find you can pay off the loan early, the lender will normally allow you a rebate of some of the interest originally agreed to cover the whole period of the loan. However, if you settle in full very early on in the agreement you may still find that you have to pay more than you originally borrowed.

Refused credit?
'I recently tried to open an account with my local department store. I filled in all the forms correctly but I got a letter last week refusing to let me have an account. I don't understand why, I've always paid my bills on time. I feel that someone somewhere has blackened my name. How can I find out what's going on?'

Under the Consumer Credit Act 1974 you have the right to find out and challenge information held about your credit worthiness.

Before anyone lends you cash they will have to decide whether you are a good or bad risk. To do this many suppliers, especially large companies, use a system known as 'credit scoring'.

You will be given points according to your answers on the forms you were asked to fill in. The supplier will know from previous experience what sort of people (perhaps depending on their job, other credit facilities, age and so on) are most likely to make the repayments. The supplier will set a 'pass' mark. If you get sufficient points you will be accepted. The information used and the scoring attached to it varies from trader to trader. Under this system there is usually no *single* reason for acceptance or rejection.

If you are refused credit, the trader does not have to tell you why you were rejected. But you do have to be informed whether a 'credit reference (or reporting) agency' was consulted and which one it was. These are organizations which collect information and compile records on individual people's financial standing; for example, whether they've ever been taken to court over an outstanding debt. The agencies don't normally give an opinion on whether you are suitable to lend money to. Traders won't necessarily base their decisions on the information they receive. You have the right to find out about that information and correct it, if you think it is wrong.

If you decide to challenge the decision you *must* act quickly.

Step one: Find out the name of the credit reference agency

Ask the shop, or their finance company if they consulted a credit reference agency. If they did, then ask them the name and address of the agency. You must put your request in *writing* ✎ and within *twenty-eight days* of the time you last dealt with them about the matter. Don't feel embarrassed or awkward about asking for this information. It is a perfectly reasonable request.

The trader or their financial company has *seven working days* within which to reply.

Step two: Write to the credit reference agency

Once you have the name and address of the agency ask them for a copy of the file. Again your request *must* be in *writing* ✎ and you *must* include a nominal non-returnable fee. (Contact the agency or your local advice centre to confirm the current fee.)

In your letter, you must give the agency as much information as you can to help them trace your file. Include:

- Your full name and any change of name in the last six years.
- Your full address including postcode and the details of any previous addresses in the last six years.
- The full name and address of your business if you run one, since separate information might be held about you in your business capacity.

The agency can ask you for any additional information that they need in order to trace your file.

Step three: The agency must reply

The agency has *seven working days* from the date they received your request either to confirm that they have no information about you or to send you your file. You should also receive a statement telling you how to go about getting your file put right.

Step four: Checking the file
Read through the file carefully. If the facts are correct you cannot expect the agency to change them. If the facts are wrong you can write ✎ to the agency with the correct information, asking them to change their records.

The agency has *twenty-eight days* to reply to this first request to correct your file.

Step five: The agency's reply is unsatisfactory
If the agency either fails to reply to your letter or refuses to alter the file or gives an unsatisfactory alteration then you can write a note of correction of up to 200 words. Send it to the agency with a covering letter. Ask them to add your note to your file and to include it with any information they send out about you in the future.

If you've had no reply from the agency within twenty-eight days of your first request, then you have a *further twenty-eight days* to send them your note of correction. If you've received an unsatisfactory reply then you must send the note of correction within *twenty-eight days* from the date you received that reply.

Step six: The agency must use the correction
Within twenty-eight days of receiving your note of correction the agency should tell you that they have added it to your file. If the agency corrects the file or adds your note of correction, they must send the new details to anyone who has consulted them about you in the last six months. The correction must always be used in the future.

Step seven: Taking it further
If you have followed all the above steps and kept within the time limits and still have not heard from the agency or had your file corrected then you should write ✎ to the DIRECTOR GENERAL OF FAIR TRADING.

The Director will need to know:

- Your full name and address.
- The name and address of the agency.
- Details of the incorrect entry, why you think it is wrong and

why you will suffer if it is not put right.
- A copy of the note of correction and the date you sent it.
- Details and copies of other correspondence.

The more information you can give, the quicker your case can be dealt with.

Step eight: Getting extra help
If you need extra help then contact your local Trading Standards Department or Consumer Protection Department (p.23) or your local CAB or advice centre.

Changing your mind
'Last weekend a double glazing salesman called at my home and persuaded me to have my windows replaced. He offered me what seemed like a very good finance deal which meant that I wouldn't have to put all the cash up front. I must admit that I'd been thinking about having the windows replaced for some time, so as they seemed a reputable company I decided to go ahead. I signed the agreement then and there. But I was awake all last night wondering whether I could afford it all. Can I get out of it?'

Most credit agreements have a very limited 'cooling off' period in which you can change your mind.

As a general rule you can cancel a credit agreement if you discussed the deal face to face (not over the telephone) with the trader *and* you signed the agreement at home, at business or at a friend's — anywhere so long as it wasn't at the trader's premises. All credit or hire agreements which can be cancelled will have a box headed 'Your Right To Cancel' which tells you what to do.

When you signed the agreement with the salesman he would have given you a copy to keep. In a week or so you will receive a further copy or a notice of your cancellation rights. You have *five days* after receiving the additional copy or notice to cancel the agreement.

Step one: Write immediately to the company
Although you haven't yet received the second copy of the agreement, if you've definitely decided you don't want to go ahead, then write immediately.

Customer Number . . .
Further to a visit by your salesman, Sam Glazier on [date], I am

writing to inform you that I am cancelling my agreement with you to install double glazing at my home. I enclose a copy of our original agreement.

Would you please confirm the cancellation in writing immediately.

For peace of mind you might want to post the letter recorded delivery.

Step two: The company still sends a second copy of the agreement

Your letter may not have reached the company before they sent off the second copy or they may have chosen to ignore it, so write again. The second copy or notice will have a tear-off cancellation slip so you can use that in addition to your letter (you might want to send it in a separate envelope).

Customer Number . . .

Further to my letter of [date] I am again writing to formally cancel my agreement with you for installing double glazing at my home. I also enclose/am returning under separate cover the tear-off cancellation slip which I received this morning.

Would you please confirm the cancellation in writing immediately.

Whatever you do, you only have *five days* to do it in!

Step three: For the future

Never, never sign any agreement until you are absolutely sure that you understand its contents. Find out if you can change your mind and how long you have to do it. Don't sign any agreement that doesn't have cancellation rights. Never just sign a blank form regardless of whether the salesman or woman tells you 'it will save on paperwork'.

My creditors are harassing me

'I've got a whole lot of outstanding debts amounting to about £3500. I've now got regular work and I've made arrangements to pay them back but sometimes I slip up on the repayments.

'I'm fed up with having so many creditors on my back. They're really

beginning to harass me. When I was desperate I borrowed £150 off this moneylender down the road. The amount of interest he's charging me is outrageous. Because I haven't paid off the debt he keeps coming around to my house in the early hours of the morning and taunting me so all the neighbours can hear. My wife's on the verge of a nervous breakdown because of it.

'I saw an ad in my Sunday paper offering to clear up all my debts in one go. Do you think there would be any risk in getting involved with this sort of outfit? I've really had enough of all the hassle. I'd much rather just have one company to deal with.'

Watch that you're not about to jump out of the frying pan and into the fire. Or more precisely into the teeth of a loan shark.

Creditors are allowed to keep reminding you from time to time about your outstanding debt but it's illegal to start harassing you by, for example, phoning you late at night, constantly calling you at work or verbally or physically threatening you.

If you think you're being overcharged for credit, you can take the matter to court. If the court agrees with you they can order the lender to decrease your payments and refund you any unreasonable interest charges.

Step one: Stop your creditor harassing you

You should either call the police or contact your local Trading Standards Officer (your town hall will give you the number) and make a formal complaint. Obviously, if any of your neighbours are prepared to act as witnesses, so much the better.

If your wife's health is being affected by the moneylender's behaviour, make sure she visits the doctor to put it on record.

Step two: Dealing with extortionate credit

If you think the moneylender is charging you too much for credit look around to find out how much interest you'd have to pay on a similar loan from another institution. If you still think that the rate is extortionate, you can take the moneylender to court.

The Consumer Credit Act 1974 states that a credit bargain (this includes not only the credit agreement itself but any other provisions which relate to that agreement such as insurance, security or a maintenance contract) is extortionate if it:

(a) requires the debtor to make payments which are **grossly extortionate**, or

(b) otherwise **grossly contravenes** ordinary principles of fair dealing.

If you allege that the bargain is extortionate then it is up to your
creditor to prove it otherwise. However, you should be prepared
to produce sufficient evidence to support your case. It can be very
difficult to establish a case of extortionate credit and if you want to
pursue this you should seek the advice of a solicitor. (You might
get help under the Legal Aid and Assistance Scheme (p.242).)

If you think that your moneylender is a really dodgy character
you have one other alternative. You can find out whether your
moneylender is licensed (those lending over £30 must be). If he's
not, your agreement is invalid and you should stop making him
any payments. You should also inform the Office of Fair Trading
about his illegal activities — he can be prosecuted.

To find out whether he has a licence you need to consult the CON-
SUMER CREDIT PUBLIC REGISTER. You can do this in person or by post,
but check current opening hours and handling fees first.

Step three: Check the newspaper advert carefully

Are they offering 'secured loans'? If you own your home or a new
car, you may have to offer it as security. If there's any danger that
you might default on the repayments you could find your home or
vehicle being sold to pay off the loan. Is it really worth risking your
home to pay off debts of £3500?

You must also check what APR (p.51) they're offering. How
much is the loan actually going to cost you in hard cash terms? You
could find yourself paying back twice as much as you originally
borrowed.

However tempting the offer might seem, if it looks at all suspect,
drop it!

Step four: Other options

If you're in regular work it might be easier for you to get credit.
However, there's no point in overstretching yourself so that you
end up back at square one with even bigger outstanding debts.

Work out your weekly budget (p.64) so that you can realistically
establish how much you can afford to pay off to each of your
creditors each week.

The single factor which is likely to make creditors most angry is defaulting on agreed repayments — however small. If you find that you 'slip up', see whether your employers would be prepared to set aside part of your weekly pay so you can sort out your debts. Alternatively, perhaps you could give your wife a similar payment so that she can deal with your creditors.

If you still want to get a single loan to pay off the other debts approach a reputable financial institution to see whether they might be willing to help you.

Coping with debts

'Three months ago I lost my job. Since then we have been surviving on the bit of redundancy pay I received and the money my wife brings in from her part-time job. She doesn't earn very much and we will soon have used up all our savings. Although I am sure I will get another job soon, I'm really worried about paying the mortgage and all the bills in the meantime. I've already missed last month's mortgage repayment and I have final demands for the gas, electricity and telephone — they are threatening to cut us off. I also owe Access a couple of hundred pounds. I know that there are a couple of letters about that bill which I don't dare open. I'm terrified of getting into debt. What can I do?'

Getting into debt can be a frightening experience. It can make you feel like you are on a never-ending treadmill; no matter how much money you pay out, your debts never seem to get any less. The important thing is to act quickly before the final demands pile up. The longer you leave it, the harder — and more expensive — life becomes.

Step one: Confront your debts
Find a quiet space, a fresh pad of paper and a pencil and collect up all your bank statements, gas, electricity, telephone bills, Access statements and the unopened envelopes.

First write down a list of all the money you owe and who you owe it to.

Step two: Decide who to deal with first
You will need to decide which of your creditors (the people who you owe money to) are the most urgent. Remember, it is not always the person or company to whom you owe the greatest amount of money, that needs dealing with first.

Consider what action each of your creditors can take if you continue to fail to pay their bill. For example, the gas or electricity boards can cut off your gas and electricity and the same would happen to your telephone. It's simple and quick and the most effective method the company has. But where would it leave you? Even if you paid your gas, electricity or telephone bill an hour after they cut you off, you would then still have to pay a substantial reconnection charge to have the service restored.

Ultimately, the building society or bank could repossess your house and sell it on your behalf. It is unlikely that they would realize a competitive market price.

Access or any other credit company cannot take immediate action against you except cancel your card. Eventually they may issue a summons against you (p.260).

Your priority then must be to contact the gas and electricity boards and perhaps British Telecom. You will also need to talk to your bank or building society manager. The important thing is to tell these people about your situation. If you don't let them know the real reason why you haven't paid their bill, can you blame them for thinking it was just because you didn't want to?

Step three: Write 'holding' letters

What you need to do is put in a 'holding' letter or telephone call. The aim of this is to tell your creditors you are aware that you owe them money; that you are currently facing financial difficulties and that you will contact them shortly with an offer to settle the bill.

You will find people more sympathetic than you may think. In fact, many of the major consumer services give a telephone number on their bill for customers to ring if they have problems settling their account.

Your customer or account number

This morning I received a final demand from you for £... .

I am writing to inform you that since I lost my job three months ago I have been facing severe financial difficulties. I am currently reassessing my financial situation and I am therefore unable to settle my account in full at this moment. I intend to contact you shortly with a proposal to repay the outstanding debt. In the meantime I would be most grateful if you would not cut off my electricity/gas supply.

If they do cut off your gas or electricity after they should have

63

received your letter and before replying to you then you may be able to persuade them to waive the reconnection charge.

Step four: Making a realistic budget

Now you need to think about making a realistic budget so that you can work out exactly how much you can afford each week to pay off your existing debts. If you are out of work, then you have probably already 'tightened your belt' and cut down on luxury items. However, if your budget is going to work you must be realistic about how you spend your money. If you need money for cigarettes then you must include it.

First of all, write down all the money you have coming in each week such as your wife's pay and any state benefits you get. This is your weekly *income*.

Next make a list of all your weekly *outgoings*. Include things like: the mortgage; gas; electricity; telephone; insurance; car — insurance, maintenance, petrol; food and household goods; other necessities — cigarettes, sweets, newspapers; fares to work; any other payments you are committed to.

Now subtract your outgoings from your income. Whatever you have left over is the amount you have to divide up between your creditors. If you have very little or none left over you may have to rethink how much you can spend on each of the items you listed under outgoings. But don't despair.

Step five: Dealing with your mortgage

Your single largest payment each month probably goes on your mortgage. Make an appointment to see your bank or building society manager. Take your budget along with you.

Explain the situation to the manager and ask if they will suspend the mortgage repayments for, say, six months, until you get back on your feet. With many mortgages it is possible to extend the terms of the mortgage so that, for example, you continue paying for an extra six months at the end of your mortgage repayment period.

If you can come to some arrangement over your mortgage you will have more money available each week to pay off some of your other debts.

Step six: Paying off your debts

Having worked out how much you can spare each week to pay off your outstanding debts you might be left with a calculation that looks like that given in the example.

Example
Spare weekly income: £25   Outstanding debts:

	Gas	£ 75
	Electricity	£ 35
	Telephone	£ 55
	Access	£350

How could you divide it up? You might try:

Offer to pay each week:	Gas	£ 7
	Electricity	£ 4
	Telephone	£ 6
	Access	£ 8

This way, with the exception of Access, your bills would be paid off in just over two months. The amount you are offering may seem minuscule but it is the only realistic offer you can make. There is no point in saying you will pay more if you default in the second week.

You now need to contact your creditors with your proposals.

Step seven: Negotiating with your creditors

This part of the negotiations really needs to be done in writing. The aim of your letter is to show that you have got back in touch quickly and that you mean business!

You need to show that you have thought about your financial situation very carefully and that you have a serious proposal to pay off the money you owe.

Your customer reference number

Further to my letter of [date] (and your reply of . . .) I am writing to inform you of my proposal to repay my outstanding bill of £... .

Having lost my job, my family is relying on the small income my wife earns from a part-time job and my unemployment benefit. I have a number of other oustanding debts. I have considered carefully my essential weekly outgoings and in the circumstances I am able to pay you £ ... each week in respect of my outstanding bill.

Please confirm that this is satisfactory.

If you have a debt with a credit card company or any other outstanding loan which is accruing interest it is worth adding another line to your letter asking the company to freeze the amount of interest they are charging.

Furthermore, given my financial situation I would ask you to freeze the amount of interest accruing on my outstanding account.

Many companies will be happy to accept repayment of the money you owe them to date. They realize that if you have difficulty paying that amount you are unlikely ever to be able to repay the extra interest which will mount up.

Your creditors may write back and ask you for full details of your income and expenditure together with information about your other debts. This is in order for them to assess your means to repay the money you owe them. You should send them a copy of the balance sheet you worked out in Step four ←.

Step eight: Keeping up with the repayments

Once you have agreed a weekly or monthly amount with each of your creditors it is vital that you keep up with the repayments. If you default it will be doubly difficult to renegotiate a new rate with them.

If your circumstances do change or you face a sudden emergency then tell them immediately. That way they will be more sympathetic to your situation.

Step nine: Keeping up with your current bills

Now that you have dealt with your debts, you need to make sure that you can keep up with your weekly bills.

You may need to make changes to the way you live — how and when you use the gas and electricity, for example. If you still have a telephone, you'll need to remember to use it after 1 p.m., or better still, after 6 p.m. when it's cheaper.

Both the gas and electricity boards offer a variety of schemes to help people facing financial difficulties to pay their bills. You could consider a budget scheme where you pay a regular monthly amount and avoid facing heavy winter bills in one go. Alternatively you could have a meter installed enabling you to pay for your gas or electricity as you use it; but initially this can be an expensive exercise. If you still have any credit cards you may want to return them or lock them away!

Finally, if you and your family are relying on a very low income and are not receiving any benefits, check with your local DSS office to see if you can claim any extra cash. If you have school-aged children you could also ask the headteacher about free school meals.

Step ten: Taking it further

Despite what some lenders might tell you you cannot be prosecuted in the criminal court because you haven't paid your debts. However, your creditors can take you to the County court as a last resort, but it's highly unlikely you'd end up in jail.

If you do get a County court summons you should reply to it immediately (p.260). You must also attend any hearings you are moned to. You are usually given the opportunity to repay your debts in instalments. However, if you default, your creditors may ask for the bailiff to seize your goods.

If you are working, the court can also make an **Attachment of Earnings Order** which means that your employer will deduct money from your wages and pay it directly to the court. Your house could also be made the subject of a **Charging Order**. This means that it cannot be sold before you have paid off all your creditors.

On the other hand the court might be able to help you sort out your debt problems. If your debts are reasonably small — a few thousand pounds — you can ask the court for an **Administration Order**. This means that the court will assess your financial situation and can make an order under which you will pay the court a certain fixed amount regularly and they in turn will pay your creditors.

This is particularly useful if any of your creditors refuse to accept your offer of repayment and demand substantially more than you can afford to pay them.

Getting extra advice
The Citizens' Advice Bureau.

Your local Money Advice Centre or Debt Counsellor.

Dealing with banks and building societies

As with any other business or institution, problems do arise with banks and building societies. The majority of complaints are the result of some genuine human error or basic misunderstanding but they are aggravating none the less. And many bank errors like bounced cheques can be extremely embarrassing for the customer.

Banks have certain legal obligations towards their customers including: not to pass on any confidential information about their customers (except in a few exceptional cases); to bear the loss if it pays out on a cheque or banker's card after they had been reported stolen; to honour cheques up to the amount agreed on an overdraft.

If you think that there has been a serious infringement of your basic legal rights do seek professional legal advice (p.237) before you embark on any legal wranglings.

Building societies are very conscious about their public image as they challenge the traditional banking system for business. They tend to treat justified grievances seriously.

As a general rule of thumb, if you have a problem with a bank or building society try this step-by-step approach.

Step one: Talk to the person you first dealt with
Often if there has been a genuine human error or misunderstanding this can be cleared up quickly and effectively by the person who first dealt with your enquiry.

Step two: Write to the manager or department concerned
Explain the nature of the complaint and say what you would like done .

Step three: Take your complaint higher up the ladder
You will need to follow the appropriate 'chain of command' (p.22).

Step four: Complain to an outside body
If you have exhausted the bank's internal complaints procedure or

feel you're not getting very far, you can make a complaint to THE BANKING OMBUDSMAN.

They will only deal with complaints about their own members (most of the major high street banks). They cannot intervene if you have already started court proceedings against a bank or if your complaint relates to the bank's commercial judgement about lending or security.

You'll need to write to the Ombudsman detailing your complaint and you'll need to do it within six months. The Ombudsman can make financial awards if your complaint is upheld. However, you are not bound by the decision and retain your right to go to court instead.

The BANKING INFORMATION SERVICE might also be able to help you by taking an objective view of any dispute and advising you on standard banking practices.

For building societies you could complain to the BUILDING SOCIETIES ASSOCIATION. Although they only have limited powers and cannot force an individual society to take a particular line of action they may be able to help you resolve the dispute.

Buying goods

When you purchase something, you and the seller make a contract. If you then find out that the goods are faulty, it's up to the seller — and not the manufacturer — to sort out your complaint. However, that doesn't mean that you can't make a complaint against the manufacturer as well.

The three rules

The Sale of Goods Act 1979 lays down three basic rules.

- Goods must be of **merchantable quality**. This means that they must be fit for their normal purpose regardless of whether they were bought in a 'sale' or not. So a washing machine must wash, a pair of wellington boots should keep out the rain, food must be fit to be eaten.

Example
It's raining hard. Susie and Clarissa Mangle rush into their nearest shoe shop to buy some boots. Susie buys a pair of rubber, waterproof galoshes and Clarissa buys a pair of suede 'fashion boots' with fancy stitching. They haven't walked very far in their new boots when they both discover their feet are sopping wet. Back to the shop to complain, Susie — galoshes are supposed to keep out the rain! Bad luck, Clarissa, the suede 'fashion boots' never claimed to be waterproof, so you'll have to put up with wet feet.

- You must also bear in mind the price of the goods and how they were described — you can't expect top quality if you buy used goods at rock-bottom prices!

- Goods must be **as described**. This means that they must match any description given of them on their packaging, shop display or by the seller.

Example

Molly Flanagan buys a new cardigan in a box marked 'Cardigan, Size 12, Blue, Wool'. When she unpacks it, she finds a size 16, bright pink, polyester jumper. Straight back to the shop, Molly!

- Goods must be **fit for the purpose**.

Example

Bill Bradley asks his local shopkeeper for something to mend his teapot lid. The shopkeeper gives him a pot of 'Get Stuck Superglue' and tells him, it's just the thing for broken china. But it won't stick Bill's china teapot lid. Back to the shop, Bill!

If the seller breaks any of the three rules they automatically also break their contract with you.

If you have a complaint you must act immediately.

Find a remedy

Stop using the item at once and contact the retailer.

If the contract has been broken you can:

- Reject the goods and ask for your money back.
- Ask for a cash payment to make up the difference between what you paid and the reduced value of the faulty item.
- Providing you both agree, get a replacement or a free repair.

It is not unusual to be offered a credit note. You do not have to accept it. If you can't find anything else you want to buy, you may not be able to get the cash instead later on.

You may also be able to claim compensation if you suffer loss because of a faulty item.

Example
Terry Whitby buys a new iron. The first time he uses it to iron his shirt, it burns a hole in the fabric. Terry takes the iron back to the shop and explains that he wants his money back because there is something wrong with the iron's temperature control. The shopkeeper agrees that the iron is faulty. Terry also asks for £10 to compensate him for having to buy a new shirt.

You can't always get your money back
You are not entitled to anything if you:

- Examined the item when you bought it and should have seen the faults.
- Were told about the faults.
- Did the damage yourself.
- Changed your mind about wanting the goods (p.83).
- Got it as a present. The buyer should claim if the item turns out to be faulty although if it was bought from a major retailer you can probably take it back yourself.

Equal liability

When you buy something on credit, with the exception of charge cards (p.47), and something goes wrong, you can also make a claim against the person providing the credit. This does not apply where you have taken out a personal loan to make a purchase.

Example
Dave Andrews borrows £1500 from his bank to pay for the new carpets in his house. Holes start appearing in the carpet after two months. Dave must complain to the carpet supplier, *not* his bank.

> *Example*
> Jill Bailey buys a TV under a hire purchase agreement. The
> TV turns out to be a dud. Jill can complain to either the dealer
> she bought the TV from or the finance company with whom
> she signed the HP agreement. The finance company is entitl-
> ed to be reimbursed by the person who supplied the TV.

My shoes have fallen apart!
*'A month ago I bought a pair of quite expensive stiletto shoes from a shoe
shop in the high street. I'd only worn them twice when the left heel fell off.
I took them back to the shop but the assistant didn't believe that I'd hardly
worn them and refused to help me. What can I do?'*

Under the Sale of Goods Act 1979 you are entitled to ask for your
money back because your shoes were obviously not of merchantable quality. It is not unreasonable to expect a new pair of shoes to
last a good couple of months.

Step one: Decide what you want
Often customers are completely floored when shop assistants ask
them, 'Well, what do you want me to do?' Decide what form of
redress you want before you go into the shop. Are you after your
money back or do you want the item replaced? Once you've decided, be assertive, stick to it! (p.30)

Step two: Ask to see the manager ☺
Armed with your one and a half heeled stilettos and your receipt,
ask to see the manager. Don't be fobbed off with excuses about the
manager being at lunch/in a meeting/down with typhoid fever. If
necessary ask to see the deputy manager or make an appointment
to see the manager another time. Above all, don't get into a heated
discussion with a junior member of staff.

Step three: Make your request
'I bought these shoes a month ago. Here is my receipt. I've worn
them twice and the left heel has fallen off. These shoes are not of
merchantable quality. I want my money back/I want them exchanged for another pair.'

Speak firmly and, if there are other people in the store, quite
loudly. Don't be intimidated — you are in the right.

At this point any sensible manager would acquiesce gracefully with profuse apologies and fulfil your request. However . . .

Step four: The manager refuses

'We don't give refunds or exchanges/these shoes have been walked in/I'm terribly busy/that's nothing a bit of glue wouldn't fix.' These comments should be dismissed as either legally incorrect or just irrelevant. Keep calm.

Step five: Make your request again

If necessary word for word. However, should you feel the need to elaborate, you might add:

'Under the Sale of Goods Act 1979, you are obliged to sell me goods of merchantable quality. As you will see from my receipt I bought these shoes only a month ago and the heel has fallen off already. It is reasonable to expect that these shoes should last for a good few months. You have therefore broken your contract with me.'

You may need to go through this ritual a number of times — perhaps four or five. But if you refuse to budge from either your request or your place in the shop, you usually get your money back. Do not be bought off with an offer of a credit note or a promise to mend the shoe. Stick to your guns.

Step six: Taking it further

If you find that you're not getting anywhere with your complaint you can ask for your shoes to be sent to the Footwear Testing Centre for an independent report.

Shops that have agreed to honour the Code of Practice for Footwear (they will display a sign in the shop) will pay two-thirds of the small test charge plus postage and packing for the shoes. You will have to contribute one-third of the test charge but if your complaint is upheld your share will be refunded. The retailer must abide by the findings of the report.

If the shop is not covered by the Footwear Code, then you can still go ahead with an independent report but you will have to pay all the costs yourself. Furthermore, the retailer doesn't have to abide by the Centre's findings.

The alternative is to seek compensation in the courts (p.249). In this case, an independent report supporting your complaint would help you.

Buying goods in a sale

'I bought my hi-fi system in a sale. It had been reduced because there was a bad scratch on the lid of the record deck. When I got home and set it up, I found that the speakers weren't working properly. The shop had a notice up saying, 'No refunds or exchanges on sale goods'. Is there anything I can do?'

First of all, remember that you have exactly the same rights under the Sale of Goods Act 1979 whether you buy goods in a 'sale' or at their normal price. Secondly, displaying notices saying, 'No refunds or exchanges' is not only legally invalid, it is also a criminal offence.

However, if something is reduced because it has a defect and this is brought to your attention, you cannot claim later that it is not of merchantable quality because of that defect. So you wouldn't be able to ask for a refund because of the scratched turn-table lid but you can get your money back if the speakers are faulty.

Step one: Decide what you want

Unless you've decided that the shop is such a ropey outfit that you want nothing more to do with them, then it's worth thinking about asking for a replacement hi-fi system. The sale may be over and you may not be able to buy an equivalent system at the reduced price.

However, if you reckon you're going to have a hard time, go for a refund — you can always 'climb down' later and accept a replacement hi-fi!

Step two: Ask to see the manager ☺

You may have to set the manager straight about the illegal notices!

'I bought this hi-fi system in your sale on Tuesday. Here is my receipt. When I set the system up, I found there was a fault with the speakers and they don't work properly. I want my money back/I want an exchange.'

On the assumption that the manager refuses your request gesticulating wildly at the notice on the wall, you will need to continue... .

Step three: Keep calm, be firm

'I bought this hif-fi last Tuesday in your sale. Your assistant informed me it was reduced because of the scratch on the turntable lid. However, the speakers are faulty and therefore the system does not work properly.

'Under the Sale of Goods Act 1979 I am entitled to my money back if the goods are not of merchantable quality. It makes no difference whether I bought the goods in a sale or not. I want my money back.'

This may be the right moment to add: 'I must point out that your notice is legally invalid.'

If you have to — and only as a last resort — you could say: 'Displaying a notice like that is a criminal offence and you are liable to be prosecuted.'

Although you could succeed in getting your refund or exchange at this point you may be subjected to further attempts to lead you up the garden path. Keep to your request.

Should a barrage of misinformation about guarantees and manufacturers' warranties descend upon you read on.

Guarantees, warranties and passing the buck

'Three months ago we bought a 'Wash-Clean' washing machine from a local electrical goods shop. When it arrived we found it was slightly dented. Since that time, it's been nothing but trouble, it doesn't empty properly, it's flooded twice and the soap dispenser drawer keeps jamming.

'The 'Wash-Clean' repairers have attempted to mend the machine but evidently there's a major technical fault and they said it would be very difficult to put right. I've gone in to see the shop manager but he just says it's under guarantee and it's the manufacturer's responsibility to put it right.

'Quite honestly, we just want to be rid of the thing, but I can't exactly just dump it in his shop. What can I do?'

The problem with large domestic items like washing machines, dishwashers, fridges and the like, is that when they go wrong they usually cause a great deal of hassle. They are often expensive and bulky — not the sort of thing you can take back to the shop on a Number 17 bus.

Many shopkeepers quite genuinely believe that their obligations stop once the goods have been sold and that thereafter any problems are for the manufacturers to deal with. This is legal nonsense. Your contract is with the shop that sold it to you and it is up to the shop to put problems right.

However, if you do have a manufacturer's warranty it does provide a useful safety net. If you really think that you will have no joy with the local shopkeeper, then you may want to bypass the shop altogether and deal directly with the manufacturer. This is particularly true if, for example, a small switch goes on your fridge — it's probably much more efficient to get the manufacturer's mechanic to fix it directly.

As for the washing machine arriving with a dent, it's worth remembering that when you take delivery of goods you usually have to sign for them. Quite often the delivery or acceptance note will carry the words, 'Received in good condition'.

If you haven't got the opportunity to examine them thoroughly, then don't agree that they have arrived in one piece! Cross through the acceptance statement, sign your name and write, 'Received but not examined'.

What can you do to get shot of your non-washing washing machine?

Step one: Decide who you want to pursue

Decide if you want to continue negotiating with the shopkeeper with the aim of getting your money back or whether you want to go ahead and get the manufacturer to fix the machine. The manufacturer may well agree to replace it if mending it is very complicated and time consuming.

Step two: (a) You decide you want your money back

You will need to write to the shopkeeper.

Wash-Clean Washing Machine, Model Number 1234

I am writing to you about the above appliance which I bought from your shop on [date]. I enclose a photocopy of my receipt, number 09716.

Since the machine was delivered on [date] it has not worked properly. The water does not always empty from the drum, the machine has flooded twice and the soap dispenser drawer is jammed. Wash-Clean mechanics examined the machine on [date] and told me that there was a serious mechanical fault which would be very difficult to put right. When I visited your shop on [date] and informed you of the situation you said it was not your responsibility and that the machine should be sent back under the manufacturer's guarantee.

I entered into a contract with you under the Sale of Goods Act

1979. Under that contract the washing machine that you sold to me must be of merchantable quality. The Wash-Clean washing machine is quite clearly not of merchantable quality and therefore you are in breach of your legal obligations.

In the circumstances, I reject the goods and claim the full refund of £350 which I am entitled to. Would you please contact me immediately to make arrangements to collect the washing machine from my home. I look forward to hearing from you within fourteen days.

Step two: (b) You decide to pursue the manufacturer

You will obviously need to write ✎ or telephone ☎ the manufacturer to arrange for the machine to be repaired or collected.

You should also write to the shopkeeper to tell him what you've done and point out that you may still come back to him to claim a refund.

Use the first two paragraphs of the letter in (a) to explain the situation, then continue:

I wish to inform you that while I have decided to have the machine repaired under the manufacturer's guarantee I am formally reserving my rights to reject the washing machine under the Sale of Goods Act and to claim a full refund should the manufacturer fail to provide a satisfactory solution within a reasonable time, or if further problems arise.

Step three: (a) No refund

Should you not have had your full refund from the shopkeeper and the offending article removed, you will probably have had one of two responses. The shopkeeper will either have ignored your letter completely or he will have sent a reply saying how awfully sorry he was that you had had problems but since the machine is still under guarantee, you should take it up with the manufacturer. In either case you need to write again.

✎

Wash-Clean Washing Machine, Model Number 1234

Further to my letter of [date] (and your reply of [date]) concerning the serious faults in the above machine purchased from you on [date], I wish to remind you of your obligations under the Sale of Goods Act 1979.

The Wash-Clean washing machine is obviously not of merchantable quality and you are in breach of your contract. I am therefore rejecting the washing machine and claiming a full refund of £350. Please contact me immediately to make arrangements to collect the washing machine from my home.

If I do not hear from you within seven days I will have no alternative but to seek legal advice with a view to taking the matter further.

Step three: (b) The manufacturer can't mend it

If the manufacturer cannot repair the machine and has not offered a replacement then you have two options. You can either continue pursuing the manufacturer under the terms of the guarantee which usually means they will agree to replace the goods and in this case it should be relatively straightforward. Alternatively, you can write back to the shopkeeper demanding a refund.

Wash-Clean Washing Machine, Model Number 1234

Further to my letter of [date] concerning the serious faults in the above machine purchased from you on [date], I wish to inform you that the manufacturer has been unable to repair the machine satisfactorily.

Under the Sale of Goods Act 1979 you are obliged to sell me goods that are of merchantable quality. The Wash-Clean washing machine is obviously not of merchantable quality and you are in breach of your contract. I therefore reject the washing machine and claim a full refund of £350.

Please contact me immediately to make arrangements to collect the machine from my home. I look forward to hearing from you within fourteen days.

If this letter produces no satisfactory reply then write again, adding the bit about seeking legal advice (see above).

Step four: Taking it further

If you've checked that the shopkeeper is still in business (if he isn't then deal direct with the manufacturer) and you want your money back, then you will have to think about claiming compensation in the courts (p.249).

My mail-order deckchairs are not what I ordered!

'I ordered four deckchairs from a mail-order catalgoue. The catalogue said

they were made from red and white striped cotton canvas and I thought they'd go well with my other garden furniture. When they arrived they were really horrible. The red stripes were a washed-out pink colour and the material was nylon not cotton. They're awful; can I get my money back?'

Mail-order customers have exactly the same rights as someone buying direct from a shop. Yes, you are entitled to ask for your money back, the deckchairs clearly don't match the description given of them in the catalogue. You need to write immediately to the firm you ordered them from.

Step one: Write immediately to the catalogue company
You don't need to send the goods at this stage, particularly if they are going to take some time to pack properly. It's important that you tell the company about the problem or defect quickly. Tell them you will send the goods separately. This way you are covered if they claim that any defect occurred when you sent the goods back.

Order Number 0987
I recently ordered from you four deckchairs, catalogue number A302. I enclose a photocopy of my receipt, number 45085.

The deckchairs were described in your catalogue on page 92 as being made of red and white striped cotton canvas. When I unpacked the deckchairs I discovered that they were not made of cotton but of nylon and that the colour was not red but a faded pink.

Under the Sale of Goods Act 1979 you are obliged to sell goods which correspond with the description given in your catalogue. My four deckchairs clearly bear little resemblance to the description given and you are therefore in breach of your legal obligations.

In the circumstances I reject the goods and claim a full refund of £112 which includes: the cost of the deckchairs; your additional postage and packing charge and the cost of returning the goods to you.

I look forward to hearing from you within fourteen days.

If you anticipate problems with the company, such as they may later deny that the colour was a faded pink or it was made of nylon, then it may be worth taking a photo of the goods and getting an 'independent' witness — a neighbour or family member — to look at them before you send them back.

Step two: Send the goods back
Remember to pack the goods well and send them registered delivery.

Step three: No refund — write again
After three weeks if you still haven't heard from the company then you should write again.

Order Number 0987
Further to my letter of [date] concerning four deckchairs which I ordered from you and which did not correspond to your catalogue description, I am writing to remind you of your obligations under the Sale of Goods Act 1979. I returned the goods to you on [date], registered delivery.

Since you are in breach of your legal obligations I am claiming a full refund of £112 which includes: the cost of the deckchairs; your additional postage and packing charge and the cost of returning the goods to you.

Should I fail to receive a cheque for £112 within seven days I shall have no alternative but to seek legal advice on taking the matter further.

Step four: Taking it further
Before you consider suing the company, you could contact the MAIL ORDER TRADERS ASSOCIATION OF GREAT BRITAIN. Providing the company was a member of the association — and most of the major companies who deal through thick, glossy catalogues are — then they may be able to help you.

The newspaper ad hasn't turned up with the goods
'A couple of months ago I saw a small advertisement in my local paper for some waterproof jackets. I thought they looked good value so I ordered two, one for me and one for my son. Since then I've heard nothing. I've tried telephoning the company concerned but all I get is the unobtainable tone. It's beginning to seem very suspect. Is there anything I can do?'

Be very careful when you buy anything from newspaper advertisements. It's often worth telephoning the company beforehand if you can because that way you might get some idea of whether they are bona fide. Better still, before you send off any money check whether the magazine or newspaper in which you saw the advertisement is a member of one of the Mail Order Protection Schemes (MOPS). If they are, you may have some redress if anything goes wrong.

Step one: **Find out what has happened to your money**
If you paid by cheque find out whether it's been cashed. If it hasn't, telephone your bank and stop the cheque. If it has been cashed you need to take some action.

Step two: **Write to the newspaper advertising manager**
It's the advertising manager's job to investigate complaints of this kind.

Advertisement placed by Huff & Puff & Sons of
21, Wet Drive, Rainham for Waterproof Jackets

I am writing to you to regarding the above advertisement which appeared in your paper on [date].

I ordered two blue waterproof jackets, one medium size and one large size from Huff & Puff on [date]. I sent off a cheque for £38 which I understand from my bank has been cashed. I am most concerned that I have heard nothing from the company for the last six weeks. I tried to telephone the number given in the advertisement but it was unobtainable. Directory Enquiries could not trace the company. Please would you investigate my complaint and establish whether the company has ceased trading.

As I may wish to make a claim under the Mail Order Protection Scheme, I would be extremely if you could deal with this as a matter of urgency

I look forward to hearing from you.

Step three: **(a) The company is still trading**
You should consider drafting a letter of complaint to the company asking for the goods to be delivered within a certain time or you will ask for your money back.

Step three: (b) The company has gone out of business

Newspapers operating under a Mail Order Protection Scheme (MOPS) usually carry details about how to claim. The important thing is to get your claim in on time — within three months of the advertisement appearing in a newspaper and within two months if the advertisement was placed in a magazine.

Step four: Taking it further

If for some reason you cannot claim under MOPS you could contact the ADVERTISING STANDARDS AUTHORITY who may be able to help you.

I've changed my mind — Can I have my money back?

'I went on a bit of a spending spree last Saturday and I bought a dress which I now regret buying. It doesn't really suit me and the colour is wrong. I took it back to the shop first thing on Monday morning and asked for my money back. The price tag is still on the dress but the assistant would only give me a credit note. Can she do that?'

Legally, the shop assistant doesn't have to offer you anything; she has not broken her side of the contract in any way. The offer of a credit note is purely in the interests of good customer relations.

It's worth asking before you buy something from a retailer, particularly if it's a present for someone else, if you can have a refund or an exchange if the goods aren't suitable. Don't be surprised if the shopkeeper only offers you an exchange or a credit note.

There's a fly in my semolina!

'I'm a pensioner and my eyesight isn't very good. Last weekend I opened a packet of semolina I'd bought from my corner shop. I made the semolina in the usual way and started eating it. Suddenly I realized that there were these black insects floating in the mixture. I looked in the packet and it was full of black bits. I felt really ill and I've had to go to my doctor. There must be someone I can complain to.'

It's a horrible sensation when you realize that there was something very unsavoury about the food you've just swallowed. But you really do need to act quickly if you suspect that your meal or ingredients are tainted in some way.

Criminal law requires that food and drink, wherever it is sold or manufactured must conform to certain standards. Newspapers often carry stories about the disgusting things found in food and major retailers and manufacturers are usually terrified of such incidents finding their way into the media.

Step one: Getting the evidence

If you have been made ill by food which you suspect is off or has been tainted in some way, then visit your doctor. It is worth putting your illness on record, particularly if you intend to seek compensation. You must also keep, if you can, the food itself or at the very least, the packet or packaging it came in.

Step two: Decide what you want to do

You have a number of options. You can take the offending item back to the shop where you can complain and ask for a refund or a replacement. Or you can pursue either the manufacturer or, in the case of one of the major food stores, the company itself. It depends on how serious you think the problem is — how badly you have been affected or whether there is a major health risk to other people.

If you think your complaint is very serious and you intend to seek compensation, consider where you would be most successful claiming.

Step three: Contact your Environmental Health Officer

Whatever you decide to do, you should contact your Environmental Health Officer (EHO) whose duty it is to see that health and safety regulations are met. The EHO can be particularly helpful if the shopkeeper refuses to acknowledge your complaint.

Telephone your local town hall or council offices and ask to speak to the Environmental Health Officer (EHO). You may find the EHO difficult to get hold of, so find out their name and write to them if necessary.

Grotty Grocers, 5 The High Street,
Eatham and Yum Yum Semolina

Three weeks ago I bought a 250g packet of Yum Yum Semolina from Grotty Grocers which I believe to be contaminated and unfit for human consumption.

Last weekend I opened the packet and made myself some semolina in the usual way. Only after I started eating it did I realize that there were black insects in the mixture. I checked the contents remaining in the packet and found they were full of black bits. I felt extremely ill and have since visited my doctor.

I am very anxious to establish how the packet of semolina became contaminated and am concerned that this particular product constitutes a health risk. I have kept the remainder of the packet.

In view of the serious nature of my complaint I would be most grateful if you would investigate the situation.

I look forward to hearing from you shortly.

Environmental Health Officers are often very helpful but frequently overloaded with work, so be patient but be persistent. When the EHO does investigate your complaint and finds the shop or manufacturer to be at fault then he or she may well prosecute them. This would help with any claim you might have for compensation.

Step four: Write to the manufacturer

Yum Yum Semolina

I am writing to you concerning a packet of Yum Yum Semolina (250g) purchased from Grotty Grocers, 5, High Street, Eatham, which I believe to be contaminated and unfit for human consumption.

Last weekend I opened the packet of Yum Yum Semolina which I had bought some three weeks previously. The sell-by date on the label is February 2003. I made the semolina in the usual way. I am a pensioner and my eyesight is not particularly good, consequently it was not until I began to eat the semolina that I realized it contained some black insects. I checked the remaining semolina in the packet and it was full of black bits. I felt extremely ill as a result of eating the Yum Yum Semolina and I have had to visit my doctor. I have since contacted the Environmental Health Officer regarding the incident.

I am very concerned that this particular product constitutes a serious health risk. The whole incident has caused me much distress and discomfort and I intend to seek redress from you, the manufacturers of Yum Yum Semolina.

I await your comments with interest and look forward to hearing from you shortly.

Step five: The manufacturer's reply

There is of course a chance that they don't reply, in which case write again. If they do write back, and few self-respecting manufacturers would fail to reply, they will probably either simply acknowledge your letter saying how they regret the incident and leave it at that, or they will offer you some kind of compensation. If they do the latter, then you will have to decide if it is sufficient and reply accordingly. If they offer no compensation you will need to write back and claim an exact amount. You might want to take some legal advice about this.

What else?

If you're in a **restaurant** and you have cause to complain either about the food or service, do so immediately. Be assertive (p.30).

Complain initially to the waiter and if necessary ask to see the manager or whoever else is in charge.

If your complaint is about the quality of the food, most restaurants, cafes, etc. will usually replace your order to avoid any unpleasantness. If you think that the food is unfit for human consumption or that the preparation conditions are unhygienic contact your local Environmental Health Officer ◄.

If you cannot resolve the matter satisfactorily you could deduct what you think is a reasonable amount from the bill. Leave a note saying why you are making the deduction together with your name and address. If you do pay up but think you may want to make a claim later, make it clear that you're doing so 'without prejudice to my legal rights'.

Buying a second-hand car — How not to get taken for a ride

'I want to buy a car but I'm not sure I can afford a new one. That means buying something second-hand. Used cars seems to be a right cowboy business. I'm a complete novice when it comes to cars — how can I avoid being taken for a ride?'

Like anything else, look around first, search out someone reliable and you're less likely to get caught out.

If you want to buy a car second-hand you have a number of choices. You can buy it:

- Through a used car dealer.
- Privately through friends or advertisements.
- At auction.

Understanding the pros and cons of each method will probably narrow the field. If you know nothing about cars, then take along someone who does!

Step one: Decide how much you want to spend and what sort of car you want

If you don't set yourself a tight budget you risk spending far more than you can actually manage. Remember that car buying doesn't stop with the body and engine — it's an ongoing expense.

Fix a total budget that includes:

- The car itself.
- Any necessary immediate repair work.
- Insurance.
- Tax.
- MOT (if necessary).

Also consider the car's running costs and the expense of maintaining it — such as the cost of spare parts and servicing. What seems like a cheap car today might turn into a very expensive pile of rusting metal within a short time.

Think about what you need your car for. Do you do a lot of driving or do you intend to take it abroad? If so an ancient car, difficult to service on the Continent, might not be the best idea!

Step two: Consider your options

Option One: buying through a used car dealer

If you buy through a dealer, he or she is bound by the Sale of Goods Act 1979. Regardless of whether the car is new or a complete 'old banger' it must be of 'merchantable quality'. In addition it must be 'as described' and 'fit for the purpose' (p.70).

Sellers cannot use small print in their contracts or advertisements to avoid these legal obligations. However, if the dealer points out a specific fault to you and you go ahead with the sale you cannot later demand a refund because of that particular fault.

- Check that the dealer is a member of a recognized trade association such as the MOTOR AGENTS ASSOCIATION. These associations have agreed to adhere to a standard code of practice which means greater reassurance and benefits over and above your legal rights. Trade associations (p.23) can often help you to resolve a dispute with one of their members.

- Find out how long the dealer has been in the business — the longer the better.
- Get all the important facts about the car in writing — the price, condition, mileage.
- Some dealers offer special warranties. Read them carefully to see what they really cover.

Option two: Buying privately

If you buy from a private individual be very careful, as you have fewer rights than if you buy from a dealer. The law simply says that the vehicle must be 'as described'. Your rights will depend very much on what the seller tells you about the condition and value of the car.

- Make sure that the car is not the subject of a hire purchase or similar agreement. If you buy a car where the previous owner has defaulted on the loan repayments, you may find yourself liable for any outstanding money that is owed. You can check this out by contacting Hire Purchase Information plc, but you must do this through your local CAB — there's no charge for the service.
- The vehicle registration document is not proof of ownership. If you have any suspicions about whether the seller either owns the vehicle or has the legal right to sell it, then *don't* buy it.
- Take along someone to witness what the seller says. These statements, like any written descriptions, must be true. Make a note of what is said.
- If you think that your 'private seller' is in fact a dealer trading from home, contact your local Trading Standards Officer immediately. They may well prosecute. Dealers use this trick to make you think that you have less rights than if you were buying from an established business. If your car turns out to be faulty and you can show that the person isn't selling privately, you can make a claim just as if the dealer had been operating openly.

Option three: Buying at auction

If you are a novice at cars and car buying, auctions are probably best avoided. You do not always have the same legal rights as when you buy direct from a garage or dealer.

Some auctions are run in a pretty unscrupulous way with organized bidding rings pushing the prices up for the unsuspecting customer. In addition you have very little chance to inspect the vehicles thoroughly or give them a test drive.

If you want to go to an auction:

- Visit some auctions first and see them in action.
- Read any notices and the auctioneer's terms and conditions carefully. If you are in any doubt as to their meaning take a copy along to your local CAB or advice centre.

Step three: Checking out the car

It's in your best interest to check out any prospective purchase thoroughly. Don't ignore small chips and scratches — it'll be very difficult to come back later and complain. The seller will probably tell you that you must have done them youself.

Remember, if you are buying a second-hand car, you can usually bargain over the price if you find faults with the vehicle.

- Always see the vehicle in daylight or in a very well-lit garage or forecourt.
- Make sure you can inspect every part of the vehicle. People have been known to buy cars from the middle of a parking lot, only to discover later that one door was sprayed a different shade from the rest.
- Take someone with you, even if they are not an expert. Another pair of eyes is always useful.
- Get an expert opinion. Both the RAC and AA run car-inspection schemes. They will be able to tell you whether the car is roadworthy and any faults it might have.
- Get a copy of *Glass's Guide* or one of the other car price guides and find out what sort of sum you should expect to pay for the make, model and year that you're offered.
- Look immediately at the mileage on the clock. You can expect an average mileage of 10–12,000 a year. If you are offered a car that's done 20,000 miles in a year, the owner may well have been a rep and the car is likely to have been driven very hard — so avoid it.

  Watch out for 'clocking', which is where the mileometer is turned back or the speedometer has been disconnected in the past. If you are offered a low mileage car which looks suspect

The Assertive Consumer

check the tyres to see if any have been replaced, also look for wear and tear around the pedals, steering wheel, carpet, driver's seat, etc.

   Ask to see the log book. A six-year-old-car with 12,000 on the clock and four owners sounds very suspicious.

- Test drive the car. Never buy without trying! Listen out for a quiet engine and brakes which don't pull to one side. Is the car stable when cornering? If you're not happy about the way a car drives, there could well be something expensive wrong with it, not to mention dangerous. Get someone to drive behind you and check for blue smoke when the car accelerates — it could mean a case of rebuilding the engine.

- Try out all the electrics, lights, wipers, etc. Don't forget the rear windscreen heater, even on a hot summer's day. Breathe on it to make condensation. Also check to see if the radio or stereo actually works. Make sure that the sunroof really opens, it doesn't matter if it's raining!

- Look over the outside of the car. Check the tyres and the paintwork. Try to spot any retouching or respraying. Tell-tale paint on the rubber surrounds of the windows or mudflaps will indicate respraying. Check every nook and cranny for rust. Look under the car for leaking oil — you don't want to see any!

- Look right inside the boot. Pull up any carpet. You may be able to spot repair work.

- Don't be taken in by appearance. However, as a general rule you can usually tell cars 'with one careful' owner. Look for tears in the fabric, scratches, burn marks, etc.

- If you're buying a relatively new car, ask to see the service history. Obviously a car that has been regularly serviced by a reputable garage is less likely to be a dud buy.

- If the car comes with an MOT certificate, it does not necessarily guarantee that the vehicle is roadworthy.

Step four: Settling up

The seller will probably want you to pay by building society cheque, banker's draft or cash. *Always* ensure that you get a receipt for your money.

   In addition you should make sure that you have all the other necessary documents: log book; MOT certificate; car handbook and any written description about the vehicle.

   In fact, you could consider writing out a short letter to confirm the details of any remarks the seller has made about the condition of the car.

/

> This is to confirm that you have agreed to sell me your/the [car make and model], registration number [...] for the sum of £... .
>
> You have stated that the car has ... miles on the clock at the time of this sale and that it is in very good/average/below-average condition. You have told me that the car is ... years old and is roadworthy. I further understand from you that the car has not been involved in any accidents requiring major repair.
>
> Signed [buyer]
> Signed [seller]

Obviously you would modify this letter according to what you had been told.

Finally, before you take the car on the road — make sure it's taxed and insured (p.126).

What else?

If you're buying a **motorbike** you will need to follow much the same procedure as if you were buying a car.

Don't forget to include things such as a helmet and protective clothing when you calculate the cost of putting the bike (and its rider) on the road.

If you're a new rider, training is essential. Your dealer might be able to tell you about local schemes or you could contact one of the following for information: the NATIONAL MOTORCYCLE STAR RIDER TRAINING SCHEME; BRITISH MOTORCYCLISTS FEDERATION RIDER TRAINING SCHEME; RoSPA MOTORCYCLE TRAINING SCHEME.

Services — Getting things done

Plumbers, hairdressers, upholsterers, car mechanics and tour operators all provide services.

Sometimes the contract doesn't involve the sale of any goods. Dry cleaners, for example, usually only provide a service, they don't sell you anything. Other contracts include both a service and the supply of goods, for example a plumber installing a new central heating system.

The **Supply of Goods and Services Act 1982** protects you when you make a contract for a **pure service**, e.g. dry cleaning a jacket, or a contract for both work and materials, e.g. having a car repaired. The obligations on the trader to supply goods of **merchantable quality, as described** and **fit for the purpose** are the same as under the Sale of Goods Act 1979 (p.70).

Unless you and the trader have agreed otherwise the service must be carried out **with reasonable care and skill** and **within a reasonable time**.

Anyone supplying a service is also bound by the **Trade Descriptions Act 1968**. This makes it a criminal offence for a trader to say or write something which isn't true about the goods or services they are selling. The local Trading Standards Officer enforces this Act and should be notified immediately if you think a trader is guilty of making a false statement.

Exclusion clauses

You will often see notices or terms in contracts which attempt to exclude or limit liability for certain things such as loss, damage, injury, breach of contract and so on. There are known as **exemption** or **exclusion** clauses.

For example, you go to a party in a hotel and leave your coat in the cloakroom. On the wall is a notice stating: *The Management will not accept any responsibility for loss, damage or theft of a guest's property, howsoever caused*.

Unless the individual or organization who put up the exclusion notice can prove that it is fair and reasonable in all circumstances, then under the **Unfair Contract Terms Act 1977** it has no legal effect. So, if you handed your coat over to the cloakroom attendant only to return some hours later to find it had been stolen, you might be able to claim compensation from the hotel despite the notice.

The Act also ensures that notices which attempt to exclude liability for death or injury arising from negligence by the person supplying the service have no legal effect. You could proceed to make a claim as if the notice never existed.

Quotes and estimates

If you are shopping around for a tradesperson, watch out for the difference between an estimate and a quote.

If you can, get a firm quote (or **quotation**) — in writing, of course! Once you've been given a quote, the individual or company concerned cannot charge you a penny more for their services unless you agree.

Example
You ask an upholsterer to re-cover your three-piece suite. He quotes you a figure of £350 to include the work and the fabric. When he delivers your furniture he tells you the bill is now £400 because he'd under-estimated the cost of the material. The loss is his. You need only pay him the £350 you *agreed* to.

However, if the quoted price turns out to be excessive or unreasonable, you will have to pay it once you've agreed to it. So do your homework first!

If you are given an **estimate**, i.e. someone tells you, 'I don't know exactly how much the job will be, but it should be around £50,' then you can expect the final figure to vary to some degree. The question is, by how much? There are no hard and fast rules. The law simply states that the variation must be *reasonable*.

In the same way, if you've got neither a quote nor an estimate, perhaps because you've called out someone in an emergency, you don't have to pay the final price if you think it's excessive. Again, the cost must be reasonable.

If you're unsure whether you've been given a quote or an estimate — then ask!

If you think you are being charged too much — challenge the final bill. ➤

My central heating's cost a bomb

'Right on the coldest day of the year our boiler packed up. I immediately contacted some local central heating contractors to come and tell us what it would cost to install a new one. This guy came round and looked at our system and said it would cost about £400 to put in a new boiler including the labour charges. I asked him to put it in writing which he did. He estimated that the work would be about £400 but couldn't give a final figure because he didn't know the full extent of what was involved.

'Anyhow we went ahead and had the job done. When we got the final bill we were somewhat shocked to see it was for £845. I queried the increase with the engineer but he said that was the cost of the work he did. He only had to see to a bit of extra pipework, I can't believe it could have cost that much. Do I have to pay him the whole £845?'

Disputes of this kind over bills, where the customer is asked to pay more than they expected, are very common.

You were absolutely right to ask the central heating contractor to give you written estimate of the cost of the work. Always insist you get a *written* statement detailing not only the cost, but the work involved, the time it will take and any special requirements — like furniture to be moved.

Step one: Write immediately to the contractor

Don't simply ignore the bill in the hope it will decrease of its own accord. It won't. Inform the heating contractor that you think his bill is unreasonable and that you will be taking steps to find out what is a reasonable price.

Boiler installation at [address] on [date]

I am writing to inform you that I consider your bill of £845 for the above work to be unreasonable.

Your original estimate was for £400 (see enclosed photocopy).

Whilst I accept that there was a small amount of additional pipework, I do not think that it justifies an additional £445.

I shall be taking steps to establish what is a reasonable price to pay for the work you have completed.

Step two: Search around for a 'reasonable' price

The problem is that it can be very difficult to get another estimate. Tradespeople might be reluctant to pay you a visit if they know that you just want to check out their prices. Obviously in some situations you might be able to get the information over the phone without actually saying that you've already had the work done.

If you can, ask your family, friends and neighbours if they know of a friendly plumber who might be able to give you an idea of what they would have charged for the work. Alternatively you can contact the appropriate trade association (p.23) to see if they can help.

Step three: Offer to settle the bill

Once you've got a good idea of what you should have paid, write again to the central heating contractor. Of course he may have already replied to your first letter and reduced the bill.

Boiler installation at [address] on [date]

Further to my letter of [date] in which I informed you that I considered your bill of £845 for the above work to be unreasonable, I have taken steps to determine what is a reasonable price to pay.

I am now enclosing a cheque for £475 in full and final settlement of your bill.

Step three: Taking it further

If the contractor does come back to you refusing your offer of settlement you should always find out immediately whether or not he has cashed your cheque. If he has, you should tell him that you consider the matter ended.

Boiler installation at [address] on [date]

Further to my letter of [date] and your reply/telephone call/visit of [date] I understand that you are unwilling to accept the £475 which I offered in full and final settlement of my bill.

However, my bank informs me that you have cashed my cheque to you for £475 and therefore have already accepted my final payment. I consider the matter to be now closed.

If all else fails and you still refuse to pay the bill, legal action may be taken against you. It will then be up to the court to decide what is 'reasonable'.

Getting the job done on time

The rules for getting a job done by a specific date are very similar to those governing prices. Basically, if the trader or mechanic has agreed to complete the work by a certain time, they will have broken their contract if they fail to meet that deadline.

If no time is agreed then the work must be carried out within a 'reasonable' time. Obviously what is reasonable will vary from situation to situation. You would expect it to take longer to repair the bodywork on a smashed-up car than to balance the wheels.

If the trader agrees to supply something by a certain *agreed* date and fails to do so, you would be quite within your rights to cancel your contract and obtain the goods or services elsewhere.

You would then charge the original trader for any extra costs you incur. Alternatively, you can continue with your original contract but charge the trader for any additional expense and inconvenience you have been put to.

To protect yourself, you need to make **time of the essence**. These four words are vital if you want to get a job done on time and give yourself the opportunity to cancel or take other measures if it isn't.

Example 1
Daisy Morris asks Madame Foufou to make her a wedding dress. Daisy makes time of the essence and the dressmaker agrees to have it ready by the 24th, the day before the marriage. On the 23rd, Daisy telephones Madame Foufou only to be told by her assistant that Madame has gone to Paris for the week and won't be back until after the wedding. Daisy panics and rushes off to buy a similar ready-made dress which costs her twice as much. Daisy is then entitled to claim the cost of her new dress, plus compensation for all the upset, from Madame Foufou.

If for some reason you don't give a specific date when you make a contract, you can still make time of the essence if the garage or other tradesperson seems to be spending a very long time getting the job done. However, you must give them reasonable time, from when you write your letter, to complete the work.

Example 2

Rob Campbell takes his car into a body repair shop to have the bonnet resprayed. He's told that the job will take a week. Ten days later the repair shop tells him it'll be another week before the spraying is finished. Rob is suspicious that they still won't get the job done in the extra time so he writes to the repair shop. He tells them that he's making 'time of the essence' and that unless he gets his car back within five days he will consider that they have broken their contract and will get the work done elsewhere and charge them for any extra costs he incurs.

My car needs servicing but without it I can't go on holiday!

'My car needs servicing very badly but I'm off on a touring holiday in a fortnight's time. I'm worried that if I put my car into the garage, they won't have it ready for me by the time I go on holiday. If I don't have the car, I can't go away. The garage are very thorough but they can also be very slow. How can I guarantee that they'll have it done?'

You can't guarantee that they'll get the service done in time, but you can protect yourself against ruining your holiday if they don't.

Step one: Make 'time of the essence'

You can either tell the car mechanic or, better still, put it in writing:

Time is of the essence. I need the car for my holiday which starts on [date]. Therefore I want the car back by [date/time] at the latest.

Make sure that the mechanic agrees to this. They should sign a photocopy of your letter or put the details on the service form.

You should always make clear what the consequences will be if they don't get the job done.

If you fail to get my car back to me by the specified date, I will have to hire another car and will charge the hire costs to you.

Step two: If the garage fails to meet the deadline

If you've made 'time of the essence' it's always worth contacting the garage once or twice during the service to see how they're doing and remind them of your deadline and the consequences if they fail to meet it.

If they look as if they're not going to finish on time, ask them what they're going to do about it, given that they have agreed a completion date. Most reputable garages and dealers will usually be able to provide you with another car. Obviously don't accept one that you think isn't up to the holiday journey.

If they cannot offer you another car and they won't finish the job even by working through the night, then investigate hiring another vehicle. You would be able to charge the hire costs to your garage.

Step three: Settling up

The garage may agree quite amicably to pay your hire charges or to waive your bill for the service if it comes to the same amount or more.

If the garage won't settle up, you can offset their service bill against your car hire bill. However, in many respects, the garage has the upper hand. They do not have to hand over your car until you have paid their bill. Consider whether you can afford to be without your car. Whatever you do, *don't* continue to hire a car. You won't be able to claim those costs, simply because you are disputing the garage's bill.

Write to the owner of the garage.

Service of [vehicle make and registration]

I am writing to you about your recent service of my vehicle and your failure to complete the service by the agreed date.

I bought my car into you on [date] and gave your mechanic [name] a letter in which I explained that I needed my car back for my holiday, making time of the essence. I also said that if the car was not completed by the specified date, I would have to hire another vehicle and would charge those hire costs to you.

Your mechanic signed a copy of the letter and I enclose a photocopy for your information.

The day before the service was due to be completed, the mechanic told me that it would be at least another three days before he would be finished. I reminded him once again that I had made time of the essence and of the consequences if the job was not done. He replied that there was nothing he could do. The following day, having again checked whether the car was ready, I made arrangements to hire a similar model for the length of my holiday.

The cost of hiring the car including insurance is £240. I note that your bill to me is £260. To save any further unnecessary inconvenience to either party, I am willing to set your bill off against mine and simply to pay you the outstanding £20.

Would you please notify me within the next forty-eight hours whether this is acceptable.

You could enclose a cheque for £20 and see if the garage owner banks it. That would indicate that he's accepted your offer (p.95).

You could always write a further letter to them, including this paragraph as a last resort.

✐

If I do not receive a satisfactory answer from you I will begin proceedings in the County court to recover the money from you without further notice.

If you want someone to contact you quickly, remember to put your telephone number(s) and the time you can be contacted.

Step four: Taking it further
If the garage fails to reply or to give you a satisfactory answer and you want to sue them for the money, pay your bill immediately and get your car. You don't want them issuing a counter-claim against you for your unpaid bill (p.256, 260, 262).

Shoddy work — Getting it put right
'I've just had my flat redecorated. It all looked very nice to start with, but last weekend the ceiling wallpaper in the hall began to fall off in great big lumps. A friend who's quite a DIY fanatic had a look at it. She said that the decorator obviously hadn't put the wallpaper up properly and hadn't

used the correct paste. I've already paid three-quarters of the money I owed the decorator, but haven't made the final payment yet. What should I do?'

If you engage a decorator or any other tradesperson they are required to carry out their work with **reasonable skill and care**. If they don't, they have broken their contract with you.

If they do make a mess of what they're doing, it's worthwhile giving them the opportunity to put the job right. However, you may not want them back inside your home — or they may decline to come!

Step one: Contact the decorator

Don't assume the worst. He may be extremely embarrassed at what has happened and only too pleased to put it right before the word gets out.

Be assertive if you have to talk to him face to face. In addition:

- Hold on to any outstanding money you owe him. Say that you're quite willing to pay him in full once the job has been properly completed.
- Don't be put off by arguments such as, 'It wasn't my fault, it's the state of the walls,' or, 'It's all to do with the wallpaper you chose.' You have employed a professional and they have a duty to draw your attention to any problems that might arise whilst they do their work. If they tell you that the wallpaper will fall off unless the wall is treated with fungicide first, and you decide to ignore their warning, then you must take the consequences.
- Don't agree to pay for any additional materials needed because the work has got to be done again. If the decorator failed to take reasonable skill and care to put up the paper in the first place he must pay for the replacement paper, paste and paint.

It might also be worth pointing out that you will have second thoughts about recommending him, if this is the standard of his work!

Step two: Write to the decorator

If the decorator refuses to put the work right make your request again in writing.

Before you do so, find out from another couple of decorators how much it would cost to re-do the ceiling and also why, in their opinion, the paper fell off in the first place.

/

<u>Decoration of [address]</u>

Following our conversation on [date] when I told you that the ceiling wallpaper, which you put up in my hall, was falling off, I am writing once again to ask you to make good your faulty workmanship.

If I do not receive a satisfactory answer from you within the next five days, I will have no alternative but to employ another decorator to redecorate the ceiling.

As you are aware I still owe you £250; this is the balance for the work you have done for me. If you are not prepared to carry out your work to a reasonable standard and to redecorate my hall ceiling, I will deduct £80, which is the cost of employing another decorator to do the work, from your final bill.

If any other part of the work you carried out for me proves to be faulty and you refuse to put it right, I shall have no hesitation in having the work completed by another decorator and making a claim against you in the County court.

Step three: Taking it further

If your letter produces no results you could consider taking the matter up with the appropriate trade association (p.23). However, if your decorator is not a member of the association, they are unlikely to be able to help you.

Generally, if you do encounter problems such as this with a tradesperson and they refuse to put their work right, get a series of quotes from other skilled people who can re-do the work for you. Have the job completed and then write to your original decorator, plumber or whoever and claim the extra amount you have had to pay out to get their shoddy work put right.

If they fail to pay up, consider suing them in the County court (p.249). Before you actually start proceedings, it may be worth writing one final letter.

/

<u>Decoration of [address]</u>

I am writing to you further to my letters of [dates] regarding the decoration of my flat.

As you are aware, the wallpaper that you put up has fallen off the walls and ceiling and all the surfaces that you painted have now flaked. I consider that you failed to carry out your work with reasonable skill and care. You subsequently refused to put right your faulty workmanship.

As a result, I had to employ another decorator to repaper my living room and bedroom. I understand from other professional decorators that the reason that the wallpaper fell off and the paint flaked was that you failed to prepare the surfaces properly or to use the appropriate materials.

I am now claiming £475 from you which is the cost of the new materials and labour charges for redecorating my living room and bedroom to a reasonable standard.

Unless I receive £475 from you within the next seven days, I shall commence proceedings against you in the County court without further notice.

Give me a wig — My hairdresser's ruined my hair!

'I went to a new hairdresser yesterday to have blonde highlights put in. I explained exactly what I wanted and the stylist seemed to be quite competent. She started putting the colour on to my hair and I thought it looked a bit reddish but I didn't like to say anything. Anyway, when she'd finished and blow-dried my hair it looked really red. I think I look awful but I was too embarrassed to say anything. I feel like walking around with a wig on. What can I do?'

Many people have a love–hate relationship with their hairdresser. It's often difficult to be confident with someone wielding scissors and chemicals over your wet tresses. However, since you cannot walk away from the bungled results of an incompetent hairdresser you do need to practise being assertive (p.30).

Explain carefully what sort of style or colour you want. If you definitely don't want to emerge looking like Princess Di or Sid Vicious then say so. And if you are not convinced of the hairdresser's ability to do the job then leave the salon, even if it means asking them to dry your newly washed hair. Remember you are the client, not some torture victim — you've every right to get up and go.

If you are concerned that you've been left drowning in perming lotion for far too long, then say so — your hairdresser may have forgotten to set the timer. And if during any part of the treatment you find your scalp itching, blood dripping from your earlobes or your hair on fire, tell them — loudly.

Finally, if something drastic does go wrong at the hairdresser's (it is not unknown for someone to lose all their hair through a bad perm), then you may need to seek legal help in order to sue the hairdresser for negligence and claim compensation (p.133). Good hairdressers are usually insured in case of accidents.

If you do think your hairdresser has left you looking like a freak — go straight back.

Step one: Decide what you want done

If you've gone to a reputable hairdresser and something has gone wrong it's worth going back and giving them the opportunity to put it right. Sometimes it's not possible to remedy that particular treatment but you could accept a reduced price or free treatment next time you go. If you really don't trust the hairdresser concerned ask for your money to be refunded.

If you think that it may take time to settle any dispute, then have a passport photo taken to prove just how bad your hair looks! If the texture or colour of your hair has been affected also cut off one of your locks and keep it as evidence.

Step two: Visit the hairdresser

Go back to the hairdresser immediately and ask to see the manager. Explain what the problem is and tell them what you want them to do. 😊

'Yesterday, I came into the salon to have blonde highlights put in my hair. I explained to Jenny, your stylist, exactly what I wanted done and we went through the colour cards together. She gave every indication that she was capable of colouring my hair the way I wanted it done.

'However, as you can see, my hair is not highlighted blonde but red. It is not what I asked for and I don't like it. Unless you can successfully re-highlight my hair with blonde tints I want my money back.'

This won't necessarily be very easy to do. You are, after all, discussing a part of your body, your appearance and all that that entails. However, try to think of it as taking your three-piece suite back to the upholsterer's. Don't be put off by various hairdressers telling you that red highlights make you look thoroughly gorgeous — stick to your request.

Step three: Why didn't you say so at the time?

This is quite a reasonable comment on the part of the hairdresser.

You should have said something before you left the salon. But don't be thrown off course.

You could be bold and say:

'Yes, perhaps I should have said something yesterday but I was very embarrassed. Your stylist appeared to know what she was doing and I didn't want to contradict her. However, as you can see my highlights are red and not blonde. If you cannot put them right successfully then I would like my money back.'

Or you could save face:

'I wasn't very happy about the colour yesterday but your stylist seemed to know what she was doing. I thought perhaps it was just the light in here. However, when I got home, I realized these highlights were red and not blonde. They are not the colour we agreed to, I want them put right.'

Step four: Taking it further

Good hairdressers don't like dissatisfied customers — it's bad for business and the word gets around fast. Usually they will attempt to put things right but be prepared to spend an hour in front of the mirror with a grudging and possibly equally embarrassed stylist — no one likes to put their mistakes right.

Unless they have caused you complete trauma, you may just have to let it all grow out — and go elsewhere next time.

If they have caused you any serious harm and you want to claim compensation (p.133), seek advice from a CAB or solicitor.

What else?

If you have a complaint against a **beauty salon** or anyone else offering similar treatments, follow the same course of action.

If you are embarking on any kind of beauty treatment do make sure that the 'beautician' is properly qualified. Reliable practitioners will display their certificates. Read them. Check that they're from a recognized institution rather than a cosmetic manufacturer!

Always find out if there are any side-effects to the treatments. Tell the beautician if you have any particular allergies or medical condition.

Check around the premises — are they hygienic? Are there sensible warnings about sun-bed treatments, etc?

The dry cleaners spoilt my expensive suit

'Last week I took an expensive wool suit to the dry cleaners. There was a small stain on the lapel and the woman I spoke to said there would be no problem in removing it. When I went to collect my suit I was horrified to find a large white patch where the stain had been. I complained to the manager and they promised to dry clean the suit again but it's made no difference. The label in the suit says 'Dry Clean Only' but the cleaners claim they're not responsible. I'm really angry — the suit's ruined. What can I do?'

Dry cleaners, like anyone else offering a service, must carry out that service with **reasonable care and skill**. If they don't, you have every reason to complain and seek some remedy.

If you are using dry cleaners or launderers you can help yourself by using a business that's a member of the ASSOCIATION OF BRITISH LAUNDRY, CLEANING AND RENTAL SERVICES LTD, or ABLC, as they are commonly known. ABLC members have agreed to adhere to an established code of practice and if disputes do arise, the association will help to sort them out.

When you use a dry cleaners or launderers do point out to the manager or assistant if the garment is particularly delicate or valuable. Ask whether buttons or other trimmings need to be removed. Check with them that they feel confident about cleaning it. You could save yourself a lot of bother later on.

Step one: Visit the shop or write to the manager

<u>Damaged wool suit</u>

I am writing to complain about the damage you have done to my suit which I brought into your shop on [date] to be dry cleaned. I enclose a photocopy of my receipt.

I first brought my suit to you for dry cleaning on [date]. I explained that the suit, a navy wool, double-breasted jacket and straight skirt, had a small stain on the lapel. Your assistant assured me that there would be no problem in removing the stain.

When I returned to your shop to collect the suit on [date], I was horrified to see that where the stain had been there was now a large white patch. You dry cleaned the suit again but it made no difference. The suit is now unwearable.

Under the Supply of Goods and Services Act 1982 you made a contract with me to dry clean my suit with reasonable care and skill. Since you have obviously not done so, you are in breach of your contract.

The suite was ruined through your negligence in the dry cleaning process. I therefore claim from you £140, the cost of replacing the suit.

Unless I receive a cheque from you within the next seven days, I will seek further legal advice with a view to beginning proceedings against you in the County court.

You might find that you can communicate this face to face 😊 with the manager without resorting to threats about court action. He might be more accommodating when you outline his legal obligations. Follow up any conversation with a letter (complete with County court threats if necessary).

You may find difficulty in claiming the entire cost of replacing the suit. It would be reasonable to argue that there should be some deduction for wear and tear. In addition it would also be fair to point out that you can still wear the skirt. (You could counter-argue that you can't replace the jacket without replacing the skirt too.)

Step two: Contact ABLC
If the dry cleaner is a member of ABLC approach them to see if their Customer Advisory Service can help. You will be asked to give them written details of your complaint. If they think it is appropriate they may send the garment for independent testing. You will be asked to pay the test fee in advance but may get some or all of it returned, depending on the findings.

Step three: Taking it further
If the dry cleaner refuses to acknowledge your claim or to make a satisfactory offer of settlement and the ABLC can't help you, you could take your case to court (p.249).

What else?
Complaints against **launderettes** can be more difficult to deal with. There is no regulatory body or trade association for launderettes, although the NATIONAL ASSOCIATION OF THE LAUNDERETTE INDUSTRY does offer some advice.

If you are concerned about safety or hygiene in your local

launderette, notify your Environmental Health Officer. Alternatively, if your complaint is serious you could take the matter to court. Launderettes, like all traders, should display a notice detailing the name and address of the owner.

Avoiding travel bugs

'My colleague and his wife have just returned from a package holiday in Spain. By all accounts they had a pretty lousy time — the hotel was still a bit of a building site, the pool was half finished, the food awful and to cap it all — it rained most days! I'm just about to book our annual family holiday and this year we'd like to go abroad. How can I make sure we don't end up with the sort of holiday my colleague had?'

Like anything else a successful holiday is going to depend on a lot of forethought and careful preparation.

With most holidays you will have to sign some kind of agreement. **Once you sign the booking form it will become a legally binding contract between you and the tour operator**. So do make sure that you've read the small print and you know what your rights are if something does go wrong.

To give yourself some protection go to a travel agent or tour operator who is a member of ABTA (ASSOCIATION OF BRITISH TRAVEL AGENTS). Most well-known agents and operators are members. They have agreed to follow a code of conduct which is designed to protect you from some of the things which have been known to spoil holidays in the past, including delays in dealing with complaints.

If you're not happy with your holiday, ensure that you understand the complaints procedure and act appropriately. Whilst many holiday companies are prepared to give a small amount of compensation if the holiday is not up to scratch, getting anything substantial from them can be quite hard work.

Step one: Decide what kind of holiday you want

Make a list of the features you would like to see in your holiday. Include:

- The countries or resorts you would like to visit.
- City, mountains, countryside or sea.
- The type of holiday — relaxing and away from it all/cities, museums, places of interest/sporting/special interest.

- Particular needs of your family, e.g. facilities for children or teenagers; any health problems such as a need to avoid steep slopes or very hot weather.
- How you want to travel.
- How long you can go for and on what dates.
- The type of accommodation and degree of luxury.

Step two: Set a budget
Make sure you don't leave anything out. Work out the maximum you're prepared to spend 'all in', including travel, accommodation, food, excursions, sporting or other activities, any car hire, insurance and personal spending. Don't forget to add in any special pre-holiday purchases such as a ski suit if you need one!

Step three: Shop around for the best bargain
Go on a fact-finding expedition. Get as much information as you can about the country, resorts, accommodation and facilities.

- Visit a number of local travel agents. Remember to probe them hard about the resorts and hotels they offer. Most agents will have information about the various package holidays which the public don't see. They will often have some idea of the bad as well as the good points of any accommodation or resort.

  If you are interested in one of the holidays you are offered, ask the travel agent to reserve it for you for a couple of days so you can take your time to make up your mind. Don't be rushed into making an uninformed decision — you might regret it later.
- Contact the tourist office of the country or resort you want to visit and ask them for some literature.
- Look through as many brochures as you can. Often you will find the same accommodation offered by two or more tour operators but the prices will vary according to each brochure. There may be a good reason for this — more expensive operators sometimes have better rooms in a hotel, so do check.
- Go to a bookshop or library and browse through the appropriate travel guidebooks. See what their opinions are of the resort or hotel.
- Ask friends where they've been on holiday. You could learn some valuable 'inside information'! But do remember, their holiday checklist may have been very different from yours.

Before you finally decide on your destination, remember:

- On a miserable winter's day any glossy brochure photograph will look enticing. But the cameras are never pointed at half-finished buildings, slums or crowded beaches, so do ask about what's not in the pictures! Also make sure that you are looking at a photograph of a hotel rather than an artist's impression. You might want to check whether it'll actually be built by the time you go away!
- You only get what you pay for. Unless you're prepared to 'do your own thing', say on a continental touring holiday, and book into small pensions and restaurants with rooms, you're unlikely to find any bargains. If it's very cheap it's unlikely to be very beautiful.
- Learn to read the brochures. 'Children especially welcome', 'Nightly entertainment', 'Lively' does not mean you're in for a quiet, peaceful holiday. If it says 'a short ride from the town', ask what exactly a short ride is — you may not want to be stuck out in the sticks!

Step four: Before you sign the booking form

You are about to sign a legally binding contract, so read it carefully.

Check whether the price includes:

- Travel: transfers both in this country and to your resort; meals during the journey.
- Accommodation: with or without private bathroom, etc; meals — bed and breakfast, half-board, full board, etc.
- Extra charges for single room, private bathroom, meals, balcony, sea view, etc.
- Supplements for particular journey dates, times or departure points.
- Reductions for children or people sharing accommodation.
- Ski passes and instruction, etc. if applicable.
- Insurance →.

Find out whether you will have to pay extra for the beach, lifts or transport into the nearest resort. How much will it be?

Ask how much deposit you will have to pay and when they will expect the outstanding amount. If you are making a booking within eight weeks of departure expect to have to pay the full amount when you book.

Double-check the dates of your holiday, the departure point and the time. Can you reasonably get to the airport at 4 am with five children in tow on Christmas Eve?

If you have any doubt about the hotel or apartment's facilities, e.g. whether the swimming pool has actually been built, ask the tour operator to confirm in writing what the position is.

Also ask about cancellation procedures. All ABTA members are required to explain in their brochures the cancellation conditions and how much it could cost you if you cancel.

Step five: Get yourself insured

It's very unwise to go away without insurance and some tour operators won't let you. **It's important to take out insurance at the time you make your booking in case you are forced to cancel**.

Your travel agent or tour operator will probably offer you insurance schemes or you can look independently. If you pay by credit card you may find that you will automatically have adequate insurance (p.47).

Medical treatment abroad is extremely expensive. Many countries have special arrangements for medical cover. These details can be obtained in a Department of Social Security (DSS) leaflet available from the DSS, CAB, advice centres, etc. However, it's best not to rely on it, take your own as well.

Check that your insurance scheme covers your special needs, e.g. the age and health, including pregnancy, of any of your party; extra cover for sporting activities such as skiing.

Step six: Have you got everything?

Forward planning helps avoid last-minute panics that make holidays seem not worth all the bother.

Check:

- Your passports are valid and you have all necessary visas.
- You've got your tickets, travel documents, itinerary.
- You have had all the necessary vaccinations (check time limits).
- You've got sufficient foreign currency and travellers' cheques or Eurocheques.
- You have the required driving licence documents if you intend hiring a car abroad.
- You've got appropriate clothes, equipment, medical supplies. If you're going to a strict religious culture or you intend visiting

religious monuments and centres, you would be advised to take something other than shorts and skimpy tops.

- Also make sure that you have taken care of what you're leaving behind — home locked up, water, gas and electricity turned off if appropriate, house kept warm in winter, pets cared for, time switches set, newspapers cancelled. Leave a key with a trusted neighbour and give them the name and number of your next of kin or someone who can deal with emergencies.

Step seven: If things go wrong on holiday

Complaints fall into two main categories: complaints about the standard of service, administration (including flights), etc; and complaints about misleading claims made by travel companies. The latter, if substantial, can be a criminal offence under the Trade Descriptions Act 1968 (p.92).

If you have a complaint whilst you're away, **complain then and there** — don't leave it until you get home.

Most large tour operators have resident representatives — their effectiveness will vary according to each individual. Well-organized companies will have an established complaints procedure. If the reps can't help, talk to the hotel manager or contact the tour operator's local office and talk to their area manager. If necessary, reverse the charges and telephone their head office in this country.

Keep a detailed record of everything that happens: dates and times you complained; who you complained to; what was said or done; receipts; whether any money was paid, etc. Many tour operators require you to put your complaint in writing so keep a note of any reference numbers.

If you think your complaint is serious, be persistent, don't give up. But remember, in the end you are supposed to be on holiday. If you can, don't let the complaint ruin your time away entirely.

Common complaints

Delays

These are inevitable, especially if you're flying on a charter plane in the height of season.

Go expecting a delay and be pleasantly surprised if you leave on time. Take books and toys for the kids. If you are delayed for a considerable amount of time, tour operators usually provide free meals, snacks or food vouchers or throw in a bottle of wine during the flight. If they don't — suggest it to them!

If you are on a scheduled flight and are very seriously delayed talk to the airline officials, especially if because of the delay you will miss an important event such as a wedding or business meeting, or a vital connecting flight. If the airport is fog-bound obviously there is very little they can do. But if you think there may be a solution such as flying on another airline, put it to them. The very least they can do is contact your family or associates the other side with a message.

Try and ring the airport before you set off to find out if there are any delays. Some tour operators offer a special flight check service.

Overbooking

Unfortunately it is not uncommon for exhausted holidaymakers to arrive at their destination only to be told the hotel is overbooked.

Most operators will attempt to put you in another hotel or resort. Do not move until you find out exactly what they are offering you. Insist on being put in a hotel of at least the same standard and location. If you do have to move to inferior accommodation ABTA members must pay you **disturbance compensation**. The large tour operators will usually tell you how much this is in their brochure under their booking conditions. Be assertive (p.30).

Problems with the accommodation

Many complaints are made about the standard of the accommodation or food. Do remember that plumbing and furnishings abroad might not be what you'd expect to find at home. Local conditions often dictate the standard that's offered. But you also only get what you pay for. So, if you've booked two weeks away in Spain at the Hotel Miserable for £99, don't expect five-star treatment. However, your holiday should meet its brochure description.

If you think that the facilities you are given are actually insanitary or dangerous, demand that they are put right immediately. Take a photograph of your room if you think you will want to take the matter further when you get home.

If you're offered any kind of 'on the spot' remedy which you think is unacceptable, **don't accept it**, at least not in 'full and final settlement'. If you do, it may prejudice your chances of making a claim when you return.

Step eight: Complaining when you get home

If you've made a complaint on holiday and you want to follow it up, make sure that you write to the tour operator when you return. If you've had no opportunity to make a formal complaint whilst you've been away, then write in any case.

Booking reference: 09751435; Hotel Bella Bella, Cost Bel Sol; 8th–22nd August 2001

I am writing to make a formal complaint about the misleading description of the above hotel given in your brochure and by your agents. I have already made a complaint through your standard procedure at the resort (ref. no. A371).

On page 98 of your summer brochure you describe Hotel Bella Bella as a 'sophisticated hotel in a peaceful and tranquil position. All the rooms have a sea view and their own spacious bathroom ... the hotel is set in lavish gardens and a swimming pool is planned for this season.'

It was on the basis of your description that I booked a holiday with your company at Hotel Bella Bella. I even checked with your agent to ensure that the swimming pool was ready; she confirmed that it was.

I was extremely angry then to find on my arrival at the resort:

1. The hotel was situated on the noisy main road in the centre of town and not in a 'peaceful and tranquil position'.
2. Our bedroom did not have a seaview but looked on to another hotel which had been built two years previously.
3. The hotel's 'lavish gardens' amounted to nothing more than an oversized back yard (see enclosed paragraph).
4. Finally, the swimming pool which I had enquired about a month earlier and had been assured was in use, was in fact a pile of building rubble.

Your company has been extremely negligent in providing a misleading description of Hotel Bella Bella. Since the hotel's location, outlook and garden have remained the same for at least the past two years and since your representatives regularly stay in the hotel, it is reasonable to expect your company to give accurate details of its amenities in your current brochure.

You are obliged under the Trade Descriptions Act 1968 to provide a true and accurate description of the holidays you offer.

The information in your brochure relating to Hotel Bella Bella is false. You are therefore in breach of your legal obligations and I shall be making a formal complaint to my local Trading Standards Department.

I also wish to inform you that I will be seeking compensation for my spoilt holiday.

The point about the above letter is that the allegations are very serious. The tour operator is being accused of a criminal offence. You would therefore not want to settle any compensation offer until you talk to the Trading Standards Department. They will advise you on how best to proceed.

You should immediately put in a formal letter of complaint to your local Trading Standards Officer.

If your complaint is less serious — perhaps about the food or service you received or the fact that the hotel of your choice was overbooked — you might want to state an exact amount of compensation in your letter. If you think that you may end up taking the tour operators to court, head all your letters 'Without Prejudice'.

Step nine: Taking it further

If your complaint does not involve trading standards and you've had no joy in your dealings with the tour company, contact ABTA ←.

They will not deal with claims involving illness or physical injury and they cannot order their members to offer you compensation. If you contact ABTA they will send you a standard application form together with details of their Conciliation Service.

If ABTA can't help you, you could take your case to court (p.249). If your case involves compensation for serious illness or injury you would be well advised to seek the advice of a solicitor (p.237).

Dealing with everyday services

Disputes over telephone, electricity or gas bills are very common and account for the majority of complaints about these services. Complaints also arise about the quality of service provided.

Although each of these services has its own procedures for dealing with problems and its own consumer bodies, the rules for making complaints and getting things put right are in many ways the same.

All three services have one very simple remedy for customers who don't pay their bills — they cut you off! And what is more, they charge you for reconnecting the service when you do pay up.

If you have a problem with a bill or some other part of the service, don't ignore it. If you don't tell them why you are not prepared to pay your bill, they will assume it is because you don't want to and will take appropriate action. If necessary pay them what you think you owe them and argue about the rest later.

However, they cannot just cut you off. The gas and electricity boards have strict codes of conduct for disconnection. If you are disconnected, it should not come as a surprise. But if you think you have been wrongfully disconnected, you may well be entitled to legal redress.

If you have a problem, ensure that you make your complaint to the right person. You will usually see on your bill a number to ring if you have any queries regarding the amount you are being charged.

On the other hand, if you buy something from a gas, electricity or BT showroom and it turns out to be faulty, take it back to where you bought it. Your rights are exactly the same as when you buy goods from any other shop (p.70).

The services have special departments to deal with repairs and faults. Telephone directories will list the appropriate number to ring if, for example, you smell gas. British Telecom also have a series of numbers for reporting faults on the line or answering questions about new installations. Again, look in a telephone directory or ring the operator.

My gas bill's sky high!
'I've just got an astronomical gas bill. I can't believe it. It's twice as much as my usual quarterly bill and I haven't used the gas any more than usual. I really can't afford to pay it — what on earth do I do?'

Don't wait until you get your final notice to make a complaint, do it immediately.

Step one: Get together the evidence
Look at your bill to see whether the meter reading is estimated — it will have an E next to the reading. If it is, you need to find out what the actual reading is. It's not very difficult to do and it might be worth doing even if the gas board claim that they've read your meter — mistakes can happen!

If you've got a digital meter, simply read off the *first four numbers* from left to right.

If your meter's got dials, write down the figures on the *four bottom dials* from left to right. If the hand is between two figures, write down the lesser figure. If the hand is between 9 and 0 use 9.

Search out your old gas bills. Make sure that they're for a comparable quarter. There's no point complaining about an extortionate winter bill if you bring out your last summer one as evidence!

Before you make a complaint, have a good think about the way you've been using the gas. Have you had any new gas appliances installed? Have you perhaps been ill or had a young child to stay and kept the heating on more than usual? Has it been particularly cold?

Step two: Contact the Gas Board

The number will be on your bill.

If your meter reading is different from the one on your bill, ask the Gas Board to send someone round to read or re-read the meter. The Gas Board might be prepared to issue a new bill based on your reading.

If the meter reading is much the same as the one on your bill, you should still inform them of your complaint. Ask them to put a stop on your bill until the matter is sorted out. This should mean that you won't get a final notice.

The important thing is to inform the Gas Board that you're not simply ignoring the bill and that you will pay when the problem is resolved.

You should follow up your telephone call with a letter. Sometimes if it's a straightforward matter of getting someone to read the meter, it may not be necessary to write.

Reference number:

Further to my telephone conversation of [date] I am writing to inform you that I think your last bill is incorrect.

As you will see from the enclosed photocopies of past bills from the same quarter, my current bill shows a 50 per cent increase in the amount I owe. I cannot accept that I have doubled my gas consumption.

I am a widow and I live alone. My two-bedroom flat has gas central heating and I cook by gas. I have not acquired any new gas appliances in the last five years and I have not changed my use of the gas supply. In addition, this last winter has been particularly mild and I have not used the heating as much as I did during the same period last year.

In view of the above evidence I enclose a cheque for £85. I believe that this sum represents the money I owe you with regard to my true gas consumption.

If you do get a final notice, telephone the Gas Board immediately and explain that you have already registered a complaint. You might want to write again.

Step three: Taking it further

If your negotiations with the Gas Board prove fruitless or you encounter other problems contact the GAS CONSUMERS COUNCIL. They have regional offices throughout the country and can offer you free and independent advice and guidance on resolving your complaint. They may even act on your behalf. OFFGAS may also be able to help you with problems about supply.

The Gas Board has a range of schemes to help people who have problems paying their bills. The Gas Consumers Council will be able to advise you about what's on offer and what would be suitable.

What else?

Complaints about **electricity** should be treated in much the same way. OFFER (OFFICE OF ELECTRICITY REGULATION) are responsible for dealing with customer complaints that can't be resolved by dealing directly with the local electricity board. They will also arrange inspections of meters which may be faulty.

Disputes over **telephone bills** can be more difficult to resolve since there's no meter to read. The best thing to do is be assertive (p.30) and be persistent. Don't give up when the person on the end of the phone tells you there's nothing they can do. Follow the appropriate chain of command (p.22). Pay what you think you owe and see what happens. As a last resort you can contact OFTEL (OFFICE OF TELECOMMUNICATIONS). They may be able to help you but their powers appear to be extremely limited.

Insurance, claims and compensation

Insurance is about covering yourself against the unexpected. Some people regard insurance cover as a kind of talisman. It's always those of us who are either without insurance or vastly under-insured who get their cars bashed, homes burgled and end up with broken limbs on skiing holidays.

But the sad fact is that accidents *do* happen — homes are broken into, cars suffer prangs, limbs can fracture on snowy mountain slopes. If you are not adequately covered by insurance even a minor mishap can become a major disaster.

You can insure virtually anything, from Betty Grable's legs to your school fête, against almost any mishap — at a price. The important thing is to make sure that you have got the *right* type of insurance and that it is *adequate* for your needs.

Insurance basics

Insurance policies may look alike but they vary enormously in what they offer. It is vital that you read the small print before you accept any policy.

- Decide exactly what you want insured — your house (p.121), your luggage, your health, a particularly valuable object.
- Decide what you are insuring it against — loss, damage, the cost of medical treatment or repair.
- Decide how much **cover** (the total amount of insurance) you need. Think about how much it will cost you to replace this object or undertake emergency treatment. Do not underestimate the cost — if necessary get a **valuation** (e.g. for a small fee a jeweller will value your jewellery).
- Shop around for suitable policies or ask a **broker** (p.129) to find out what policies are on offer.

- Carefully compare what the policies cover together with their terms and **premiums** (how much you have to pay for the policy).
- Look out for any **exclusion clauses** (what isn't included in the policy).
- Check whether you will have to pay any **excess charges** (a fixed amount for the first part of any claim).
- Fill in the **proposal form** (application form) very carefully. Do not be tempted to gloss over the truth. You are responsible for the accuracy of your answers. If you give false information or tell less than the whole truth you may invalidate your policy. If in doubt, put it on the form.

  It is vital you keep a copy of the completed form. Make a note in your diary of when you need to renew the insurance policy.
- When you receive your **renewal form** look over the policy again and make sure it still gives you the cover you need.
- If your policy is **index linked** (the amount of cover goes up with inflation) don't rely on it to provide adequate cover year after year. It will not take into account new purchases you have made, for example, in your home.
- *Always* check your cover is adequate and consider updating it if you buy something expensive.
- Take good care of the things you've insured. If you let your house fall into disrepair you may find that the insurance company might not pay up if you need to make a claim.

Step-by-step guide to making an insurance claim

Step one: Inform your insurers and get a claim form
As soon as you discover the loss or damage, tell your insurers. If you think that your property has been either vandalized or stolen you should contact the police immediately.

Step two: Temporary repairs
Check with your insurers before you make any repairs, however minor they might seem. **Don't undertake any major repair work until your insurers give you the go-ahead**. You ought to take steps to limit the efects of any damage such as flooding or a leaking roof.

Start getting estimates for repairing or replacing your property — it'll save time later on.

Step three: Complete the claim form

Fill it in immediately and return it — don't delay. It can take time to get estimates so you may need to tell your insurers that you intend to submit a further claim later on.

In an emergency, such as a serious house fire, ask for an **interim payment** to tide you over.

If you've got **indemnity cover** (as opposed to 'new for old' cover) you'll have to make a deducation for wear and tear. The size of the deducation depends on the age of the property you've lost or damaged. You may also have to pay part of the costs of the repair. The aim of the cover is to put you back in the same position as you were before the accident or theft happened and *not* a better one.

If you have an unusually large or difficult claim you could employ a **loss assessor** to help you through the insurance jungle. They will charge you a percentage of the final settlement. They will prepare the claim, get valulations and negotiate with the insurance company on your behalf.

It's best to get them involved right at the start of your claim as they may not be willing to take over a half finished job. The INSTITUTE OF LOSS ASSESSORS will be able to give you names of their members in your area.

Step four: Inspector or loss adjuster calls

If you've got a large or complicated claim the insurance company may send round a claims inspector or an independent expert — a loss adjuster. They will be checking details of the claim.

They may recommend that your insurers offer you less than you've claimed. If you think that that would leave you in a worse position, don't be afraid to explain why you think that they're wrong and your claim is right. Be persistent. Insurance companies aren't renowned for their generosity!

Step five: Settling up

When you get your cheque from the insurers — which might take some time and repeated reminders — you may be asked to sign a **discharge receipt** or **satisfaction note**. These will say that the money you've received is in 'full and final settlement' of your claim. Add the words 'so far' which means that you can make another claim if you discover further loss or damage.

Step six: Taking it further

If you're not happy with the way your claim has been dealt with, perhaps because of the settlement you've been offered or because your insurers seem to be taking far too long, you should complain to the person you've been dealing with. If that fails and you took out insurance through a bank, building society, motoring organization or broker, ask them if they can help you.

If you still find that you are getting nowhere, take your complaint to one of the professional organizations for the insurance industry. Most insurers are members of at least one of the following:

- The ASSOCIATION OF BRITISH INSURERS (ABI). They can intervene on behalf but they can't force members to pay up.
- The INSURANCE OMBUDSMAN BUREAU (IOB). The Ombudsman's decision is legally binding but you will have to exhaust your insurance company's own complaints procedure before approaching them. If you disagree with the Ombudsman's decision you can take the matter to court.
- The PERSONAL INSURANCE ARBITRATION SERVICE (PIAS) can only arbitrate on claims up to a certain limit. Their decision is legally binding on both you and the insurance company, so if you disagree with their decision you won't be able to take the matter to court.

House insurance — What's it all about?

'My friend and I hope to be moving into a flat we are buying. We're slightly confused over all the different types of insurance that we're supposed to have. Is there anything we can cut down on?'

If you are about to join the great home-owning population you need to think about *three* types of insurance. Although, if you have been previously living in rented accommodation, you may have already come across a couple of them.

It's a difficult dilemma when you are setting up a home to work out where you can afford to cut corners. You will have to decide what sort of risks you are prepared to take. Unless your flat is gutted by fire or flood or a burglar steals or vandalizes your every belonging you are unlikely to make a claim for the total value of the contents of your home. However, it is not beyond the realms of possibility.

Whatever you decide to do, do make sure that if you have a really expensive piece of jewellery or equipment that you value and simply couldn't afford to replace, get it adequately insured. Insurance is not only about eliminating nasty surprises, it's also about peace of mind — how well do *you* sleep?

Buildings insurance

This means the actual house or flat — the bricks and mortar itself — along with the interior decorations and the fixtures and fittings (built-in wardrobes, fitted kitchen, bathroom suite and so on).

If your property is unusual, for example it has a thatched roof or elaborate stained glass, then you may need to seek advice from professional valuers.

If you are buying a **leasehold** flat it is usually the owner, or **freeholder**, who arranges the buildings insurance. However, you should check this out thoroughly. It is not uncommon for the freeholder, particularly if they are absent-minded, to have failed to get adequate insurance. You also need to make sure that not only your flat but also the 'common parts' — entrance hall, stairs, etc. are insured.

If you are buying the flat with a mortgage from a building society or bank they will normally insist on buildings insurance as a condition of the mortgage. Most building societies will arrange such cover for you but if you think you can get a better deal elsewhere then you should tell the society concerned. Providing it offers at least as good a policy as the one they propose, they will usually accept it.

Buildings should be insured for their full rebuilding costs and not what you would normally expect to sell them for. Your surveyor will tell you how much this should be. Alternatively most insurance companies provide a guide to rebuilding costs.

Contents insurance

This covers your furniture, carpets, domestic appliances, clothes and other belongings. Don't forget to take into consideration books, pictures, large plants and 'knick-knacks', all of which could be very expensive to replace.

- Make a list of your belongings; this will help you to value them and also give you an idea of what is missing if unfortunately you are burgled or your home gutted by fire. Keep the list up to date.
- Keep a list of the make and serial numbers of more expensive things.
- Check whether your policy has an upper limit on the value of

any single item insured. For example, you may have to insure single items worth over £400 separately; this might include the hi-fi, video recorder or items of jewellery.

- Decide whether you want a **new for old** policy where the insurance company will provide the full cost of replacing stolen or destroyed items. Or you may opt for a policy that takes into account wear and tear and will only give a reduced amount towards replacing the goods. **Make sure that the policy you choose gives you the cover you want.**

Insuring individual or portable items

If you own something expensive (it can be anything over £250) and/or you intend to take an item out of the house, for example an engagement ring or camera, you may need to insure it separately.

- Work out how much it would cost to replace the item — you may need a professional valuation, for example from a jeweller who will give you a proper valuation certificate.
- Make a note of the make and serial number, for example of a computer or camera.
- Take a photograph of the item.
- If you borrow or hire an expensive item, for example a television or video camera, make sure you have insurance for it.

My flat has flooded!

'I live in a flat on the first floor of a converted house and one evening last week I was running my bath when I heard this awful racket outside my front door.

'I went to have a look and found next door's cat chasing a bird around the hallway. As I tried to save the bird my front door slammed shut and locked me out. I panicked but eventually I got hold of my neighbour who has a spare key.

'By this time the water had flooded over the bath and out into the hall. Not only are my bathroom and hall carpets ruined but the person who lives downstairs has water trickling down her walls. The place is in chaos. It's all so embarrassing — what shall I do?'

If you have any kind of flood you need to be concerned about two things: limiting the damage the flooding has caused and making a claim for what has been damaged and any other necessary repairs.

Getting things back to normal after a flood can take a very long time. If you have wet carpets and timber or walls it may take weeks or months before your home dries out and the smell can be quite unpleasant.

Step one: Make a record of the damage

If you have been flooded you are likely to have to start moving objects and household furnishings around. It can be easy to forget exactly what has been damaged and how bad the damage was.

If possible take a photograph of the affected area. Write down exactly what happened and make a list of what has been damaged. Don't throw anything away.

Step two: Limit the damage

You have a responsibility once you discover any flooding to limit the damage the water is likely to cause. Left to its own devices, water and dampness can do a great deal of harm, so if, for example, a pipe had burst you would immediately turn off the water at the mains.

In the same way, if your carpet is sopping wet you should try and mop up the excess water and if possible hang the carpet up to dry or at least put extra heat into the room. If necessary take advice from a carpet fitter or upholsterer on the best way to deal with your furnishings.

It's possible to hire special commercial heaters to help dry out your home. Of course you would add their hire cost to any claim you made.

Take down and store any items, for example paintings, that are likely to become damaged if they remain in damp conditions.

Don't undertake any repairs without first checking with your insurers (p.119–21).

Step three: Make a claim on your insurance (p.119-21)

Don't forget that your neighbour may make a claim on your policy, so you'll need to get quotes for the repair to her flat as well.

My home's been burgled

'I've just arrived home to find that the place has been burgled. My back door's been smashed and there's glass everywhere. The cupboards are all open and everything's been tipped out of the drawers. The TV, stereo and video seem to have been taken and I think some jewellery's gone too. The place is in such a mess, it's hard to tell what's missing. What shall I do first?'

Discovering that someone has broken into your home, gone through your personal belongings and taken your possessions affects everyone differently. The common reactions are shock, anger, distress, a feeling of revulsion and often fear and loss of self-confidence. If you can, get the support of your family, friends or neighbours in trying to sort things out.

Step one: Getting help

If you think that someone has broken into your home or office and may still be inside, use a neighbour's or public telephone to contact the police.

In any case, if you suspect that something is not quite right, try and get someone to go into the house with you.

Step two: Don't touch anything — call the police

If you've had a break-in it's vital not to touch anything. The only clues the police might have as to the identity of the burglar might be fingerprints or footprints — and you want to avoid wiping them off. Call the police immediately. Wait with a neighbour if you feel nervous or shaken.

Burglaries are so common that often the police don't follow the incident through although they may come and take fingerprints. A scene-of-crime officer may visit you, usually within twenty-four hours, so you may be advised to spend a night somewhere else if you have to, particularly if you're on your own.

Step three: Make a list of everything that's missing

Go through your home systematically, making a note of everything that you think's been taken. The police (and the insurers) will want details of the items — make, model, serial number, colour or perhaps a drawing or photograph of any jewellery.

It can take days or even weeks before you remember or discover everything that's gone.

Step four: Make your home secure

If the burglars have broken a window or forced a door to get in, then you will need to make it secure before you leave it unattended or go to sleep. The police usually have the names of carpenters and locksmiths who deal with emergencies. Don't forget to keep any receipts so you can claim the money back from your insurers.

Step five: Clear up any mess

Clearing up after intruders can be very distressing, especially if they have fouled your home. Do get other people to help you if you can.

It's not unusual to want to obsessively 'spring clean' or wash whatever the burglars have been through or to throw out personal things such as cosmetics which you think they may have touched.

Step six: Make an insurance claim

Contact your insurers and ask for a claim form. Remember to claim for everything you have lost and include any repairs to broken windows, doors or locks.

Step seven: Making your home more secure for the future

If you've had a break-in you might be wondering whether you need to think again about protecting your home.

Most police stations have a **Crime Prevention Officer** who you can talk to about the best way to make your home safer.

There are some very simple changes that you can make:

- Move the bolts or locks on your doors; one bolt a third of the way down the door and one bolt a third of the way up the door is much stronger than just a bolt in the middle.
- Put your lights and TV on time switches so that even when you're out the house doesn't look unattended.
- You can buy a range of DIY security equipment such as window locks quite cheaply or you can get quotes from established security companies.

Alternatively, if you think that security is a problem in your locality talk to your neighbours about setting up a **Neighbourhood Watch Scheme** — your local police will be able to advise you.

Step eight: Reassess your insurance cover

If the worst has just happened, you may well have discovered that in fact you were under-insured. Do check your insurance policy and make sure you have enough cover.

Car insurance — Where do I start?

'My parents have just bought me a car for my birthday but they've said that I'll have to be responsible for the tax and insurance. I've heard of "ful-

ly comprehensive'' and ''third pary'' insurance but I'm not sure what I should do. I'm a student and I don't have much money so I'm keen to keep any outlay to the minimum.'

If you have a car then you are required by law to insure it. If you don't have the appropriate insurance you may be charged with committing a criminal offence.

Step one: Decide what sort of policy you want

Car insurance usually comes in three packages: **Fully Comprehensive; Third Party, Fire and Theft;** and **Third Party Only**. The type of cover you decide on will depend largely on the value of your car and how much you can afford.

Fully Comprehensive

Fully comprehensive cover can cost more than twice as much as Third Party, Fire and Theft but if you have a new car or one that is worth quite a bit this may be your best option.

Fully comprehensive cover will cover you for:

- Injuries or damage you cause to other people, their vehicle or their property.
- Loss or damage to your car even if the accident was *your* fault.
- Loss or damage to the contents of your car, e.g. radios, clothing or a camera.
- It will also normally cover you for other costs such as getting your car to and from a garage after an accident, car hire costs and some medical costs. These 'extras' will vary according to each individual policy.

Third Party, Fire and Theft

This type of insurance covers you for any injury or damage you do to other people or their property, i.e. 'third parties' and gives you limited cover for your own car.

Third Party, Fire and Theft will cover you for:

- Injuries or damage you cause to other people, their vehicle or their property.
- Loss or damage to your car, and the things fixed in it, like a car radio, providing the loss or damage occurred as a result of lightning, fire, explosion, theft or attempted theft.

Third Party Only

The cheapest of all types of car insurance it will *only* cover you for injury or damage you cause to other people, their car or their property. It will *not* cover your car or its contents. So, if you have an accident or your car is stolen or broken into and you can't claim against anyone else you will be responsible for repairing the damage or replacing the car yourself.

If your car is not worth very much you could consider either Third Party Only or Third Party, Fire and Theft. Within a few years you might find that the extra premium you would have to pay to take out Fully Comprehensive insurance will add up to more than the market value of the car.

Step two: Other things to take into account

The amount you pay for car insurance will depend not only on the company you choose but on their assessment of how likely you are to make a claim.

The company will start with a basic premium based on the type of cover you want ←, where you live and the car you drive. They then add and deduct different percentages for various things which they think may increase — or decrease — your likelihood of making a claim.

These usually include:

- What you use your car for. They will add a percentage loading if you use your car for work.
- Your age. They will add a percentage loading for drivers under twenty-five and give you a discount if you are over fifty.
- Age and price of car. They will deduct a percentage for an older car and add a percentage loading for a very expensive car.
- You occupation. Teachers, civil servants and bank employees tend to get discounts and publicans, musicians and journalists usually get increased premiums!
- Any previous claims or convictions will add money on.
- They will also deduct a percentage for No Claims Discount →.

Step three: Finding the right policy

Once you've decided what type of insurance cover you want then you will have to find the right policy. There are a number of ways of doing this:

- Find out from the major insurance companies what they can offer you.
- Use a **broker**. Insurance brokers are essentially people who advise on and arrange insurance. They usually earn their money from commission paid to them by the insurance companies with whom they do business. If you do use a broker remember that although they may have shopped around to find a suitable policy it does not necessarily mean that it will be the best value one available.
- Ask the AA or RAC what they suggest.

Car accidents — What to do and who to claim from

'I was driving back from town yesterday when I got into a traffic jam and had to stop. All of a sudden there was this tremendous bump — the person in the car behind me had driven into me.

'I was in a right state, but I got out of the car and gave the driver my name and address. He gave me his name and telephone number but not his address. I've got his registration number. When I tried to telephone him he was really offensive and wouldn't give me his address. I looked in the telephone directory but I couldn't find his details.

'Although the car doesn't look badly damaged, my garage says it will cost about £600 to put right. I now don't know whether to claim through my insurers or try and claim against the other driver. Also is there anything else I should have said or done at the time of the accident?'

The two most common immediate reactions to car accidents are shock and anger. Yet it's vital that if you are involved in an accident and are not badly injured, you keep a very clear head. The best thing you can do is keep an emergency checklist in your car of everything you should do and say in case the worst happens.

If you have to make a claim, only claim off your own insurance company as a last resort. Even if the accident is not your fault you still stand to lose some or all of your **No Claims Discount (NCD)** → if you make a claim.

Step one: Make an accident checklist

Keep the following list somewhere handy in the car. It's even better if you can keep a couple of typewritten photocopies. If you've already had an accident then fill in the details as best you can.

ACCIDENT CHECKLIST

VEHICLE REGISTRATION NUMBER
VEHICLE MAKE & MODEL
VEHICLE COLOUR

DRIVER'S NAME
DRIVER'S ADDRESS
DRIVER'S TELEPHONE NUMBER

DOES THE VEHICLE BELONG TO THE DRIVER?
IF NOT, WHAT IS THE OWNER'S NAME & ADDRESS?

DRIVER'S INSURANCE CERTIFICATE NUMBER
AGENT OR BROKER

DATE OF ACCIDENT
TIME OF ACCIDENT
PLACE OF ACCIDENT

NAME(S) OF WITNESS(ES)
ADDRESS(ES) OF WITNESS(ES)
TELEPHONE NUMBER(S) OF WITNESS(ES)

DESCRIBE WHAT HAPPENED — DRAW A DIAGRAM
IF NECESSARY

WRITE DOWN DETAILS OF ANY CONVERSATIONS
THAT TOOK PLACE

Step two: What you need to say and do at an accident

Whatever else you do, *don't* lose your temper even if you think the other driver was totally at fault and has just written off your pride and joy.

If anyone is injured or property damaged, even a dent in the car, in an accident you are required by law *either* to give the other driver your name, address and insurance details *or* to report the accident to the police within twenty-four hours.

- Call an ambulance for the injured. If you are suffering badly from shock or perhaps whiplash, don't be reticent about getting help.

- If the accident is serious, people are injured or you suspect that the other driver was behaving illegally in some way, e.g. driving whilst drunk, call the police immediately.
- Get all the other driver's details using the checklist above. Ask to see their driving licence and insurance certificate.
- Give the other driver all your details.
- Unless the accident is trivial don't move the cars until the police turn up. If you have to move them, then try and make chalk marks where the cars were positioned.
- If you have a camera with you take a photograph of the accident.
- Get hold of your witnesses before they disappear.

If you think that the accident was the other person's fault:

- Be very specific about what you say — 'You have just driven into the back of me,' or 'You just stepped out in front of me without looking.'
- *Don't* say, 'Sorry' if it wasn't your fault!
- If they disagree, don't get into an argument.

If you think the accident was your fault:

- *Don't say anthing*. Certainly don't admit responsibility.
- Just give your details.

Step three: Tracing the other driver
Depending on the amount of information you are given, you have a number of choices:

- Some drivers won't give you their insurance details because they would prefer to know what the cost of the damage is and pay you directly rather than lose their No Claims Bonus→. You should give them this opportunity.
- If you suspect that the driver has no insurance, you should contact the police immediately. It's illegal.
- If you have their name and telephone number, call them and if they refuse any further information, point out their legal obligations. The conversation might go like this:

DRIVER A:Mr Brown, it's Mrs Angel here. I'm calling about the accident yesterday when you drove into me. I intend to make a claim against your insurers for the cost of repairing my car which is £600. Please will you give me your insurance details?

DRIVER B: I don't want you bothering me again. I've told you I'm not going to give you the information.

DRIVER A: Mr Brown, you are required by law to give me this information. If you don't, I will have no alternative but to go to the police.

DRIVER B: Stop threatening me, lady. I'm not interested.

DRIVER A: I'm not threatening you, Mr Brown. Since you won't give me your insurance details, I will have no alternative but to go to the police.

- If you do go to the police, find out if the other driver has reported the accident. Do make it clear that you gave the other driver your details. The police may well help you to trace the other driver.
- If you still haven't got anywhere but you have the vehicle registration number, write to DVLC (DRIVER AND VEHICLE LICENSING CENTRE).

Step four: Whose insurance company should I claim from?

Before you make a decision you need to think about your **No Claims Discounts (NCD)** which is an area that can cause some confusion for car drivers.

No Claims Discounts (NCD) basically mean that the longer you go without making a claim on your insurance policy, the greater the discount (or bonus) the insurance company will give you on your next premium. The discounts usually range from 30 per cent for one claim-free year to 60 per cent after more than four claim-free years. If you do have to make a claim after three years you usually won't lose your entire NCD. However, since an NCD can be worth a considerable amount of money it's worth making sure that you hang on to it.

Even if you have an accident which isn't your fault you could end up losing your NCD if you make a claim on your insurance policy. This is because the NCD is a no *claim* discount and not a no *blame* discount. This means that before you make a claim you should always work out whether it would cost less to repair the car yourself or to pay the extra pemium you would incur through losing all or part of your NCD.

Most insurance companies have a 'knock for knock' agreement with each other. This means that when there is an accident in which all the drivers involved have comprehensive cover (p.127), the insurers will each pay their own policyholder's claim instead of first trying to claim the money from the other insurers. Unless you can prove that your claim would have been met by another insurer had the knock for knock agreement not existed, you will lose all or some of your NCD.

Some companies offer special NCD Protection Schemes. By paying an extra premium these allow you to make a limited number of claims without losing your NCD. If you are offered one of these schemes make sure that the policy itself still compares favourably with others you are offered.

It is for this reason that you should always try and claim off the other driver's insurers if you think they were to blame.

However, if you do have an accident, it's worth informing your insurers, in case you have to claim off them as a last resort. Always make it clear that you don't intend to make a claim for the time being.

Step five: Make a claim (p.119-21)

Hurt in an accident — Can I claim compensation?

'I was out shopping the other day in my local supermarket when I slipped and fell on some spilt yogurt. I was badly shaken up and my arm was very painful.

'The sales assistant was really kind and he called the manager who took me into his office. He offered to call an ambulance but I said I didn't need one so he paid for me to go home in a taxi instead. Anyway, that evening my arm was so painful that my neighbour took me to the hospital. They discovered I'd broken my elbow and kept me in overnight.

'I'm going to be off work for at least two months and although my firm are being very good about sick pay I wondered if I could claim anything for all the pain I'm suffering?'

If you suffer injury because of someone else's carelessness you are entitled to claim **compensation**. This means that you can claim money for any income you've lost or extra costs that you've incurred through your injury. You can also claim an amount for 'pain and suffering' and the effects of any lasting injury.

If you are involved in any kind of accident, however trivial it might seem, always make a point of ensuring that someone in the shop or organization knows what has happened. It is not unusual to hurt yourself and think that it's really nothing, only to find out later that in fact you've injured yourself quite seriously. Most large companies and shops have special procedures for dealing with accidents that happen on their premises, and staff are trained to keep a record of the incident.

However, if you are injured somewhere else — perhaps you fall over an uneven paving stone or you're thrown violently when the bus stops — don't be embarrassed about calling for help if you are in serious pain and get the names of anyone who witnessed what happened.

Personal injury claims can be very complex. Although CABs and advice centres can tell you how to go about making a claim, you should really seek the advice of a professional lawyer (p.237) who specializes in these cases to tell you *how much* you should claim. You may, however, decide to accept an offer made by the shop or organization and finish the matter.

If you are very seriously injured and you don't know what the long-lasting effects of your injury will be, avoid stating a final figure for your claim until you know exactly what will happen to you. You can get an interim payment of compensation but this is best dealt with by a professional lawyer.

Step one: Write to the store manager

Accident, Upper Heights Superstore, [date]
On [date] I was shopping in your store at about [time] when I slipped on some yogurt which previously had been spilt on the floor.

Your sales assistant, Clive Sedley, kindly came to my assistance and took me to your office. I was very shaken and complained that my arm was hurting. You offered to call an ambulance but as I thought at that time that my injury was not serious, I agreed to go home in a taxi instead.

However, later on that evening I was in considerable pain and my neighbour took me to Upper Heights Hospital. There they discovered that I had broken my elbow and I was kept in overnight. My arm is now in plaster and I have been advised to stay off work for two months. I am in a great deal of pain. At the moment the doctors do not know the long-term effects of my injury.

I am writing to inform you that I consider the accident was a result of negligence by Upper Heights Superstore. I intend to make a claim against your company for the pain and suffering which I have been caused. Please will you forward this letter to your insurance company and notify me of their details.

Step two: The company contacts you

If you are dealing with a large retail chain you will probably hear from their head office claims department, otherwise you will get a letter from the company's insurers.

You will probably get one of two responses:

- A claims form for you to fill in giving details of the accident and your injury.
- An offer of settlement.

Step three: What kind of offer should you accept?

You may have done a rough calculation of how much you have lost in wages. You should also make a list of any other extra costs you've incurred such as: the cost of a daily help; perhaps the cost of going to the hairdresser; using minicabs and buying more expensive pre-packed food. You should also include an amount for pain and suffering.

If the offer meets your expectations then consider accepting it. Remember that insurance companies rarely break the bank when they offer you a settlement — you can be sure it won't be over-generous!

If you do start negotiating, head all your letters '**Without Prejudice**'. This means that should your case ever go to court, the letters you've written headed with the words 'without prejudice' won't be able to be used as evidence.

If you are not sure what to accept or to ask for, then consult a solicitor (p.237).

Step four: Taking it further

If you find that the company concerned refuse to admit the accident was their responsibility or refuse to make what you think is a sensible offer you may have to consider **suing** for compensation (p.249).

Once again, make sure of the validity of your case by talking it through with a solicitor. Consider using the **Fixed Fee Interview Scheme** (p.245).

Home sweet home

Only a footstep away — neighbours

Is your life an endless round of all-night parties? Do you lie in bed on Sunday mornings listening to the beat of the latest pop tune? Do smoky bonfires give a lift to your washing day? If these are not your usual pleasures, you could be suffering with a case of 'the neighbours'.

Disputes with neighbours can bring out the worst in normally peace-loving citizens. And the problem with them is, they are not always that simple to solve. Neighbours can be a complete nuisance.

The law defines two types of nuisance:

- **Private nuisance** which includes excessive noise or smell or inconvenience. If you think someone is causing a private nuisance you must establish that the nuisance has a degree of *continuity* and that it is *interfering with the enjoyment of your property*. Private nuisance is a civil matter. If you want to take out an action against another person you must do so as an individual. Legal action can be extremely expensive (p.265).
- **Public nuisance** is one that affects the public at large. What constitutes a nuisance is defined by various Acts of Parliament and by-laws. In general, public nuisance is a crime and the responsibility and expense of taking an action will be borne by the local authority.

To find out whether the nuisance is private or public contact your Environmental Health Officer.

The best way of sorting out disagreements is by being assertive (p.30) and talking to your neighbour before the problem gets out of hand.

Often disputes arise because one or other person is unaware of the legal position, or because the person causing 'the nuisance' is unaware that there is a problem.

Example

Helen Bates is studying for some exams. She has to work at home in the afternoons. Her neighbours Mr and Mrs Jameson are both in their late eighties and deaf. Consequently they tend to keep their television on very loud during the day and early evening. Helen finds the noise very distracting and is unable to study properly.

Helen visits her neighbours and explains what the problem is. Mr and Mrs Jameson weren't aware that their TV was disturbing Helen. Helen realizes that the TV is very important to them so she asks them to experiment with the volume and see how low they can turn the sound and yet still hear it. The noise is more tolerable for Helen. They finally agree to keep the TV turned right down until after Helen's exams.

If you have a complaint about one particular person or complaint in your neighbourhood it's always much more effective if you can get together a number of residents to make a complaint. Ask your immediate neighbours if they've been bothered by the noise, smell, etc. and find out whether they'd support you in making a complaint.

Ask your Residents' or Tenants' Association to put out a 'Good Neighbour Guide'. You might include guidelines such as:

- Keeping TVs, steros, radio, etc. turned down especially during the summer months when noise travels through open windows.
- Not mowing the lawn with an electric mower very early or very late in the day.
- Keeping the noise from parties down after midnight.
- Tying rubbish up securely to stop cats and dogs scattering litter around the street.
- Not lighting bonfires during the day especially at weekends — and asking neighbours to take their washing in first!

- Visiting elderly or disabled neighbours particularly in the winter to check if they're okay.

Finally, if you have a dispute with one of your neighbours, do remember that you may have to live next door or near to them for many months to come!

My neighbour's tree is messing up my garden

'My neighbour has a very old greengage tree which is completely overgrown. It's overhanging my garden and I'm fed up with having to continually clear up the mess from all the leaves and fallen fruit. I don't mind cutting the branches down but I want to know if I can legally do this.'

Quite simply you are entitled to cut off any branches or roots that are encroaching on to your property. However, you must not trespass on to their property to cut off the offending branches without getting their permission first. Your only legal obligation is to return the cut-off branches or the fruit to the owner. In the interests of good neighbourly relations you ought to give your neighbour the opportunity to chop them off first.

Approach your neighbour ☻

Make it friendly: 'I don't know whether you've noticed, but the branches from your greengage tree are overhanging my garden. I'm concerned that the leaves and the fallen fruit are giving me extra work to do. Please could you cut them down.'

If you get no satisfactory answer or your neighbour is non-committal, continue: 'I'm quite happy to cut the branches down myself but I thought I'd give you the opportunity to do it yourself if you wanted to.'

If necessary you might need to add: 'Legally I'm quite within my rights simply to cut off the branches but I wanted to be neighbourly and check with you first. If you don't want to do anything about it, I'll go ahead myself.'

You should also find out what your neighbour wants you to do with the cut-off branches. Dumping a lot of old wood on their front lawn might not be the answer!

What else?

If you find that your neighbour's **tree roots** are affecting your house and it's clear that the roots are causing the damage, then you can claim compensation from your neighbour.

If you're buying a house (p.145), remember to ask your surveyor about any trees in the garden or the neighbouring gardens that might affect your house.

The dog next door is out of control

'My next-door neighbour has got this horrible yapping dog which she fails to keep under control. The dog has managed to pull up her fence, which was only wire mesh and not very stable. As a consequence the wretched dog keeps burrowing into my garden and digging up all my prize flowers. In addition it makes a mess all over my lawn. This makes me very cross, not least because my nieces and nephews come to play and it's not exactly hygienic. What can I do?'

Dog owners are subject to a number of legal obligations to keep their animals under control. These include: not allowing their dogs to foul the footpath and not letting them be unreasonably noisy. In many areas local authority by-laws make it an offence to commit one or both of these things. However, you may not always be able to get the authority to prosecute the culprit.

Ultimately you could sue your neighbour for the damage the dog has caused.

As with all neighbour disputes, it's always best to try and sort things out amicably.

Step one: Decide what you want done
The simplest solution would probably be to get your neighbour to erect a sturdy fence. Obviously you want to avoid legal action if you can, although you might want to use it as a threat.

Step two: Approach your neighbour ☺☺
Make it friendly but be very specific about what you want done.

I've come to talk to you about your fence. As you know the fence is broken because your dog keeps burrowing underneath it. As a result your dog is frequently in my garden and has dug up all my prize flowers which I find very upsetting. In addition he fouls the lawn. I'm very concerned about this because my nieces and nephews come to play.

I'm sure that you'll agree that the best way to stop this happening is for you to put up a sturdy fence.'

Be pleasant but be very firm. Repeat youself if necessary. Your neighbour might agree totally with you and set about doing something practical.

Or you might get one of the following responses:

- *Neighbour*: 'My dog's such a handful, it's impossible to keep him under control.'

  You: 'Yes, it's obvious that he's a handful and you find him very difficult to control. That's why it's very urgent that you put up a sturdy fence so that he doesn't cause any more damage.'

- *Neighbour*: 'I'm sorry that he's got into your garden but I don't see that it's really my responsibility.'

  You: 'Legally, it is the owner's responsibility to control their dog. Your dog is doing a great deal of damage to my garden and it's your responsibility to see that he stops it. The simplest way would be to erect a sturdy fence.'

- *Neighbour*: 'I'm awfully embarrassed about it but it was only a few flowers, I'm sure they'll grow again. As for the mess, a little dog muck never hurt anyone. I'll make sure he doesn't do it again.'

  You: 'The flowers may well grow again but that's not the point. I'm very upset that after carefully cultivating them, your dog chewed them up. They meant a lot to me. I also don't want my family having to play on a lawn fouled by your dog. If this happens once more I will again have to ask you to replace the fence.'

Step three: Write to your neighbour
If your neighbour agrees to take some action confirm it in writing.

I am very pleased that you have agreed to have the mesh wire fence in your back garden replaced with a sturdy wooden one.

As I told you the other day I am very concerned that your dog is not under your control. Having burrowed under your fence he spends a lot of time in my garden and has done considerable damage to my prize flowers as well as fouling the lawn. I am very worried about this as my family come to play in the garden.

I would be most grateful if you could have the fence put up as soon as possible. Perhaps you would let me know when you expect the work to be carried out.

Thank you for your co-operation.

Step four: Your neighbour does nothing

If your neighbour refuses point-blank to do anything or after a number of letters has not done the work they promised to do, you will need to write a stronger letter.

> Further to our conversation/my letter of [date(s)] I am very concerned that you are not prepared/have not done anything about replacing your back garden fence.
>
> I am concerned that you are not controlling your dog. He has burrowed under your fence and consequently spends a lot of time in my garden where he has caused considerable damage to my prize flowers and fouled the lawn. I am worried about this as my family come to play in the garden.
>
> Legally you are required to control your dog. Unless you erect a sturdy fence in the next month I will have no alteranative but to take legal action. I will be claiming compensation for the damage your dog has caused and for putting up a proper fence.

Step five: Taking it further

If your neighbour still refuses to take any action you may want to consider putting up a strong fence and then claiming compensation in the County court (p.249). You would be advised to seek the advice of a solicitor which you could do under the Fixed Fee Interview scheme (p.145).

The people over the road are causing a racket

'A few months ago some people moved into the house that backs on to our house. We've chatted to them over the fence and they seem quite pleasant. But recently they've started playing their stereo at full blast at all hours during the day and night. They also turn their TV up to full volume. The noise is driving us mad, particularly my wife who works from home. Is there anything we can do about it?'

Noisy neighbours can be incredibly irritating and trying to put a stop to the noise can be extremely frustrating. But there are remedies.

You say that your new neighbours seem quite pleasant — apart from the noise. Before the noise gets worse, it's worth having a word with them. They may not realize the extent to which they're disturbing you.

Step one: Talk to your noisy neighbours

Ask your immediate neighbours if they've been affected by the noise. Remember there's strength in numbers. Be assertive when you visit the noise makers (p.30) and also be friendly.

'You may not realize it but the music from your stereo is so loud that we can hear it inside our house. My wife works from home and it really is disturbing her. Please can you turn the music right down.'

If you get an apology and the noise stops, it's worth dropping them a note to thank them for their co-operation.

Step two: Taking it further

If the noise continues you should do three things.

- Put your complaint in writing to your noisy neighbours. Make sure that you date the letter and keep a copy. Ask other neighbours to do the same.
- Contact your Environmental Health Officer and ask them to come and listen to the noise. They will be able to tell you whether they consider the noise bad enough for them to do something about it. Again, it's much more effective if a number of local people ring the EHO.
- Keep a diary of when the noise occurs, how long it lasts and the effect it has on you; e.g. if it stops you working, wakes you up or stops you sleeping, prevents you relaxing or watching TV. Get your neighbours to do the same.

Step three: Going to court

If the Environmental Health Officer is unable to take action on your behalf you can take the matter to court yourself.

You will need to know the full name and address of the person you are complaining about and you should have a fairly comprehensive record of the noise. Generally you need to have a couple of months' worth of diary entries to make the case stand up in court, but this will obviously vary according to the nature and severity of the noise.

Go to your nearest **Magistrates Court** and explain that you want a summons issued against your noisy neighbour under **Section 59 of the Control of Pollution Act 1974.** A member of staff will advise you about the procedure. Always ring in advance to check the best time to go to the court. Take your diary evidence with you.

If the magistrates decide you have a case, you will be given a date and time for the hearing and a summons will be issued and served on your noisy neighbour. You will have to pay a small charge for issuing the summons.

Continue to keep your noise diary up to date and bring it with you to the hearing. Ask your other neighbours to come along too; you may need their evidence.

One word of caution. If your action isn't successful, you may be liable to pay court costs. If in doubt do seek the advice of a lawyer under the Fixed Fee Interview Scheme (p.245) or visit your local CAB.

Can next door simply extend their house?

'The family living in the house next to me want to build an extension to their kitchen. I think it's going to be a complete eyesore. What's more, it's going to block out much of the sun from my patio. Can they just go ahead and build regardless of the effect on their neighbours?'

The laws and regulations governing planning permission are quite complex. Basically you can go ahead and build an extension on to your house provided it meets certain rules.

You don't need planning permission if the proposed extension does not add more than either 50 cubic metres or 10 per cent of the existing building (with a maximum of 115 cubic metres) whichever is the greater. The existing building is taken to mean the *original* size of the house. Future extensions must not take the house size above the total specified limit.

In addition, the extension mustn't increase the original height of the house and it mustn't extend towards the road at the front of the house.

You also don't need planning permission to build a porch outside an existing door providing it doesn't exceed 2 square metres or is more than 3 metres above ground level.

Step one: Ask to see the plans

Visit your neighbours and tell them about your concerns. Ask to see their proposed plans for the extension. You might in fact find that the new building won't affect you at all.

Step two: Taking it further

If you think that your neighbours need planning permission for their extension or that the new building will seriously affect you in some way you ought to seek the advice of a solicitor (p.237).

If your neighbours have made an application for planning permission you will probably get a notice from the council telling you. If you object you should write back to the council immediately. Send the letter recorded delivery.

However, in both these cases, it is not enough simply to object to the new building. You will have to prove that there is some sound reason for your objection, such as it will block out your light or will be an eyesore.

If someone does put up a building illegally, they can be told to pull it down.

What else?
What else do you need consent for?

- Some **internal building work** such as a new bathroom or toilet. Your local building control department will be able to advise you.
- If you **change the use** of a property you need planning permission. So if your garage becomes a workshop for your business or a granny flat for your mother, you need planning permission.
- You can keep a small van at your house but if you want a large lorry or a fleet of **commercial vehicles**, you'll need planning approval.
- You can keep a **caravan** in your drive, you can even sleep in it there. What you can't do is allow someone else to stay in a caravan on your land without planning permission.
- Finally, if you live in a **conservation area** or in a **listed building** you may find severe restrictions on what you can do with your home and land.

Complaining about local services

If you are concerned about services in your neighbourhood — street cleaning, refuse collections, lighting, etc. — you should contact your local council.

The services offered by local authorities vary from area to area. Your town hall or civic centre will be able to put you in touch with the right department.

Once you've made a formal complaint either over the phone or in writing you might want to try other tactics such as writing to your local paper or contacting your councillor. ✎ 📞 👓

If that doesn't work there's always scope for starting a campaign or getting involved with a local pressure group or political party (266-73).

What else

If you have a complaint about your local authority — for example, you feel you've been unfairly treated by their action (or inaction), you can ask the Local Ombudsman to investigate your case. You should exhaust all other channels first and you must put your complaint in writing ✎ and ask your councillor to pass it on to the Ombudsman for you. The service is absolutely free and there is a free booklet about it, obtainable from your local CAB or council offices.

Buying your own home

We want to buy our own home — How can we avoid the pitfalls?

'My sister and I want to buy our own property, perhaps a small house or a flat. We currently rent a flat in the centre of town but we'd like to move further out into the suburbs. We've heard some nightmare stories from friends buying their home.'

Buying and selling property is very rarely a picnic. Think of it more as negotiating an army endurance test. If you begin by accepting that the whole process may take many months and be fraught with disappointment and delays, you're far less likely to end up with a major headache. However, there are ways to make the experience less painful.

The Purchaser is the person buying the property.
The Vendor is the person selling the property.
The Conveyancer is the person — a solicitor or licensed conveyancer — who undertakes all the legal transactions.

Step one: Decide how much you can spend

First work out the total amount of money you have available to spend on actually buying and setting up your own home.

Your resources will comprise any cash you have plus a mortgage (p.49). You should shop around the various banks and building societies to see that they can offer you, both in terms of the amount they are willing to lend and their interest rates. Don't necessarily be tempted by the highest loan — work out whether you can actually afford the monthly repayments. Consider if you would still be able to make those repayments if interest rates went up another three or four per cent.

By this point you will have a fair idea of the maximum amount you can spend on the actual property. Before you begin looking for the home of your dreams make a list of all your house purchase costs. Exclude the estimated price of the property but include:

- Legal fees. Many solicitors and licensed conveyancers offer special 'packages' to home buyers so ask around your high street to see who can offer you the best deal. On the whole these 'package deals' give you a very basic service, so find out exactly what is on offer.
- Stamp duty (currently 1 per cent of the total purchase price for properties over £30,000), Land Registry fees (based on a sliding scale) and any local authority search fees (allow about £30).
- Survey and valuation fees. Your bank or building society will insist on carrying out a valuation of the property, the fees for which are assessed on a sliding scale according to the value of the property. In addition you would be advised to have a full or part structural survey of your own. The bank or building society can arrange for this or you can get an independent surveyor. Ask around for some guide to costs.
- Moving costs. Whether you decide to move yourselves, perhaps with a hired van, or get in professional movers, you must include their costs. Telephone a couple of companies to get a rough estimate — explain to them why you're asking.

Add up all the above costs and subtract them from your resources. You now have a more realistic guide as to how much you can spend on the property.

That figure can only really be a guide because you will also need to think about things like buying a cooker, fridge, carpet, curtains and so on. The more of these things that either come with the house or you have already, the more you can spend on the actual bricks and mortar.

You will also need to think about cash for the deposit. It's usual to put down a deposit of between 5 per cent and 10 per cent of the purchase price. You can get 100 per cent mortgages but you might find that it's not the best deal for you. Alternatively, you might be able to negotiate a 95 per cent mortgage, leaving you with less cash to find for the deposit.

Get a mortgage agreed in principle with a building society or other financial institution.

Step two: Decide what sort of property you are looking for

Home buyers hardly ever end up with exactly what they want but it does no harm to make a list of all the features you'd like. Include:

- Location — in a certain part of town, near transport, park, shops, schools, etc. If you rely on public transport, location might be crucial to you.
- Special requirements — minimum number of bedrooms, garden or balcony, garage, ground floor flat (for ease of access), top floor flat (for security), work room, own front door.
- Modern or period property. Conversion or purpose built.
- Also consider how much work you are prepared to do. If you're not a great DIY person and you haven't got the spare cash to pay a professional then steer clear of unmodernized properties.

Step three: Explore potential locations

If you're not familiar with an area then drive around or, better still, walk around it. What does it feel like? Do you feel safe? Can you smell a sewage works near by? Are there any trees or parks? Where are the nearest shops, bus stops or station? Can you park? Are the houses well looked after? Can you hear traffic/trains/old cars being crushed?

Don't just look at individual streets, find out what they back on to. There's no point in getting excited about an idyllic cottage with roses creeping around the front door only to discover later that it backs directly on to a bus depot, the gas works and two smoking factories.

Step four: Register with local estate agents

Estate agents are much maligned and as far as many are concerned that's quite justified. On the whole, older established agents who are also qualified surveyors tend to be more reliable.

It's not unusual to give your name and address to the same estate agent half a dozen times without ever hearing from them. The secret is to pester them. If you're really interested call them up three times a week, every day if necessary, to see what they've got on their books.

To begin with, it's useful to see as much property as you can even if it's not exactly what you're looking for. That way you'll get a good idea of what is actually available in your price range in a particular area. It's a good way to stop yourself chasing rainbows. You'll soon find out if you're being over-optimistic about what your money can buy.

Looking around will also give you an invaluable insight into 'estate agent speak'. You'll know for sure what a nine foot by eight foot double room looks like — cramped, and that an Ascot water heater with butler sink usually means a distinct need for modernization.

Once you've established for yourself what's available you'll have a better idea what you are *really* looking for and where you'll have to compromise. You'll probably know the streets to avoid and which house has a nasty view over everyone else's washing lines.

Step five: Looking at property

Unless you insist on a 'ready to move into' home, *ignore* the wallpaper and paint. For a start they might disguise all sorts of nasty structural horrors. Secondly it doesn't cost very much to redecorate — it costs a lot more to change the room sizes and you can't change the outlook and the location.

Here are some guidelines to looking at homes:

- Sniff the air. Does it smell damp?
- Look for staining on the walls and ceiling. Feel the walls if necessary.
- Take a sharp implement and (if you can) prod it into the window frames, skirting boards and other wood. Is it soft?
- Open all the doors. It's amazing how many 'fitted wardrobes' haven't a shelf or rail inside.
- Ask whether there's been any dampproof treatment/new roof/rewiring; how old the heating system is, etc.
- Go out the back of the house — look for crumbling brickwork, cladding coming away, leaking gutters, missing tiles off the roof.

If you smell damp, feel soggy wood, see tiles missing from the roof, crumbling brickwork and you haven't got spare cash for renovations maybe this home isn't for you!

Step six: You find something you like
Make an offer. It won't necessarily be accepted outright. You may have to negotiate.

Step seven: Your offer is accepted
The offer is accepted **subject to contract** which means that either side can pull out at any time before the formal contract is signed.

You may be asked as a token of good faith to make a nominal **preliminary deposit**. Make sure this is held by the vendor's estate agent or conveyancer. You have a right to have the preliminary deposit back at any time before you sign the formal contract, although if you do ask for it back the vendor is going to doubt whether you are a serious purchaser.

Step eight: Sorting out the formalities
You now need to do three things:

- **Secure your finance**: Go back to your mortgage provider←and make a formal application for a mortgage. They will take up references and will have the property valued ←.
- **Have the property surveyed**: You must find out whether the property is structurally sound. You can ask your building society surveyor to carry out a part or full survey at the same time as they do the valuation — you might save yourself money. Alternatively, contact the ROYAL INSTITUTE OF CHARTERED SURVEYORS to find a surveyor in your area.
- **See your convenyancer**: ←. You need to instruct your conveyancer. They will start making the necessary **searches** and finalizing the terms of the formal contract.

Step nine: Carrying out the searches
There are three main categories of searches for the vast majority of land transactions:

- **Local searches**: These will reveal who is responsible for the road and the mains, whether the house has been condemned, if it's the subject of a compulsory purchase order and many other matters which are under the control of the local authority. It can

149

take quite some time for these searches to come through, so the sooner you start the better.

- **Bankruptcy searches**: You will want to make sure that you're not buying from a bankrupt and your mortgage provider will want to know what they're not lending to a bankrupt. These searches are normally done just before completion → so that they are as up to date as possible.
- **Inspecting the entries at the Land Registry**: The vendor's conveyancer will provide your conveyancer with a copy of the entries at the Land Registry. This will show who owns (has **title** to) the land you are buying and whether there are any special restrictions over it.

Your conveyancer will also ask the vendor a number of questions about the property; this is called **Enquiries before Contract**. You should make sure that these confirm what the vendor is going to leave behind — carpets, light fittings, domestic appliances, etc.

Step ten: Signing the contract

When you sign the contract you hand over a deposit, which is normally 10 per cent of the total purchase price but it can vary ←. You are now committed to buying the property. If you pull out you will forfeit your deposit.

At the time you **exchange** (signing and swopping the contracts) you will agree a day to **complete** (move in).

You should also arrange with the vendor where to collect the keys on the day you complete.

Step eleven: Preparing for completion

First make sure that you have got adequate **insurance** (p.121). You will then need to organize the following:

- Hire a removal company. Contact the British Association Of Removers to find someone in your area. Or you could hire a self-drive van.
- Start packing. The earlier you begin the less hassled you'll feel as the big day draws closer. Even if you're getting a removal company to pack for you, it's worth going through cupboards and drawers in advance and throwing out the accumulated rubbish!
- Write to the Gas Board, the Electricity Board, the Water Board and British Telecom and tell them where you're moving to.

This is to inform you that on [date], I shall be moving to [address]. Please arrange for the meter to be read on that day.

Please can you continue to supply [service] to the above address.

Don't rely on the vendor to notify these services for you.

- Send out change of address cards or notify all your family, friends and colleagues of your new address. You may also want to arrange with the Post Office to redirect your mail for a limited period of time.

Whilst you are doing this your conveyancer will have confirmed that all the searches remain up to date.

Step twelve: Completion
Your conveyancer will arrange for the balance of the purchase price to be sent to the vendor. The property is yours. You can now move in!

- When you move in try and label all your boxes according to the rooms they should be put in. You could even put different colour stickers on them to ease identification.
- Keep your tools, cleaning materials and a kettle (along with coffee, tea and other essentials) handy.

Step thirteen: After you've completed
You'll probably be asked to settle your conveyancer's bill if you haven't already done so. You'll also have to pay your **stamp duty** (tax) and **Land Registry fees** (to register you as the owner of the property).

You should also think about getting a standing order to pay your mortgage and associated life or pension policy.

Can my spare room earn me money?
'I've recently bought my own flat but I really can't manage to pay the mortgage all by myself. I thought that I'd rent out my second bedroom. However, I'm a bit concerned about getting the right person and I'm not sure how formal I need to be about rent, bills and so on. Also I want to know what happens if it doesn't work out. Will I have to keep the person on even if I don't like them?'

Renting out a spare room is a good way to help pay the bills. If you think it through you can avoid the many pitfalls that flat sharing can set up for you.

Before you go ahead and look for a lodger, check with your mortgage provider (your bank, building society or other financial institution) that they don't object to you taking in a lodger.

Step one: Decide what sort of lodger you want

If you're used to living by yourself or in someone else's home and now want to rent out one of your own rooms, you may have to think hard about yourself and the way you live. Unless you can offer someone self-contained facilities they will be sharing your bathroom, kitchen and probably your living room.

Make a list of the things that are important to you. Think about the following:

- Does it matter what sex or age they are?
- Is their background, job or the hours they work important?
- Do you want someone who is away most weekends?
- What about their girl/boyfriends? How do you feel about extra people staying over?
- Do you have any particular dietary or religious requirements? For example, if you're a vegetarian are you prepared to accept a meat eater cooking in your kitchen?
- How do you feel about someone sharing your main living room with you?
- Do you need to use the bathroom at a certain time in the morning?
- How about noise? Do you go to bed very early?
- How fussy are you about cleanliness and tidiness?
- Are you prepared to let them use your cooking utensils, etc?
- Do you have any very strong religious, political or moral viewpoints?

Once you have some answers you'll have a clearer idea of: who you are looking for; where you might find them; the questions you want to ask when you meet them; and the basic ground rules you want to lay down.

Step two: Decide what you can offer and make some ground rules

What facilities are you offering your lodger? These might include:

- Room.
- Shared/own bathroom.
- Shared kitchen.
- Shared living room.
- Use of washing machine/dishwasher/garden, etc.

You also ought to think about ensuring you have all the essentials such as a bed, curtains, chest of drawers and a wardrobe. Also, what do you intend to do about bed-linen, etc? Will the lodger be expected to provide their own? In addition you need to consider what to do about buying things such as tea, coffee, cleaning stuff — will you have a household kitty?

At the same time make yourself a set of ground rules which you expect your lodger — and yourself — to keep to. For example:

- The flat must be kept clean and tidy. No dirty china, newspapers or clothing lying around. The lodger is expected to clean their own room, do their own washing up and clean the bathroom after they've used it. Other cleaning to be split between both of us.
- Lodger's friends can stay over only by prior agreement and for not more than two nights at a time.
- I expect to have the flat to myself occasionally to entertain in and will give good notice of this.
- I go to bed at 11 pm and don't want any noise after this time. No telephone calls after 10.30 pm.

You can always change the ground rules as you go along — as long as you both agree to keep them. But it's definitely worth getting down on paper what you expect. It's much fairer, no one is left guessing.

Step three: Decide how much to charge

You will need to shop around to find out what the going rate is in your area for a flat share. You will then decide whether to charge rent including all bills or rent plus bills. It's usually safer to charge a basic rent then ask for a half (or a third depending on how many people are sharing) of gas and electricity bills.

You will also need to consider how to deal with the telephone. It is possible to get telephones with a device that records the time taken for any call.

Step four: Advertise for a lodger

Write out a basic advertisement which you can change according to where you use it.

'Wanted. Female, 25–30 to share comfortable flat with one other woman, Lower Balham, near station. Own room. All mod cons. £50 per week plus bills. Tel: 071 123 4569'

'Flat share, centre of town. Professional, male or female for own large room. Share kitchen, bathroom, etc. £45 inclusive. Call Bill after 6 pm, 0722 8716.'

The best way of finding someone suitable is of course the great grapevine of friends, colleagues and family. The chances are you will get a lodger who someone you trust already knows.

The problem with this or any situation where your lodger was recommended by someone you know is that if things don't work out, it can become quite messy having to tell your closest colleague's best friend that you no longer want her living in your flat!

Alternatively, try advertising:

• At work.
• Local shop windows, church or community centres.
• Through clubs or organizations you belong to.
• Local or national papers and magazines.

Step five: Interview prospective lodgers

If you are at all concerned about having strangers in your home, do ask a friend to come along as well. Another opinion from someone you trust can be valuable but you might want to ask them to keep in the background at least to start with.

You ought to find out as much as you can about your prospective lodger, not only whether they can actually pay the rent but their habits and attitudes. Don't go by immediate impressions. Someone who seems very arrogant when they walk in might just be very nervous about meeting you.

To get information out of people you need to ask 'open ended questions'. If you ask, 'What do you do — do you enjoy it?' you might well get the reply, 'I'm a teacher — it's all right.' Try saying things like: 'Tell me about your job — what do you enjoy most about it?'

You also need to sound interested in what they are saying, so look at them when they are talking. The more you find out about them — their job, hobbies, ambitions, where they grew up, what they do in their spare time, their tastes in literature, music, politics, films, etc., the easier it will be to make a decision about them.

Remember you are not choosing someone to be your best buddy, you're trying to find a person you can tolerate living in your home. Tact and consideration for others are not bad qualities to go for!

Finally, you must be prepared to talk a bit about yourself. It is, after all, a two-way deal. Give the other person your ground rules and ask them what they feel about them.

Step six: The paperwork

At the very least you need some form of letter confirming your arrangement, even if you are renting out your room to a friend.

Room for rent, 36b, Roof Road, Overhead

This is to confirm that I have agreed to rent to you a room in my flat at the above address as from 5th April.

The rent will be £50 a week, payable fortnightly in advance. In addition I will require a further £200 as deposit to be paid with your first four weeks rent; this is returnable. You will be expected to pay for or replace all your breakages.

The rent excludes the electricity and gas bills and these will be split equally between the two of us. You will be responsible for keeping an accurate record of any telephone calls you make and reimbursing me for them.

If either one of us wishes to terminate this agreement we can do so at any time giving two weeks' notice.

Please would you confirm that you accept the above by signing the enclosed copy and returning it to me.

You might want to add any details about washing, linen, cooking utensils, cleaning, etc. that you feel are relevant.

Step seven: Making the flat share work

Don't expect to get on like a house on fire within a few minutes. The other person might be extremely shy and reserved, so if you're a boisterous extrovert avoid overwhelming your new lodger — give them time to get settled. Again, don't make value judgements about their behaviour — you know how everything works in your home, they don't and will need to find their feet.

If, on the other hand, you find yourself with a bounding fire raiser, then you might have to be very firm about marking out your own space. For example, you may need to point out that certain parts of the flat such as your bedroom are yours alone and that your lodger isn't welcome there.

Whatever you do, be very straightforward about things that bother you such as untidiness, noise or failure to put the lids on bottles and caps on tubes. Don't leave your lodger to guess what is wrong by your sulks or tantrums. Say that you expect the same from them. Be assertive! (p.30).

Make lists, rotas, funny regulations but above all make sure you both know the rules of the game.

Step eight: What happens if things go wrong

With any luck your flat share will end quite amicably when one or other of you decides to move on to pastures new.

However, if you find that you really don't get on with your lodger you can ask them to leave, giving them two weeks' notice (or whatever else you specified). You may find that if the feeling is mutual or if your lodger tells you that they want to move out, one or other of you might decide to forfeit some rent. Remember to refund them their deposit if appropriate.

If you give your lodger notice and then they still refuse to go at the end of the notice period, you can apply to the Magistrates Court for a **Possession Order**, whereby the court will order your lodger to leave.

If your lodger leaves without paying rent, you could recover the money they owe you through the County court (p.249).

If you find that your lodger has left some of their belongings in your flat after they've moved out, you can't simply throw them away. You'll need to write to your former lodger and give them a reasonable time within which to collect their things before you dispose of them.

What else?

If you **rent** a property and you are given some kind of agreement or licence to sign, make sure that you understand it fully before you put your signature on it. A CAB or advice centre will go through it with you.

If you live in a self-contained flat or house, landlords do not have the right to come into the property without your permission except in an emergency.

If you think your landlord is harassing you or trying unlawfully to evict you, get advice immediately. You cannot simply be thrown out on the street, neither can the landlord withhold your belongings.

Family matters

Getting along with family members and close friends is obviously very different from dealing with shop managers and personnel in bureaucratic organizations.

If you're having to cope with a particular crisis, such as divorce, illness or death, you'll need not only to understand what can be complex procedures and laws but also how to handle strong emotions. Even the pleasant things in life — birth, watching children grow up and marriage — are not free from trauma and stress.

The important thing is to know when to turn to others for help. Build up a strong support network of family and friends (p.160), you never know when you might need them — even just to have someone to listen to you.

There are numerous organizations and self-help groups ready to offer practical advice, a sympathetic ear and even physical help. Some of them are listed in the back of this book, you'll find others through your local library, CAB or Social Services. Don't be afraid to use them, their services are usually free.

Getting on with the family

A great deal of unnecessary resentment and ill feeling builds up in many families because people are reluctant to be absolutely honest with themselves and those around them. They hide their true feelings, are afraid to make demands on others or ask them to change their behaviour.

This doesn't mean you should become totally insensitive to those around you but it does mean you should learn to recognize your own needs.

Make a list of your personal needs. They might include practical things such as 'the need to be given help around the house' or 'the need to have time or space to get on with my hobbies'. They might include more general things such as 'the need to be listened to' or 'the need to be respected'.

Now change the word 'need' to the words 'I have the right to…'. Before you can get other people to recognize your needs you have to believe that you have the right to them. If you are at all in doubt ask yourself, 'why not?' It's often hard to find a good reason. It won't be easy to change habits of a lifetime and with it people's expectations of you but it's worth doing. Practise being assertive (p.30).

Where can I find someone to look after my baby?

'I had a baby two months ago and I've every intention of going back to work, at least part time. What's really bothering me at the moment is how I can find someone reliable to look after my child whilst I'm working. I've heard such horror stories that I'm now beginning to have second thoughts about it all. Where do I start looking?'

The seemingly never-ending cycle of dilemmas, soul-searching and compromises is something which many working mothers and, increasingly, fathers face. On the one hand there is a need — financial or personal — to return to work, on the other an intricate set of complexes and concerns about leaving the child, missing its first steps, words, etc. and giving over the precious bundle to someone else to care for. Will my child be scarred for life? Will my child realize I'm its mother? etc., etc.

The solution seems to be to accept the fact that you may never feel completely guiltless ever again and to find a carer in which you have almost total if not absolute faith.

There are many options and the one you choose will obviously depend largely on your resources and your ideas about the needs of your child. Remember that you might not find the ideal solution right away and it may be a case of trial and error before you find something which is suitable.

Step one: Before you start looking

Make a list of all the important points about your work and child-care arrangements.

These might include:

• How much you can afford to spend.

- Whether you have a spare room in your house and if you are willing to put it aside for live-in help.
- The kind of job you will return to. Does it involve shift work or awkward hours? How flexible can you be?
- Is it important for your child to socialize with other children? Does your child have any special needs?
- What hours do you need a carer for? Is it important to have a carer in the evenings and at weekends?
- What kind of support do you have in emergencies, e.g. if the child or carer was ill?
- How good are you at getting up and organized in the morning rush?

Step two: Build up a support network

You may already have a large circle of family, friends and neighbours who support you. If not, you need to start building one. Of course if a support network is going to be successful it has to work both ways and be reciprocal.

Making new friends and renewing old acquaintances is not necessarily easy to do especially if you feel very shy. Try to be assertive (p.30). You will have to take a few risks. You may find yourself rejected a couple of times but it is more likely you will find some very good friends. If you do feel rejected, remember, it's probably because the other person was harassed/had just had a row/was too shy to talk to you; nine times out of ten it has nothing directly to do with you.

Make contact with your neighbours, especially those with children. Ring their doorbell, invite them over for coffee. If they don't come (it's probably because their kids are driving them mad), call again.

Join a local mother and baby group. Your library, town hall or community centre will have details.

Join the local branch of an organization like the NATIONAL CHILDBIRTH TRUST or more general women's organizations such as the NATIONAL WOMEN'S REGISTER, TOWNSWOMEN'S GUILD or NATIONAL FEDERATION OF WOMEN'S INSTITUTES. Obviously each local group will depend on its members, but don't write them off before you've met them — you might be pleasantly surprised!

Find out if your church has a mother's group or perhaps the vicar can put you in touch with other young mums or an older person who enjoys looking after children.

Step three: Your options

Although you will want to ask about professional qualifications, the general rule of thumb seems to be, if the carer feels right and the atmosphere they create makes you feel confident and relaxed, then that counts for far more than official pieces of paper.

In general, if you have someone to care for your child in your home you eliminate many of the travelling and timing difficulties. It also means you probably won't have to make other arrangements if your child is ill. However, you will have to organize emergency cover if the carer is ill.

If your carer is outside your home, you will have to consider the distance you'll need to travel and in the case of nurseries, strict opening hours. On the plus side, especially as far as nurseries are concerned, your child will get a rich social life and plenty of stimulation from other children and a variety of carers. However, they may end up catching more illnesses from the other children — and you might have to organize emergency cover! (You can't win!)

Leave yourself about two months to find a carer. You might find that you have to register with some nurseries as soon as the child is born in order to secure a place.

Option one: member of your family

The carer is likely to be someone your child already knows. However, you would need to think about the willingness and ability of that family member to undertake the role of carer on a regular basis. Even if a member of your family cannot fulfil the carer role permanently perhaps they would help out in emergencies.

Option two: registered childminder

These are usually women with their own children who look after a limited number of other children in their home. All childminders have to be registered with the local council. They will usually care for the child between 8 am and 6 pm with any extra hours by arrangement.

Always visit a prospective childminder with your child. Look at the toys she has available and discuss with her your attitudes towards child care to see if they are compatible. Try and speak to the parents of the other children she cares for.

For more information about childminders, average fees, etc., contact the NATIONAL CHILDMINDERS ASSOCIATION. In addition your local Social Services or health visitor should have a list of registered childminders.

Option three: nurseries

Unfortunately it is almost impossible to get places in local council-run, heavily subsidized nurseries. Although a growing number of employers such as banks are introducing workplace nurseries, your best bet is going to be a community or private nursery. However, the most expensive are not necessarily the best.

It can be quite difficult to find a place for a very young baby. Some nurseries require children to have reached a certain stage before they will accept them.

When you visit the nursery ask about the qualifications and number of staff. Find out about play provision and the type of food provided. Look around to see if all the other children seem happy and cared for.

Again, your local social services should be able to provide you with a list of nurseries in the area.

Option four: nannies

Nannies come in about as many varieties as Heinz! — from the highly trained, uniformed Norland nanny who may well expect you to keep other 'staff' to a young girl with no formal qualifications but the experience of bringing up numerous brothers and sisters.

Most trained nannies will have a **National Nursery Examination Board (NNEB)** qualification. However, personality and your confidence in them to do the job are usually more important. Remember, if you're out at work all day, you need someone who's capable not only of looking after the child but won't panic if the freezer starts defrosting or a strange man comes to the door.

Nannies can live in or out. They are not expected to do any housework or other chores except those directly concerning the child. Neither can they be expected to spend all day in a wreck because you failed to clear the house up. If you have a live-in nanny you have many advantages but consider carefully whether you want an extra person living in your house — you might find you have to cope with an additional set of emotional problems.

The other option is to share a nanny with someone else. You would have to decide which house the nanny would work from and recompense that family accordingly. You will also have to think about holiday arrangements and what happens if one child is ill. Use your support network ← to see if anyone is interested. Do make sure that your views are compatible before you start looking for a nanny.

You can find a nanny either by advertising — *The Lady* seems to be *the* magazine to use — or through an agency. Before you use an agency always check what their terms are. Or you could try word of mouth.

In your advertisement be very clear what you expect the nanny to do, the accommodation (if any) you are offering and any peculiarities about your work situation, e.g. shift work, freelance working at home, etc. Avoid slushy phrases such as 'darling cherub boy needs devoted angel nanny' — it won't get you anywhere and it's a waste of money. Try something along the lines of:

NANNY required from May for six month old girl. London N3. Own room, shower. Some housework. Four weeks paid holiday. Mother works from home. References. Tel: [   ]

When you interview your prospective nannies find out as much as you can about their background — home life, contact with parents, religion, boyfriends, as well as their professional skills including ideas about play and learning, feeding, etc. Always take up references personally — telephone the other families, ask about the nanny's bad points as well as her good.

If you employ a nanny, you must give her a statement of her terms and conditions including notice period. You will also be required to deduct tax and National Insurance contributions from her pay and pay employers' National Insurance, too. It is highly unlikely that the Inland Revenue will accept a nanny's claim that she is self-employed. Contact your local Inland Revenue office — their address will be in the phone book — and explain that you are about to start employing someone. They will ask you a few basic questions and will then send you the appropriate forms and other literature.

Option five: mother's helps
Mother's helps will often help with the housework as well as childcare. They may not have an NNEB qualification and their rates are usually cheaper. You would need to advertise and interview in the same way as you would for a nanny.

Option six: au pairs

The majority of au pairs come from western Europe, although some come from further afield and a few are British. They are usually very young, filling in for six months or a year before they go to work or college. For most of them their aim is to learn or better their English.

You should be prepared to accept the au pair as a member of the family. Her housework and child-care routine is limited and she must have time to study. Au pairs have all their accommodation and food provided by their employer and in addition are entitled to 'pocket money' — usually considerably more than you might give your teenage offspring.

Au pairs from EEC countries are not subject to any restrictions, those from outside the EEC may be — check with the HOME OFFICE.

Au pairs can be found through recommendation, agencies or by advertising in a foreign newspapers. Do remember that these girls are young and often inexperienced. For many it is their first time abroad. Avoid disasters — don't expect them to take on too much responsibility until you have assessed their capabilities.

Step four: Making the relationship work

Whatever you finally choose to do, remember that it won't be perfect all of the time.

- Do be very exact about your nanny/mother's help/au pair's duties. If you leave someone else in your home, spend a couple of days with them going through everyday routines. Write down any important details such as how to operate the central heating system or burglar alarm.
- Whoever looks after your child, make sure that they understand the child's diet, sleeping patterns, peculiarities.
- Always leave a telephone number for emergencies with your carer. And if you have a nanny or similar carer, telephone once a day to see that everything is okay.
- Finally, don't take your carer for granted. She's also got a job to do.

What else?

If you're looking for any type of **domestic help**, **carer** or perhaps **companion** for an elderly or disabled person, the same rules about advertising, interviewing and employment apply. Whether or not you will have to deduct tax and National Insurance will depend on how much your employee earns. Your local tax office will be able to advise you.

I think my son's taking drugs

'I'm really concerned about my fourteen year old son. Recently he's been behaving very strangely. He's very pale and he seems lifeless a lot of the time. When I ask him if anything's wrong he just avoids me. His whole behaviour has changed. I'm worried that he might be taking drugs. Is there any way of telling? What do I do if he is?'

The first thing is not to panic. Your son might not be on drugs. The second thing is to understand the facts about drugs and drug taking.

Any drug used to excess, including 'socially acceptable' drugs like tobacco and alcohol, can have destructive effects. There's little evidence to suggest that the sort of drug use most common amongst youngsters — glue sniffing, smoking cannabis and the odd sniff of amphetamine powder — will develop into a damaging drug problem in the future.

Although it's unlikely, those youngsters who do move on to stronger drugs and who perhaps end up as confirmed 'hard drug' addicts, often have a range of other social and psychological problems that have not been resolved.

Always think carefully about what it is your child might be involved in. Is it simply a part of experimental and rebellious growing up? Or is your child facing other problems — low self-esteem, romantic break-ups, bullying or work problems at school, crises in the family? Have you given your child a real chance to talk to you? Are you prepared to listen?

Step one: Find out the facts

Below is a brief summary of the kind of drugs children may be involved in. To ensure you have a balanced picture ask for more information and advice from the agencies listed in the reference section at the back of this book under 'Drugs and Addictions' (p.284).

Solvent abuse is commonest amongst youngsters. It's not illegal, it's relatively cheap and not that difficult to obtain. On the whole 'glue sniffing', as it's commonly known, is indulged in by small groups of adolescent boys as the latest craze usually during the spring and summer months. Although some individuals become compulsive 'sniffers', even they seem to suffer no long-term detrimental effects. Solvent abuse does not create a physical dependency.

A wide variety of household and domestic products are inhaled to produce an intoxicated effect not unlike that of alcohol. However, the effects are immediate but short-lived — about half an hour. There are three types of products likely to be sniffed:

- Solvents where the vapour evaporates to leave a solid base, such as impact adhesives and glues.
- Liquids that give off vapour, such as petrol and nail varnish.
- Compressed gasses, such as butane-gas lighter refills or aerosols.

Often the intoxicating substance is poured on to a rag or clothing or put into a small bag, such as a crisp packet and inhaled.

The main dangers of glue sniffing are:

- Suffocation by placing a plastic bag full of glue over the head.
- Sniffing in dangerous places such as beside railway lines or canals where an intoxicated youngster out of control might fall, or in isolated spaces including alone in their own bedroom where help is unlikely, or in confined or high places.
- Suffocating due to inhalation of vomit after sniffing to the point of unconsciousness.
- Experimenting sniffing with new or combinations of substances such as glue and alcohol or glue and pills.

Heroin is an 'opiate' which derives from the opium poppy. Many opiates such as morphine and codeine as well as heroin are used for quite legitimate medical purposes.

Most heroin is mixed with similar looking powders such as glucose and sold in small bags. The powder mixtures can be various shades of grey, pink, brown or white. It can be dissolved in water and injected, sniffed or 'snorted' up the nose or smoked. 'Chasing the dragon' is a method of smoking heroin by heating it (usually on a piece of foil or a spoon) and breathing in the fumes often through a small tube.

Heroin is now cheaper and more widely available, but its use appears generally limited amongst young teenagers.

Heroin generally induces feelings of warmth, well-being and euphoria. Unpleasant side-effects such as vomiting quickly disappear with regular use. Someone 'high' on heroin will usually function relatively normally although they may appear a little drowsy and their speech may be slurred.

The main dangers of taking heroin are:

- Addiction. It's possible to become addicted to heroin *no matter how it's taken*.
- There are greater health risks from injecting heroin. These include the dangers of overdosing; using infected needles and introducing damaging bacteria or viruses including AIDS directly into the bloodstream.
- Taking impure drugs of an unknown strength.
- Breaking the law.

Cannabis is the subject of much controversy and some people want to see it legalized. Cannabis is usually taken in the form of herbal cannabis (a green or brown mixture made by drying and shredding parts of the cannabis plant) or cannabis resin (a brown solid that must be heated and crumbled before use).

Cannabis is often smoked sometimes with tobacco or combined with other food and drink.

The most common effects are relaxation, talkativeness and sense of well-being, although not everyone is affected.

Users cannot become physically dependent on cannabis but may develop a psychological dependence on it as a way of relaxing or coping.

The dangers of taking cannabis are:

- Possible respiratory diseases as a result of long-term, regular smoking.
- Consequences of becoming intoxicated and attempting to drive or cross a road or undertake some other activity.
- It's illegal.

Barbiturates are probably the most dangerous form of sedatives. Like tranquillizers they help reduce anxiety and induce sleep. But in large doses, if the user stays awake, they have an intoxicating effect.

The dangers of taking barbiturates are:

- They are extremely addictive and unsupervised withdrawal can be not just unpleasant but also dangerous.
- They are easy to overdose on, particularly if taken with alcohol or injected.

- Users can injure themselves whilst 'high'.

Tranquillizers such as Mogadon and Valium have similar effects to those of barbiturates, but their effect is less dramatic.
The dangers of tranquillizers are:

- They are the most frequently prescribed drugs in Britain but can create dependency if not monitored.
- They can be reasonably accessible to young people if left lying around the house.

Cocaine or 'coke' is a stimulant which gets rid of tiredness for a time and produces a feeling of alertness and confidence.
Consisting of a white powder which has sometimes been mixed with other substances such as milk powder, it is sniffed into the nose.
Although more widely available, it's still expensive.

Amphetamines are more commonly used stimulants. Known as 'speed', amphetamine sulphate is a white powder that can be eaten, smoked or injected but is usually 'snorted' like cocaine.
Often amphetamines are used in a 'run' lasting several days. There are no dangerous withdrawal symptoms.
The dangers of using amphetamines are:

- Unpleasant side-effects, such as disturbed sleep and loss of appetite, feelings of anxiety or paranoia.
- Sometimes amphetamines are mixed with barbiturates before being sold. The user may not know this and the consequences are potentially very dangerous.
- They are illegal.

Hallucinogens such as **LSD** or 'acid' and **Liberty Cap mushrooms** are not addictive and cause few known health hazards. The effects vary greatly but range from joyous or mystical experiences to grotesque fears or visions.
LSD is absorbed in minute quantities on to paper, sugar cubes or some other material before being swallowed. Liberty Cap and other hallucinogenic mushrooms grow wild in Britain and can be eaten fresh or cooked.
The dangers with hallucinogens are:

- Psychological rather than physical, particularly if someone has a frightening experience or already has a disturbed personality.

- Poisonous mushrooms rather than the hallucinogenic varieties might be picked by mistake. This could be fatal.

There are medicines which can be bought **over the counter** which, if taken in sufficient quantities, can be used to get high.

These include: cough medicines containing opiates; motion sickness tablets; decongestants containing antihistamines which have a sedating effect; and some nasal decongestants which can act as stimulants.

Step two: Recognizing the signs of drug taking

An observant parent will immediately notice any changes in their child's behaviour and wonder what has caused it. There may be a host of 'normal' reasons, so eliminate those first.

Any evidence of drug taking will obviously depend on the type of drug your child may be using. You must consider to what extent the effect 'prying' (as it may be seen) into your child's affairs including searching their room or pockets will provoke unnecessary hostility. This would be counter-productive.

- Changes in behaviour — listlessness, restlessness, disinterested in food or other activities, secretive, aggressive, depressed, acting as if intoxicated.
- Changes in appearance — pale, losing weight, cold-like symptoms, a rash like cold sores around the mouth and nose, unusual scars, constipation, irregular menstruation.
- The apparatus — evidence of solvents, pills or other substances which cannot be accounted for under normal circumstances, pieces of silver foil, crisp packets that smell peculiar, the smell of solvents on clothes, blood stains on clothes, needles.

Do not search for evidence that isn't there.

Step three: Confronting drug taking or addiction

There are no hard and fast rules about how you should confront the issue. Your actions are going to be very different if, for example, you simply suspect your child of glue sniffing than if you find him comatose from a concoction of barbiturates and alcohol. Consider these three things.

- What are your own attitudes? How do you feel? If you think you feel angry look back at the anger ladder on p.31. Get the situation into perspective.

- Do you know enough about the subject?←Can you distinguish between fact and fiction about drugs? Do you know where to go for extra help?
- What sort of relationship do you have with your child? Can you talk openly? Or will sitting down and talking together make either of you feel uncomfortable?

Above all, don't be afraid to talk about the subject of drugs and drug taking.

You have a number of options — one or a combination of them might be appropriate.

- Talk to your child. Be direct and be assertive (p.30). Beware of creating a battleground.
- Seek medical advice. A doctor might be able to put both your minds at rest about any ill effects or advise you about any necessary treatment.
- Talk to teachers at your child's school. They may also be aware that there is a drugs problem amongst their pupils and might want to try and eliminate it. Local youth club leaders might also be approached.
- Talk to other parents; they may well be experiencing similar problems (or have failed to recognize that there is a problem).
- Contact one of the many specialist organizations or counselling groups←. Some give you the opportunity to talk to a counsellor over the telephone rather than face to face. They are used to dealing with these problems.
- Get support from family members, friends, other parents.

If you can, don't let the problem get out of hand. Ask for help *before* you find you can no longer cope with it.

Your legal responsibilities

You don't need to use or supply illegal drugs to commit an offence, you can fall foul of the law by simply allowing someone to produce or supply drugs on your 'premises'. So if you know that your child is sharing illegal drugs with a friend in your home, including cannabis or opium, and you do nothing about it, you have committed an offence.

If you find drugs, you must destroy them or hand them over to the police. What you do depends on the situation.

- If your action will prevent another person committing an offence with the drugs, you can either destroy the drugs *or* hand them over to the police (see Example).

> *Example*
> Jenny Travers finds a small packet of what she presumes to be cocaine in her daughter's bedroom. Jenny thinks that if she leaves the packet there, her daughter will use the stuff. She is therefore allowed by law to destroy the drug and does not have to involve the police.

- In any other situation, you must ensure that the illegal drugs are handed over to the police.
- You do not have to tell the police if you suspect your children, or anyone else, are taking or supplying illegal drugs.

What else?
- If you're concerned about your own or someone else's dependence on **tranquillizers**, even if they've been prescribed by a doctor, contact an organization such as TRANX who can provide support for those wishing to live without relying on tranquillizers. They can also offer help to people experiencing problems coming off these drugs.
- If you think you may have a drinking problem — you can't get through the day without at least one drink — or you are concerned about someone close to you, an organization such as ALCOHOLICS ANONYMOUS or AL ANON may be able to offer you support and advice.

My boyfriend is battering me and my children
'I'm really frightened but I've no idea who to turn to. I've been living with this man for five years and we've got a boy of three and a girl of eighteen months. My boyfriend used to be very caring and kind towards me and the children. Recently he's been having some trouble at work and he's started drinking. I know that he behaves perfectly in the office but once he gets home he becomes really abusive.

'Usually he just makes verbal threats but last week he started pushing me around. Two evenings ago he hit me in the stomach and I had to go to the doctor. I'm really afraid that he'll start on the children next. I'm worried that if I say anything he'll just get more violent. I can't talk to his family or friends — they'll never believe me.'

171

Living with a violent partner can be terrifying and also very lonely. A great deal of abuse is suffered in silence. So why don't women say anything?

Often they are frightened of the consequences, that no one will believe them, that their partner will become more violent or hurt the children. Sometimes women continue to suffer abuse because they want to cling on to their relationship or because their partners are full of remorse after each bout of abuse.

If you are in such a situation you should act immediately to take yourself and your children out of danger. The law isn't foolproof but it can offer some protection. Although there are still some people around who think that wife battering is part and parcel of a relationship, you will find there are many who will listen to you and try to help you.

Step one: Get out of the house

Don't worry that your partner will be able to evict you or claim that you have left the house for good — he can't. Take the children somewhere safe. A neighbour, friend or member of your family might give you somewhere to stay. It's surprising how willing people are to help in times of emergency.

If this isn't possible contact your local Women's Aid Refuge or Battered Women's Home. Your police station, CAB or advice centre will have a telephone number. For obvious reasons refuges don't make their addresses public.

If you find yourself trapped in the house or your partner threatens to become violent, call the police. Sometimes they are reluctant to intervene in 'domestic rows' but they will usually wait until peace is restored. They may offer to take you to a refuge but they can only remove the children if they think their safety is being threatened.

Step two: Apply for an emergency injunction

An **injunction** is a court order to either bar your partner from all or part of the house (known as an **Ouster Order**) or to stop him abusing you (known as a **Non Molestation Order**).

You can apply for these without first having to leave the house but in practice it is often less harassing to do it from somewhere safe where you are not worrying that your partner might come home drunk any minute.

Although you can apply for the injunction yourself by going to your nearest County court, it may be easier if you use a solicitor (p.237). If you are in conflict with your partner, their financial position is irrelevant. So if you have no or very little money of your own you may qualify for legal aid.

You can obtain an injunction in a matter of hours. This is known as an **Ex Parte Order** which means that your partner does not have to be notified or heard in court. However, he can contest it at a later date. Injunctions can be obtained at weekends or after hours. If you find yourself unable to contact a solicitor, ask the police for the number of the Duty Judge or Magistrate. Be persistent, you are quite within your rights to ask for it.

Your application for an injunction is presented in the form of **affidavits** — sworn statements of your evidence. If you can, take along any witnesses or doctor's letters if you have them. You may need to show your injuries. If you are abused, do visit your doctor, so that your injuries can be put on record.

If you have been actually physically harmed by your partner ask the judge to attach **Powers of Arrest** to the injunction. If your partner then forces his way into your home or threatens you with abuse, call the police. The police have greater authority to take action to protect you.

Step three: Making an injunction work

Injunctions are only pieces of paper — they cannot keep the wolf from the door. If you are abused again, call the police. Your partner may well be arrested and charged with breaking the order and possibly assault.

Whatever you do, don't be persuaded to let your partner back in again. When you do, you will invalidate the injunction. If the situation deteriorates, which it usually does, you may find the courts less sympathetic to grant another order.

Step four: Deciding what to do next

You may feel that you need some emotional as well as practical support. Friends and family might be willing to believe and help you. Alternatively, you could get in touch with a local women's centre or group.

If you decide to stay in your home you should consider getting your home put into your name and sorting out the financial consequences. If you decide to leave make sure that you get your share of any property you own or have put money into. A solicitor will advise you what to do.

If you are not married your children have only one legal parent — their mother. If you separate from your partner you can ask the court to make orders for custody, access and maintenance as if you were married. That means that it is possible for fathers to get court orders for custody and maintenance of their children.

Organizations for single parents
GINGERBREAD ASSOCIATION FOR ONE PARENT FAMILIES
NATIONAL COUNCIL FOR ONE PARENT FAMILIES

We want to get divorced
'My wife and I haven't been getting along for some years now — I suppose we've just grown apart. We've decided to go our separate ways. We've got a little boy of four and have agreed that our son should stay with his mother. What are the legal requirements regarding divorce procedures? As we are still on very amicable terms do we need to do anything formal about custody and maintenance of our son?'

If you end your marriage on friendly terms that's really good news. However, to safeguard all your interests, particularly your child's, it's worth formalizing your arrangements through the courts. There is always the chance, however slight, that your relationship may not be so amicable in the future, perhaps if one of you finds a new partner or you have a disagreement about your son's schooling or upbringing.

As you and your partner are in complete agreement over the division of your property, maintenance, custody and arrangements for your child then you can go ahead and manage the divorce yourselves. If there are any doubts or disputes seek the advice of a solicitor immediately (p.237).

The Petition: The application to court requesting a divorce.
The Petitioner: The person who files the petition.
The Respondent: The person sued for divorce.
Co-respondent: In cases of adultery this is the person with whom the respondent has had a sexual relationship.

There is only one ground for divorce in this country — that the marriage has broken down irretrievably.

There are five ways of proving this:

- **Desertion**. The respondent has deserted the petitioner for at least two years.
- **Two years apart with consent**. The parties have lived apart for a minimum of two years and the respondent agrees to a divorce.
- **Five years without consent**. The parties have lived apart for a continuous period of five years. No consent is needed.
- **Adultery** and you find it impossible to go on living with your partner. Providing the respondent doesn't contest the petition this is often the quickest and easiest way of achieving divorce. However, in most cases if you resume normal relations with the offender after the adultery you may be seen as having forgiven it.
- **Unreasonable behaviour**. The respondent has behaved in such a way that the petitioner cannot be expected to continue living with him/her. It can be very difficult to categorize but includes violence, public humiliation, insanity, excessive or unnatural sexual desires, meanness with money. If you are filing for divorce other than on the grounds of physical abuse, you would be wise to seek the advice of a solicitor.

You cannot get divorced if you have been married for less than a year. You or the respondent will also have to be either legally domiciled (the country which you regard as your permanent home) or resident in this country for a year before you can start proceedings.

Step one: Get copies of the application form

You can get these from Divorce County Courts, legal stationers and CAB. You will need *four* copies of the form — one for you, one for the respondent, one for the court and one for the co-respondent (who need not be named if the petitioner does not know their name) in cases of adultery.

If you have children you will also need to obtain at the same time another form called the **Statement as to Arrangements**. On this form you will have to explain your proposals for your children — where and with whom they will live, education, access, maintenance, etc. You will need *three* copies.

The forms are reasonably straightforward to complete. Take a photocopy of the blank form and write a draft so that you can think through carefully what you want to say.

You can either take the forms or post them to your local Divorce County Court — look for the address in the telephone directory. In

London the petition is filed in the Divorce Registry. You will need to include the current fee and a copy of your marriage certificate.

Step two: The petition is circulated

The court sends out copies of the petition to the respondent and where necessary the co-respondent. If neither indicates their intention of defending the case you will be sent a copy of the acknowledgement together with two new forms to complete.

The first is an **Affidavit of Evidence**, the second a **Request for Directions to Trial** which is an application for the case to be heard by a registrar. You can send these both back by post but if you do, you will have to go first to a solicitor to have the **affidavit** (a formal statement witnessed by a solicitor) sworn; the solicitor will make a small charge for this.

If there are children involved the registrar will fix a date to meet the custodial parent — the parent with whom the children will remain. This informal hearing, the **Children's Appointment**, is where the registrar considers the arrangements for the children.

Step three: Granting of a Decree Nisi

Once the registrar is satisfied that the petitioner is entitled to a divorce, they will announce a date on which in the absence of any objection, a **Decree Nisi** will be granted. This is the first part of the divorce decree but you cannot remarry yet.

The registrar will also decide which party ought to pay costs. Even if the costs are minimal you can always ask for them to be paid by the respondent.

Step four: Granting of the Decree Absolute

After six weeks, the petitioner can apply for the **Decree Absolute**. The form can be obtained from the court office. If, after three months, the petitioner still fails to apply for it, the respondent can apply instead.

Useful organizations

For single parents, see p.174.
RELATE (formerly the Marriage Guidance Council)

My father's becoming senile — How can I safeguard his interests?

'I'm concerned about my elderly father. Until recently he was physically

quite frail but mentally very alert. Now whenever I see him, he appears to be getting very confused although for some of the time he seems quite lucid. The doctor just says it's senility which will get progressively worse.

'*He's quite a wealthy man and he seems to have numerous bank accounts, shares and so on — I think it's one of his hobbies! What worries me is that he soon won't be able to cope with all his business affairs, not to mention looking after his house, paying the bills, etc. Is there anything I can do to make sure everything is kept in order?*'

If you want to safeguard your father's interests you must act quickly before his condition declines to the point where he is considered mentally incapable.

You say he is 'quite a wealthy man' and therefore it is doubly important that you check whether he has made a will (p.179). Whenever someone has a substantial estate — property, savings, valuables, etc. you would be strongly advised to seek the help of a solicitor, not least because it may save you money in the long run when it comes to paying inheritance tax and so on. Since the value of property has increased dramatically over the last ten years, it doesn't take much for a home-owner to possess a substantial estate.

You may have already come across the term **Power of Attorney**. This is a legal agreement which means that you give someone else the power to handle your affairs on your behalf.

The Power of Attorney can be limited to specific things or it can be general.

If you have a relative or friend who you think might become mentally incapacitated, you can apply for an **Enduring Power of Attorney**. This means that the **attorney**, (the person who is given the power), can continue to act on behalf of the **donor** (the person

---

Example

Mick and Josephine Bennet are going on a two-month holiday to South America. They want to make sure that if something happens to them — for example, one of them is taken ill or their house floods whilst they're away — their daughter Rebecca can deal with any emergencies such as withdrawing money from their bank account. They therefore give Rebecca Power of Attorney before they leave.

---

who gives the power), after they have become mentally incapable of handling their own affairs.

The vital thing is to ensure that the Enduring Power of Attorney is made *before* the donor becomes incapacitated.

Step one: Secure an Enduring Power of Attorney

It might not be the easiest task to persuade your father to make you his attorney. You hardly want to tell him outright that he is becoming mentally incapable of handling his affairs. You could suggest that by making you his attorney it would save him a lot of bother having to go to the bank, building society, etc. and that you could handle all the tedious things like any insurance renewal, repairs to his house, bills and so on.

If there is any doubt about your father's mental state, talk to your doctor and explain what you are trying to do.

There are three types of power that you can be given:

- **General power**, which means you can carry out any business on your father's behalf which he is legally able to delegate to you.
- **Specific power**, which enables you to carry out only certain business as specified by your father.
- A **general or specific power with conditions and restrictions**. This authorizes you to deal with all your father's property and affairs except certain specified exceptions, e.g. you would not be allowed to sell your father's house.

There is a standard form you will have to complete. You can obtain it from a legal stationer or a solicitor will prepare the exact words for you. The form will have to be signed by both you and your father and be witnessed. You then have the power to act on your father's behalf until he becomes mentally incapable. You must then register the power.

Step two: Registering the Enduring Power of Attorney

As soon as you or the doctor believe your father has become mentally incapable, you must register the power with the COURT OF PROTECTION. Until you do so, your authority to deal with your father's affairs will be very limited.

You will have to complete a standard form giving notice to your father and to certain close relatives. You must then complete a standard application form and send it along with your original enduring power and the current fee to the court.

Step three: If there's an objection

If someone objects to the registration, the Court of Protection will fix a date and place to hear the objection. They will instruct you with further details.

If you want to find out whether an Enduring Power of Attorney has been registered you can apply to the court for a search to be made. There is a small fee for this.

Do I need to make a will?

'I'm a single parent with one daughter aged five. A friend of mine died recently, she was the same age as me. She didn't have any children but it's made me think about what would happen to my daughter if I died. Will my daughter automatically inherit everything I have? Do I actually need to make a will?'

Yes, you should make a will. If you die without having made one, your **estate** (everything you own) will be divided up according to the rules of **intestacy** (strict legal rules governing the division of an estate). The result may be very different from what you had intended.

Your estate would be held in a trust for your daughter until she reaches the age of eighteen. The rules governing trusts are especially rigid and may not be sufficiently flexible to meet your daughter's needs.

You should also consider who you wish to appoint as **testamentary guardians** — people to take care of your daughter. And also who you want to administer your estate for the benefit of your daughter, known as **trustees**.

Step one: Decide what you want to happen with your estate

Make a list of everything you own. Include:

• Your home and its contents (you don't have to list everything individually).
• Any particular items of value, sentimental worth — jewellery, silver, antiques, paintings, etc.
• Money, bonds, shares, etc.

Then decide who you want specific items to go to. For example, you might want your sister or a close friend to inherit a certain piece of jewellery or a sum of money.

Once you have made a list of the specific gifts you will have what is known as the **residue** — the rest of the estate. This is presumably what you want your daughter to inherit — make sure that this is sufficient for her.

You may also want to express specific wishes about your funeral arrangements or the disposal of your body (p.182).

Step two: Appoint executors

Executors are the people who administer the wishes expressed in your will. The job is more than a mere formality. Executors may have to arrange for your house to be cleared, clothes, etc. to be dispensed of and undertake some general running around depending on the complexity of your estate.

Normally two executors are appointed and are essential if you have young children who will benefit under a trust.

No one can be forced to act as an executor, so always check that the people you want to appoint are in fact willing.

You might want to consider appointing your solicitors as one of the executors, although of course they will charge for their services. Banks are also willing to be appointed as executors but they are even more expensive.

On the whole, solicitors and banks, although they should be very efficient, will not necessarily understand the subtleties of your wishes, which a close friend or family member might. If your executors don't stand to inherit anything under your will, you might want to consider leaving them something for carrying out the job.

Step three: Appointing guardians

These are the people who you want to look after your daughter if you should die.

If you do not appoint guardians under your will and your daughter is under eighteen when you die, it will be up to the court to appoint someone to look after her.

Think carefully who you want as guardians. Do they have the same views on child rearing as you do? Will they be able to offer your daughter a happy and stable home life? Can they give her the support she'll need if you die?

You could have the same people to act both as executors and guardians. Make sure that they're willing to take on the task before you appoint them.

Step four: Drawing up a will yourself

There is nothing to stop you drawing up a will yourself. There are plenty of books to tell you how to do it. You can get a pre-written form from stationers but they are generally best avoided since they can never be appropriate for all situations.

However, if your affairs are at all complicated — if you own your own business or you have a child under eighteen, you should ask a solicitor to draw up your will. In some circumstances you can still get legal aid (p.242).

Step five: Changing your will

You should review your will regularly, especially if your circumstances change, to ensure that it still represents your estate and the needs of your daughter.

If you want to change your will you don't need to write out the whole document again, you can simply add **codicils** or supplements to it. However, any supplements must be witnessed, as was the original will.

Step six: Administering the will

In order to carry out your wishes, your executors will need to get **probate** after your death. This is where the court confirms the appointment of your executors. Generally banks and building societies will not release any money from your accounts until probate has been granted.

If you don't make a will or your executors are unable or unwilling to act, the court will appoint one of your relatives or beneficiaries to act as an Administrator instead.

Step seven: Making other provisions

You might also want to think about taking out life assurance to provide for a sum of money or income for your daughter if you should die. If you're in good health this need not be very expensive.

What do I do when my aunt dies?

'My aunt who's in her late eighties lives with me and quite honestly I don't think it'll be that long before she dies. The thing that terrifies me is what to do when she does die. I've never had to face such a situation before and I'm really worried about dealing with all the funeral formalities. What do I have to do?'

Of all the ceremonies and rituals we go through during our lifetime, death is perhaps the one most shrouded in mystery and is therefore often the most difficult to deal with.

Not only are there strict legal procedures to be dealt with but also funeral rituals and other religious rites to confront, not to mention coping with what can be profound grief. For a bereaved family member or close friend, the process of death does not stop with the burial; there are very real practical as well as emotional problems to overcome which may take months or even years to solve or come to terms with.

Although it may not be a pleasant thing to do, think through what you would want to happen in the event of your own death and talk to those closest to you about how they feel. The more direction you can give to those who may survive you and the more ordered you leave your affairs, the easier the task will be for them.

Where the death is sudden, perhaps through an accident, not only will the shock and perhaps grief be more acute, but the procedures for the funeral arrangements may be more involved. Whatever your situation, remember that as with most other things there are professionals whose job it is to deal with deaths and funerals. Above all, try and seek support from people around you — family, friends, neighbours, your minister of religion, special support organizations for the bereaved.

> **Note**: When you are confronted with a death and have to make funeral arrangements you will find that things happen very fast. The following goes through what you need to consider and do step by step. However, in the early stages at least, you may find yourself needing to deal with a couple of steps at one time.

Step one: Think ahead

Find out from your aunt whether she has any special ideas about the way she wants her funeral organized. This may not be the easiest thing to ask outright but you may be able to introduce the subject, if for example someone either of you knows dies or there's a piece in a newspaper about a funeral or death. You could even talk about your own feelings.

Try to establish:

- If she wants to be buried or cremated and where.
- Whether she has made any special provision for her death, e.g. by paying into a friendly society or similar fund and in reserving a plot of burial ground.
- If she wants any special flowers, prayers, music, etc. or perhaps donations to a particular charity.
- If she wants a religious ceremony and what kind.
- Anybody she particularly wants notified.

You might want to find out if she is interested in leaving any part of her body for medical use. She may already carry a donor card.

You are not obliged to, or, in the case of becoming a donor, may not be able to, adhere to any of these wishes but it might help you when you have to make the funeral arrangements.

In addition, check that she has made a will (p.179-81).

Step two: Death happens

If your aunt dies peacefully at home, you should ring her doctor. If the doctor has been attending her regularly and had seen her a short time before she died, he may not come immediately.

If your aunt dies in hospital, the ward sister will usually inform you. You will be asked to go to the hospital to collect her belongings. You will only be asked to identify the body if, for example, your aunt collapsed whilst she was out shopping and was taken to hospital where she then died.

If you are at all suspicious about a death, call the police.

Step three: Get a medical certificate of cause of death

Without this you cannot proceed. The doctor will give you a medical certificate stating the cause of death. There's no charge for it.

If you intend to have your aunt cremated, you will need to have her death certified by *two* doctors. Your own GP will usually help you.

Any sudden death will have to be reported to the coroner who may then recommend that a post-mortem or inquest is held. After the coroner has completed their investigations, they will issue the medical certificate.

Step four: Decide what to do with the body

You can either bury the body or cremate it.

Burial

You can be buried in one of the following places:

- Your parish churchyard. Ask the vicar or rector.
- In a cemetery. Many are non-denominational and are run by local authorities or private companies. Some have certain ground consecrated and reserved for specific religious denominations.
- You can bury bodies in other places, e.g. a private garden but the burial must be registered and you'll need permission from your local planning authority — which may not grant it.

It might seem a simple process to dig a hole and bury a body but the various types of graves available can be bewildering. Graves come in many different categories and therefore prices. Their cost largely depends upon their size, location and whether they are reserved or not. The vicar or cemetery administrator will be able to advise you on what is available. Before you make a decision, do find out whether what you have chosen will restrict your choice of headstone or memorial plaque or has any other stipulations.

Cremation

Each **crematorium** has its own scale of charges and they can vary considerably. There is no need to have a religious ceremony but crematoria have non-denominational chapels and usually keep a roster of chaplains of different religions.

There is no law regulating the disposal of cremated remains. The crematorium will usually keep the ashes for you free for a limited time and then having notified you will bury or scatter them. You should always get a certificate confirming that the cremation has taken place. You will need this if you want to scatter or bury the ashes elsewhere, such as a churchyard.

Step five: Contact an undertaker

There is nothing to stop you organizing the entire funeral yourself. However, it is probably advisable to contact an undertaker at the earliest opportunity. They can deal with all the necessary arrangements from registering the death → to organizing refreshments after the funeral.

Since funerals can be incredibly expensive, it's worth spending time thinking about what you actually want before you start talking to an undertaker — you may find yourself with a bigger bill than you had anticipated.

Undertakers, like any other traders, can vary enormously in the service they offer. To safeguard your interests look for an undertaker who is a member of the NATIONAL ASSOCIATION OF FUNERAL DIRECTORS (NAFD). They have drawn up a code of practice which they have agreed to adhere to with regard to both the service they offer and their professional conduct including confidentiality. As with other professional and trade associations you have more comeback if something goes wrong.

Do remember that, however emotionally upset you feel, you are dealing with a pure business transaction with the undertaker. Whilst they should certainly not be taking advantage of you, their role is not that of a counsellor or confidant.

Tell the undertaker how much you want to spend on the funeral. NAFD undertakers will provide a simple basic funeral including: coffin; a hearse; one following car; bearers and conductor. There are then additional costs such as removing the body from the house or hospital to the undertakers, 'laying out' the body which means washing and preparing it and a shroud. You will also need to think about extras such as flowers.

The things that will really add to the cost are fancy wood coffins and brass handles. For cremations it's usual to have the simplest unadorned coffin as it will go into the cremator with the body. If you have a cheap coffin you can ask for it to be covered with a 'pall' or heavy cloth throughout the funeral.

The undertakers may offer to **embalm** the body — some do it automatically. Embalming cannot be done until you have a medical certificate of cause of death. The process which is sometimes called preservative treatment is intended to delay the process of decomposition and involves replacing the blood with a chemical solution. In this country embalmers tend not to use cosmetics but try to create an appearance of sleep. If you don't want this done — and some religions such as Judaism forbid it — then make this clear.

Arrangements for the funeral can be discussed but should not be confirmed until you have the burial or disposal certificate from the registrar or coroner→.

Always remember to get any estimate or quotation in writing (p.93).

Step six: Talk to your minister of religion
If you want a religious service (you don't have to have one), then

get in contact with your local minister. Obviously if you have close ties with your religious community, the funeral arrangements will often be a lot easier.

You will want to think about the sort of prayers, music and hymns you would like. If the person officiating didn't know the deceased well, they will often want to ask you details about their life.

If you want to have some kind of ceremony but of no particular denomination you can write one yourself. Ideally it should be no more than twenty minutes to half an hour. You might include your aunt's favourite poems, writing or songs. Involve other people who knew her well and ask them to speak about their memories of her. Alternatively, contact a non-denominational organization like the BRITISH HUMANIST ASSOCIATION who have produced a booklet suggesting forms of service you could use.

Step seven: Registering the death

Once you've got the medical certificate, you should immediately register the death with the Registrar of Births, Deaths and Marriages. You must register the death in the registration sub-district in which it occurred. Your doctor will be able to help you or else ask at your local post office, library or town hall. You don't need to make an appointment; just go along during opening hours (they may shut for lunch).

Only certain people can register the death — they are known as the **informants**. Basically it's anyone who knew the deceased well, was with them when they died or who discovered the body.

You will be asked some very simple questions about the date of your aunt's death, her full name, her maiden name if she was married, etc. To save yourself trouble later on, make sure that the name you give for your aunt is the same as on all her official documents — birth certificate, bank and pension books, etc.

Make sure that you carefully check the entry in the register to see that it is accurate, then sign it. The registrar will then give you a certificate of registration of the death, which is free. The registrar will also issue you with a burial or cremation certificate, commonly known as a 'disposal certificate'. Without this you cannot bury or cremate the body.

At the same time you will be able to obtain copies of the entry in the register which are known as death certificates. There is a small charge for these.

You should also take along your aunt's medical card.

Step eight: Notify family and friends

You will probably have contacted some people immediately after your aunt died. Make a list of everyone who needs to be told of her death and the funeral arrangements.

It's probably best to telephone people but try to get someone else to do the ringing around for you. You can send official cards out but you may choose to write letters after the funeral is over to those who live too far away to attend the ceremony.

If you feel it's appropriate put a notice in the deaths column of one of the national papers or alternatively a local paper. Write out what you want to say. A simple notice might read:

> BROWN: On 11th November, Elizabeth Mary (née Jones) of 2, Honeysuckle Cottages, wife of the late William Brown. Sadly missed by all her family.

Some of the national papers are very specific about what they will and won't allow you to say. Again, this can be done over the phone.

Step nine: Make arrangements for after the funeral

It is usual to have some kind of refreshments after a funeral. People who have travelled some distance to the funeral will welcome the hospitality and it's important to give everyone the opportunity of talking to the bereaved and the family away from the cemetery or churchyard. It's all part of the mourning process. Obviously customs and traditions vary according to each religion and family.

You could organize simple drinks in your own home. Again this is something that you could get other people to help with.

Step ten: The day of the funeral

By this time you will have arranged with the undertaker where the hearse and the following cars are going to travel from. Check that all your close family and friends know the place and time of the funeral. Tell those people who are travelling in the following cars what time they have to be with you — or any other pick-up point.

Step eleven: Settling up

Remember that unless other provision has been made, all the funeral costs will be taken from your aunt's estate (her money, valuables, etc.).

Your final accounts should include:

- Any doctors' fees (for signing cremation forms — this might be included in the undertakers' bill).
- Fees for copies of death certificates.
- The undertakers' bill.
- The bill from the cemetery or churchyard, which will include the costs of the plot, grave and gravedigger.
- Minister's fees — sometimes you are asked to make a donation to a church or charity.
- Flowers.
- Food and drink for the refreshments.
- Bill for any newspaper advertisements.
- Any out-of-pocket expenses.

Step twelve: Settling the deceased's affairs

Once the funeral and official mourning time is over you will need to sort out your aunt's affairs.

If you have not already done so, open and read the will. If you are not the executor of the will, pass it on to the person who is (p.180).

If necessary you will have to get probate (p.181) or **letters of administration** (if there was no will) before any bank, building society or other financial institution will deal with you. When you register a death you will get a booklet telling you where you can obtain the necessary application forms.

If the will looks very involved or there are other complications such as a large estate, trusts or other financial provisions, then do seek the advice of a solicitor.

- Claim any state benefits you are entitled to. Contact your local DSS.
- Return any pension or allowance books to the DSS — the address will be in the book. Keep a note of the pension or allowance number.
- If you receive any other pensions or other allowances, do not cash them but send them back with an explanatory note.
- Arrange to have any unwanted clothes sold or given to a charity. Go through pockets and bags *very* carefully before you give anything to someone else.

Step thirteen: Memorial stones and services

Before you commission a monumental mason, find out about any restrictions imposed by the church or the cemetery on the size or shape of the headstone or other memorial. You may also find that you have to wait a certain amount of time before you can actually erect a memorial over a grave.

Don't be bulldozed into ordering a headstone by an unscrupulous mason calling you on the day of the funeral or immediately after. For a list of established local monumental masons contact the NATIONAL ASSOCIATION OF MASTER MASONS. Always remember to get any estimate or quotation in writing (p.93).

If you decided to restrict the number attending the funeral or people couldn't come on the day, you could hold a memorial service sometime later. Some religions, e.g. Judaism, hold a memorial service when they erect the headstone.

A memorial service doesn't have to be an elaborate religious affair: it could be a simple get-together of the deceased's family and friends. Ask certain people to prepare some kind of short address or tribute to the deceased.

Organizations that help the bereaved

CRUSE (the NATIONAL ASSOCIATION FOR THE WIDOWED AND THEIR CHILDREN)
HELP THE AGED
AGE CONCERN

Feeling better about the medical profession

Doctors, dentists, medical specialists like any other 'professional' hold a certain power over ordinary mortals. Not only do they supposedly understand more about our bodies and minds than we could ever hope to, but they usually get us when we feel most vulnerable — ill, stark naked or with our mouths clamped firmly open (or all three)! Consequently it can be difficult to be assertive with the medical profession.

If you are not happy with your doctor, dentist or optician, you are under no obligation to stay with them. Find another practitioner who is prepared to take you on and ask for your records to be transferred. Obviously it will not be to your advantage to keep changing and you may find good practices unable to take on more patients.

If you need to consult a medical professional then write down before you go exactly what you want to say or ask — and don't leave the surgery until you've had some answers. There's nothing wrong with going in with a 'shopping list'.

If you're unhappy with the answers you get or you think that a course or treatment or operation may be unnecessary, ask for a second opinion. After all, it's your body and it's the only one you've got!

If you feel concerned take someone else with you to the consultation. If the consultant asks them to 'wait outside' for you and you want them in the room with you ask whether there is a medical reason as to why the can't stay with you. (There rarely is.)

Always ask what your consultant is doing and why. They might not like you asking, they can proceed far more quickly and think less with quiet, submissive patients. If you don't understand what they say ask them to repeat it in short, one-syllable words.

Our doctor refused to treat my son

'When we moved to a new part of town my family registered with a local doctor. Shortly after this, my teenage son came down with what we thought was a bad dose of flu. He seemed really ill, so we rang our doctor and asked him to make a home visit. The doctor was very abrupt and said he didn't make home visits for everyday colds. We tried to explain that our son seemed to be having difficulty breathing but he just ignored us. Anyway we took the boy along to the surgery. The doctor didn't bother examining him, he said it was nothing very much and gave him a prescription for various cough medicines.

'That night, the boy was desperately ill, feverish and couldn't get his breath. We rang the doctor again and got an emergency locum, who did come round. He said my son had pleurisy and wanted to get him into hospital immediately, which he did.

'I'm livid about the way our doctor treated us. I want to make a complaint about his behaviour and none of us want to see him ever again. What can we do?'

Complaints about GPs and other medical professionals usually fall into two categories.

First of all there is serious professional misconduct. This might include:

- Indecently assaulting a patient.
- Having an improper relationship with a patient.

- Being drunk whilst attending a patient.
- Disclosing confidential information.

Then there are more general complaints about the standard of service. Examples of poor service include:

- Dirty surgery.
- Rudeness by doctor.
- Failure to attend a patient when asked to do so.
- Rudeness by a receptionist attempting to give medical advice over the phone.

In general complaints of serious misconduct are dealt with by the doctor's professional body, the GENERAL MEDICAL COUNCIL (GMC). Complaints about the standard of service are dealt with through your local FAMILY PRACTITIONER COMMITTEE (FPC) — the NHS body that administrates GPs, etc.

Making a complaint about a doctor is not the simplest, most straightforward thing to do. You may need help to guide you through the maze of committees and complicated procedures. It is proposed to simplify the system. Your local COMMUNITY HEALTH COUNCIL will give you advice and may well assist you through the case.

Step one: Write to your Family Practitioner Committee
You'll find the address in your local telephone directory. You must do this immediately as there are strict time limits enforced. You will need to give details of the exact nature of your complaint.

Re: Dr John Gall, 2 Little Artery Road, Malaise on Thames

I am writing to complain about Dr Gall's failure to attend my son, James, during his recent illness.

On April 5th, my son was taken ill with what my wife and I thought was a bad case of flu. His condition became progressively worse and we telephoned Dr Gall and asked him to make a home visit. My son had a high temperature, difficulty in breathing and was obviously not fit enough to leave the house.

Dr Gall refused to visit us, saying that he did not make home visits to treat a common cold. This was despite the fact that we had described our son's symptoms to the doctor.

Later on that day we were so concerned, that we took James down to the surgery. Dr Gall did not bother to examine him and said it was nothing to worry about and gave him a prescription for some cough linctus.

That night, James got worse and we telephoned Dr Gall's emergency number. This time a locum, Dr Michael Cure, visited us. He immediately diagnosed pleurisy and arranged for my son to be taken into St Gore Hospital. James remained in hospital for a further week and has been at home convalescing for the past fortnight.

We believe that Dr Gall's failure to attend to my son at home when asked to do so and subsequent failure to examine him properly was not only totally unprofessional but also negligent. Would you please investigate our complaint further.

Step two: Your doctor replies
Your letter will be forwarded to the appropriate committee dealing with complaints about GPs. They will find out what your doctor has to say to your allegations. You will be sent your doctor's reply and asked to comment on it. You have only *two weeks* to do this.

Step three: The FPC decides to hold a hearing
The committee will look at all the correspondence and will decide if the case is worth pursuing. If they do decide to investigate it further they will hold a formal hearing where each side will put their case — lawyers are not permitted. Alternatively they will carry out an informal investigation without a formal hearing, to decide what action should be taken against the doctor.

If, after looking at the correspondence, the committee decides that there is no case for the doctor to answer then you will be told. However, you will be asked if you want to take the case further by submitting an additional statement.

Step four: The FPC make a decision
The FPC cannot award you any compensation but they can recommend that your doctor should receive a warning from the Secretary of State or have some of his pay withheld. Obviously their recommendations will depend on the nature of the case.

Both the doctor and the patient have the right to appeal to the Secretary of State against the FPC's decision.

Step five: Making a formal complaint to the General Medical Council

If you believe that the doctor is guilty of serious professional misconduct then you should also write to the GMC.

Once again they cannot offer you any compensation. If they find the doctor guilty they can decide on some form of disciplinary action.

Step six: Taking legal action

If you want to pursue a negligence case against a doctor you would have to prove that the doctor was not only wrong in what they did but that other competent doctors would not have acted as they did.

Taking a claim of negligence by a doctor through the legal system can be an incredibly expensive and drawn-out process. Always seek the advice of a solicitor before you embark on such a course of action.

Step seven: Change your doctor

Ask neighbours and friends whether they can recommend their doctor. Go and visit the surgery and see what the atmosphere is like. Find out whether the new doctor will accept you on to their list.

Many doctors now work on the basis of group practices. This is to your advantage since you have more chance to consult a different doctor if you find you don't get on with the one you see on your first visit. It also means for example, that if a woman wants to see a female doctor but is registered with a male doctor in the practice she usually can.

What else?

For complaints against either **dentists** or **opticians** follow the same procedure through the FPC.

- If you think that your dentist is guilty of professional misconduct write to the registrar of the GENERAL DENTAL COUNCIL.
- If you think your optician is guilty of professional misconduct contact the GENERAL OPTICAL COUNCIL. You could also write to the BRITISH COLLEGE OF OPTHALMIC OPTICIANS or the ASSOCIATION OF OPTOMETRISTS, but not all opticians belong to these two organizations, so check first.

If you have a complaint about **hospital services**, then make an informal complaint first.

- Formal complaints should be made in writing to the Hospital Administrator who will see a proper investigation is made. You may have to present your case in front of a tribunal set up by your Area Health Authority.
- If your complaint is against a **consultant** or **member of the medical staff** and you cannot resolve the dispute by talking to them directly write to the Regional Medical Officer at your Area Health Authority.
- If you are not satisfied with the response you get then you should contact the HEALTH SERVICE OMBUDSMAN. They will not investigate complaints that have already been dealt with by a tribunal or court; complaints about a diagnosis itself; complaints about GPs and others covered by the FPC or anything to do with the internal working of a hospital such as staff appointments.

  There is no charge for this service and if you want to make a complaint to the Ombudsman write to the Health Service Commissioner for your area — the address will be in the telephone book.

Other organizations that can help
The PATIENTS ASSOCIATION
ACTION FOR THE VICTIMS OF MEDICAL ACCIDENTS

All in a day's work

The laws relating to employment are very complex. They include amongst others: the Employment Protection (Consolidation) Act 1978 as amended by the Employment Acts 1980 and 1982; the Equal Pay Act 1970; the Sex Discrimination Act 1975 and the Race Relations Act 1976.

This chapter can only deal in very general terms with problems and complaints relating to employment. If you have a serious complaint, do seek the advice of a qualified lawyer with specialist knowledge in this area (p.237).

Looking for the right job

You may have a very clear idea of your skills and qualifications and the type of job you are looking for. But if you are searching for your first job or you're about to return to the workforce after a career break you will need to think carefully about the skills you have and the sort of position you want.

At some point you will probably be asked to complete a job application form or send off a **Curriculum Vitae (CV)** (a statement giving general details of your eduction, employment history, skills, etc.), so it's worth finding time to complete the following exercises.

What are your skills?
Make a list of *all* your skills. Include:

- Your eductional qualifications — CSEs, 'O' and 'A' levels, GCSEs, Degrees.

- Other qualifications or membership of professional bodies.
- All the jobs you've ever done and what they involved.
- Any voluntary, charity, political work you've ever done — think about your responsibilities and the projects you've undertaken.
- Other skills such as typing or driving.
- Personal qualities such as patience, ability to get on with people or listening skills.

What sort of job do you want?

You will probably have to be very flexible when it comes to taking on a job but it does no harm to start out with a clear idea of what you're after. Think about:

- Which of your skills you most enjoy using.
- How much responsibility you want.
- What kind of hours you are prepared to work.
- What kind of career path you are looking for.
- Would you be happiest in a large company with all the fringe benefits or a small company where everyone knows each other?
- Do you need to work in a certain geographic area, for example to ease travelling?
- What is the minimum salary you want?
- How important are fringe benefits, e.g. car, subsidized mortgages, private health care, sports facilities?

Writing a CV

It's worth writing out a CV even if you eventually have to fill in a standard application form. At least you'll have the information at your fingertips!

The knack of writing an effective CV is to turn your skills list ← into a professional piece of sales literature about yourself. The important thing is to make all your skills relevant to the job for which you are applying.

Remember — you don't necessarily need 'professional' qualifications to prove you can do a job. If you can show you have the necessary *skills* and *experience* which you may have learnt outside a paid job then that usually counts for more than mere pieces of paper.

Example

Julia Larch wants a job as a Personal Assistant to an MD of a large company preferably in the advertising/public relations world. Julia has been bringing up her young family for the last six years so she has not done any paid work but she has been active in her local community.

Julia decides that to get the Personal Assistant job in the kind of company she wants she will need to highlight:

- That she is intelligent (her 6 'O' and 2 'A' levels).
- That she has the right professional qualifications (RSA typing and shorthand certificates).
- That she has relevant work experience (she concentrates on her previous jobs first as a secretary in a publishing company and then as a PA to a Marketing Director).
- That she has initiative and good organizational skills (she set up and ran a successful local toddlers group).
- She has proven interest in advertising/public relations (the fact that she worked for a Marketing Director and in a voluntary capacity was responsible for publicity for her church charity group).
- That she is prepared to work outside normal hours if necessary. She may be asked about this at the interview and will make a better impression if she can show she has thought through her child-care arrangements.

How to lay out a CV

CURRICULUM VITAE

(A) NAME
(B) ADDRESS
(C) TELEPHONE NUMBER

(D) PRESENT POSITION:

(E) EDUCATION:

(F) OTHER QUALIFICATIONS:

(G) WORK EXPERIENCE:

(H) ADDITIONAL EXPERIENCE:

(I) ADDITIONAL SKILLS:

(J) INTERESTS:

(K) REFERENCES:

Notes on writing a CV

- Don't put yourself down or be over-modest, but do make sure you are writing fact not fantasy.
- Your application form or CV is your 'foot in the door'. Make sure you create the right impression — good presentation is vital. Use a typewriter or word processor. Double-check there are no spelling mistakes.
- A — Give your full name. It is not necessary to indicate your sex or marital status unless you want to.
- B — Include your postcode.
- C — Give a day and evening number if appropriate.
- D — This is about the job you currently hold. Give your title and an outline of your chief responsibilities. If you are not working at the moment say so. For example:

    'I am currently searching for a job following a career break to raise my family. However, during the past few years I have been involved in unpaid activities (see below). At the moment I am taking a course at my local college on computers and word processing in order to become proficient at these new skills.'

- E — Give details of schools and colleges attended since the age of eleven. Where appropriate list the exams you have taken and the results gained. The higher up the educational ladder you go, the less need there is to be specific about early exam details; the same applies to work experience.
- F — State whether you are a member of a professional body or if you have taken any further tests or exams.
- G — List all your work experience *in reverse order*, i.e. start with your most recent or second most recent job depending on whether or not you are currently working. Include details about your job title and your responsibilities.
- H — This gives you space for listing all your accomplishments for which you have not been paid! For example:

    'Chair, ''Young Ruffians'' — Under 10 Football Club. Responsible for running this successful club including encouraging and training young footballers and organizing fixtures. I also set up a sponsorship deal with local firms worth £750.'

- I — Include details about other skills you have, e.g. driving, typing, computer skills.
- J — This section gives the prospective employer some opportunity to see that you are a real person — with life outside work! State your interests very succinctly, e.g. Cinema, Reading, Badminton, Skydiving, etc.
- K — Almost all employers will want references and you should put down two or three names. At least one of your referees should be from work or college. Make sure you give their job title and address. However, if you don't want them contacted until you get a firm job offer, don't put down a name, instead write, 'Provided on request.'

Where to look for jobs

- Newspapers. Many have special sections for particular job areas.
- Specialist magazines.
- Careers offices.
- Employment bureaux. Some of the big ones now offer special training packages for particular groups of workers, e.g. women returners.
- By applying to specific companies. You will need to send a letter with your CV to the company's personnel department telling them the kind of position you are looking for and asking whether they have any vacancies. /

Example
Julia Larch← meets Bob Allen at a party. He suggests she writes to a friend of his, Gerda Graham, who runs an advertising agency and might be looking for a PA. Julia sends off her CV← with the following letter.

Dear Ms Graham
   Bob Allen of Allen Communications suggested that I contact you. I would like to talk to you about the possibility of working for your company as a Personal Assistant.

As you will see from the enclosed CV I have experience of working in marketing. I have all the necessary professional secretarial qualifications. I am familiar with word processors and I am an excellent organizer. I am currently looking for a challenging PA post in an advertising agency such as yours.

I realize that you may have no vacancies at present. However, I would appreciate the opportunity of meeting you to discuss possible openings in the future.

I look forward to hearing from you shortly.

Yours sincerely

Julia Larch

- Always follow up your letter with a visit or telephone call.

Attending an interview

Being good at interviews is a skill in itself. Here are some basic tips. Think of yourself as a product, a new vacuum cleaner perhaps, which you are trying to convince someone else (the employer) to buy!

- *Do* find out as much as you can about the job and the company before you go.
- *Do* sound enthusiastic.
- *Do* remember to make your skills and experience *relevant* to the job and the company.
- *Do* dress appropriately.
- *Do* look at the person when they are talking to you and you are replying to them.
- *Do* prepare some questions in advance.
- And whatever else you do — *don't* be late!

Problems at work?

Work always has its ups and downs. A promotion or project well completed gives a great sense of satisfaction and self worth. Bearing the brunt of unpleasant office politics or doing a job without a purpose can make Monday mornings seem like absolute hell. On the whole we 'play the game' and ride the storms. But there are occasions when someone else isn't playing by the rules, when it's time to blow the whistle and do something positive.

Work problems usually fall into two categories:

(a) Personal complaints and general grievances such as disliking the way the company is run, or the behaviour of a particular manager. On the whole, at least to start with, these kinds of problems have no legal consequences.

(b) Infrigements of legal rights. As a last resort these can be dealt with by an **Industrial Tribunal**→or the courts (p.249). These infringements include:

- Unfair dismissal.
- Racial or sex discrimination.
- Infringement of maternity rights and pay.
- Un-itemized pay statements.
- Prohibition of union membership and activities.
- Certain problems with redundancy.
- No time off for public duties.

Before you embark on any claims against your employer you must be aware that strict time limits and restrictions apply in taking a case to an Industrial Tribunal→or in claiming maternity rights (p.217-19).

Organizations that can help

Trade unions

Trade unions can be particularly helpful in dealing with grievances that may not have any legal consequences, particularly if they have implications for a number of workers.

The ability of any individual union to help you will obviously depend on their resources and the capabilities of their local representative.

If you belong to a union it's always worth contacting them for their advice — after all, that's what you pay your union dues for!

ACAS

ACAS — the ADVISORY, CONCILIATION AND ARBITRATION SERVICE — is an independent body which aims to promote better industrial relations.

ACAS runs a series of conciliation, arbitration and mediation services. They cannot compel either employer or employee to accept their recommendations.

ACAS have issued a Code of Practice about disciplinary procedures which all employers should keep to but are not obliged to do so by law. However, if they fail to keep to the code, this can be brought as evidence in any Industrial Tribunal hearing. Copies of the code are available free from ACAS.

There are no formalities to go through if you need help. You simply write to or telephone your nearest ACAS office.

Industrial Tribunals

Industrial Tribunals are independent judicial bodies. The tribunal hearing is intended to be more informal than a court hearing but it can still be quite an involved process.

The tribunal usually consists of a legally qualified chairman or woman and two lay members who have knowledge and experience of employment in industry or commerce.

There are no fees involved and you may be able to claim certain allowances, such as travel costs.

You are entitled to be represented at the hearing. This could be by a professional lawyer, a trade union representative or a friend or spouse. Alternatively you can represent yourself. However, if you do employ a lawyer you will not be able to get help under the Legal Aid Scheme (p.242). You may, though, be able to get some advice under the Legal Aid and Advice Scheme (p.242) as to whether you have a valid case.

Costs are not usually awarded against an applicant in an Industrial Tribunal. However, if the tribunal decides that the applicant has acted 'frivolously, vexatiously or unreasonably' in bringing the case, it has the power to award costs against him or her.

Even though they are intended to be informal, the tribunal can only work within the scope of current employment law. Before you begin proceedings you must make sure that you have a case in law — your trade union, ACAS or legal adviser will be able to confirm whether you do. The hearing will not go in your favour just because the tribunal feels sorry for you or because your employer has acted unprofessionally.

If you decide that the tribunal has the power to deal with your case *you must act quickly*. There are very strict time limits, usually three months, within which you must submit your application.

The Department of Employment has prepared a series of leaflets about Industrial Tribunal proceedings and employment law. Copies of these are available from your local employment office, job centre, CAB, advice centre, etc.

Finally, the amount of compensation an Industrial Tribunal can award you is restricted (p.233). You would probably be much better off trying to settle the case 'out of court'. To do this you may well need extra advice and help from a CAB, advice centre or solicitor.

For a step-by-step guide to making an application to an Industrial Tribunal, see p.229.

Getting on with the job

Many work problems are caused by a simple breakdown in communications.

Example

Person A has a good idea for a new project but only half explains it to person B. B gets 'the wrong end of the stick' because A didn't spend enough time going through the project and fails to check that B fully understands. B goes off to C and D and tells them to get on with the new project. C and D think the project won't work (it won't, they haven't got the right instructions) and therefore work unenthusiastically. The project fails. A shouts at B who shouts at C and D who get fed up and leave the company.

The example shown here is simplistic, perhaps, but unfortunately it's not far from reality for many work situations.

• If you are giving instructions — of any kind — double check that the person you are talking to fully understands and preferably agrees with them.

• If you find yourself in a situation where you don't fully comprehend how and what you are supposed to be doing, *ask*! Be assertive (p.30). If you think you haven't been briefed properly or you see a problem in completing a task then say so!

• Learn to say 'no'. If you think a colleague is making unreasonable demands on you then tell them so. You don't need to sound unenthusiastic or nasty.

• Be prepared to find a compromise solution to a situation or problem but don't end up compromising your self-respect or sanity.

• Don't underestimate the power of praise. Give it whenever you can and give it immediately. Praise given long after it's due won't

Example 1

Alan Bridges is a teacher in a secondary school. He teaches geography but he's also good at sport and at drama, so he's been roped in to take some extra classes. It's near the end of the summer term and Alan's worrying about marking exam papers and writing reports, not to mention helping to organize the annual sports day. One day the headteacher stops Alan in the staff room and asks him to 'have a think about putting on an end of term play'. Alan is somewhat alarmed at the thought of this extra commitment so he decides to confront the headteacher. He makes an appointment to see her.

'I'm really pleased that you asked me to have a think about an end of term play. I've considered it carefully and I've decided I can't take responsibility for one this year.

'My priority must be the exams and writing reports. In addition I've already agreed to organize the sports day which is taking up a considerable amount of time. I imagine that you'll feel let down but I really don't think that it's reasonable to ask me to take on another major responsibility this term. Next year I'd be perfectly happy to put on the end of term play providing someone else organizes the sports day.'

have the same impact and its sincerity may well be doubted.

• If you are criticized for doing something wrong, think before you leap to your defence or else crumple into a heap. If the criticism is justified admit your mistake with grace. But if you think the criticism isn't justified or someone is simply trying to put you down then say so.

• If you have to criticize someone else prepare in advance what you're going to say if you can. Avoid labelling them, 'You're so stupid/ignorant/hopeless'. Try and be positive about some aspect of their work or behaviour. Be specific about what is wrong and offer a sensible, workable solution. Ask them why they think the problem has occurred and what they imagine would be an effective solution.

In the example given here, Melinda's boss, if he'd been assertive, might have confronted her in this way.

Example 2
Melinda Sykes is a secretary and she's just been hauled into her boss's office where he's complaining about some letters she has typed.

BOSS: 'What's this rubbish you've just typed up? It's full of spelling mistakes and typing errors. You obviously haven't bothered to spend the time to do it properly. Also, what's all this nonsense about a meeting on the 3rd? The meeting's on the 6th. Can't you take dictation?'

Melinda is flaming mad by what her boss has said. But before she opens her mouth she stops to think.

MELINDA: 'Yes, you're right about typing up the letter in a rush. I did it before I went to lunch. I'm sorry about the spelling mistakes. I'll have to use a dictionary. I'll type it again. However, you know my dictation is excellent. You quite distinctly said the meeting was on the 3rd, in fact you confirmed it in your diary. If the date's been changed, I'm quite happy to amend the letter.'

'Melinda, you're usually so conscientious about your work but I'm very cross about this letter you've just typed. It's full of spelling mistakes and typing errors. It looks as if you didn't take much care about doing it. A dictionary might help with the spelling. If you don't have one, I'll get you one.

Your dictation is normally excellent, so I don't understand why you wrote the meeting is on the 3rd, I think it's on the 6th. Is that right? Please retype the letter.'

Good working relations

'I started working for a tour company about a year ago. When I joined them I was put into the bookings department but I recently moved to the office that plans the tour itineraries. It's a good move for me as there's far more responsibility. The only problem is that although they promised to train me, no one has really bothered to even talk me through the job properly.

Within the first week, I was given sole responsibility for planning a week's tour programme. Because I wasn't familiar with the job and didn't know which were the best hotels to contact, I made a complete mess of it. I got a real dressing down from my boss and was made to feel a complete fool.

I think that my boss is partly to blame for the mess because she hadn't given me any training. We get on reasonably well but she still expects me to do my job without understanding how I'm supposed to do it. I can see myself getting into deep water all over again. How can I stop this happening?'

Step one: Decide what you want your boss to do

Before you approach your boss, think about what it is that you want out of her. The chances are that if she didn't train you properly in the first place, she may not be aware of what it is she's supposed to do. Think about what kind of information you need to know and how you feel you can best learn it. Write out a short training proposal.

I need to learn about the following:

The best way to learn it would be: [This might include: reading appropriate background material; 'shadowing' someone more experienced; going through a project stage by stage and having it monitored continually by a more senior manager.]

Timetable: [You might want to suggest how you go about this, e.g. daily meetings with your manager to discuss your progress and any meetings.]

Step two: Make a convenient time to see your boss

You don't want to try to tackle this in the middle of a busy corridor with telephones ringing and people rushing about. If necessary suggest meeting for a quiet drink, undisturbed after work. You might approach your boss by saying: 'I'd like to make a time to see you to talk about my work. I'm very concerned about what happened the other week and I would like to sort things out so that I can work effectively in future. I'd appreciate it if we could talk undisturbed for half an hour/an hour. Would [date] at [time] be convenient?'

Consider the possible responses:

'You know you can talk to me any time.'

'If you want to talk to me, talk now.'

'I'm extremely busy, I don't think I've got time to see you.'

'I can't imagine that there's anything to say.'

If you're confronted with that kind of reply, don't be put off. Be assertive (p.30), repeat your request. You could add something like: 'It's very important to me to speak to you urgently. I recognize that I didn't complete the last itinerary properly but I want to do it properly in the future. I can only work efficiently if you/someone spends a short time training me. That's what I want to speak to you about and I don't think it would be appropriate to discuss it here/now as you are obviously involved with other matters/leave it for another few weeks.'

Step three: The meeting

Think over what you want to say before you go in. Be very specific about what is wrong and what you want done in the future. You can modify the following as appropriate.

'I was very upset/distressed/concerned about what happened to the tour itinerary I was given to organize and your reaction to the situation. I quite accept that I didn't complete the job well.

'But I do feel that it was unreasonable to have been given such a task to do without having had any training or someone more experienced there for support.

'I'm keen to work in this department and to do the job competently. I don't want to make the same mistake again and therefore I have a proposal for a training programme which I'd like to discuss with you.' [Go through your plan ←.]

Listen carefully to the response you get and acknowledge what your boss says. For example:

BOSS: Your plan sounds very good. However, I don't think that I've really got the time to spend with you. We expect you to pick up the job as you go along.

YOU: I'm glad you think the plan sounds good. Look, I know how busy you are so perhaps we can spend just fifteen minutes each morning together. That way you can give me some direction as to what I'm supposed to be doing. I know I'd be much more useful to the department if you'd spend just a short amount of time with me going through things. I think it's only reasonable that having got me in the department and asked me to undertake important projects, you train me. Can we agree to fifteen minutes a day?

If you seem to be getting nowhere you could suggest that someone else in the department is asked to train you.

If your boss still refuses to give you any commitment you might want to say something like: 'I'm very disappointed that you're not willing to give me any training in my job. If you want me to pick up the job as I go along I'll do my work as best I can. However, if I make a mistake, I'd rather be told quietly where I went wrong than be shouted at as I was last time. I found it very disconcerting and not at all helpful.'

Step four: Put any decision in writing
Write your boss a memo confirming what was agreed in the meeting — even if it wasn't very positive!

Step five: Taking it further
If your boss does agree to your request, then obviously you will need to be assertive and keep her to her agreement. Do remember to be positive about any help she gives you. Remind her how much better you work now you have some advice!

If your boss doesn't agree to your request and you still feel strongly about it you could approach your personnel department or a more senior manager to see if they might help you. Whatever you decide to do, don't forget about the unwritten rules of office politics or you may find yourself in deeper water.

A new job — what about the paperwork?
'The week before last I got a new job working as a foreman at a small factory. I thought that I would have to sign some papers and give them details of my National Insurance number and so on but no one seems in the least bit interested. I want to make sure that everything is above board. What should I be doing?'

Providing you're not working for the company on a freelance basis or employed for less than sixteen hours a week you need to be concerned about getting a written statement about the principal terms of your employment. In addition you should make sure your employer intends to pay your National Insurance and tax contributions.

Step one: Getting a written statement
Your employer is obliged by law to give you a written statement of

your principal terms and conditions within *thirteen weeks* of you starting work.

The statement should include:

- Your name and your employer's name and address.
- The date you started work.
- Details of your pay — how much and how often you will be paid.
- Details of the hours you are expected to work.
- Details of holidays and holiday pay.
- Terms and conditions relating to sickness and injury.
- Details of any pension schemes.
- The amount of notice of termination to be given by your employer and by you.

In addition you should receive a written statement about the company's disciplinary and grievance rules and procedures.

If the company has no guidelines or terms for some of the above it should tell you.

If your employer refuses to give you a written statement of your terms and conditions you can ask an Industrial Tribunal (p.229) to produce one for you. However, you should be aware of an important fact. In practice you have very little job security for the first two years of your employment with a company. So, if your current employer thought you were 'being a nuisance' by asking for a written statement he could dismiss you without necessarily giving a reason and you would have no comeback.

However, *all* employees have the right not to be wrongfully dismissed. This means that if you are dismissed you are entitled to work out your notice and be paid for it or to receive pay in lieu of notice. If neither of these things happen you could sue your employers for **wrongful dismissal**. You would do this through the County court (p.249). You might want to seek advice first from a CAB, law centre or solicitor to make sure you have a valid case.

You cannot claim wrongful dismissal if you've been dismissed for 'gross misconduct' such as theft or assaulting a member of staff.

Step two: National Insurance contributions

You are required by law to make National Insurance contributions (NIC). The amount you will pay will depend on how much you earn and what your working arrangements are. Even if you decide to make your own pension provisions, you will still need to pay NIC. If you don't pay your contributions, you may well find yourself facing penalties. You may also have some state benefits curtailed.

If you don't have a National Insurance number contact your local Department of Social Security immediately.

Step three: Paying tax

Most employees pay tax on the basis of **PAYE (Pay As You Earn)**. This means that your employer deducts a sum of money directly from your salary equal to the amount of income tax you're liable to pay. For people paying above basic rate tax, you may find there is some difference.

Your employer deducts PAYE according to the tax code given to them by the Inland Revenue. If your tax code is wrong, you might find that too much or too little PAYE is being deducted. If your employer doesn't know your tax code they will deduct tax according to the emergency code. It's in your interests to get the correct code.

The code is made up by adding up all the income tax allowances to which you're entitled. They then knock off the last digit from this total figure and replace it by a letter. This letter represents your personal status — married, single, lone parent, etc.

The code is then adjusted so the Inland Revenue can collect any unpaid taxes owing from previous years or to reflect changes in your status.

If your circumstances change in any way — you get married or divorced or you get extra income by renting out a room — you are under an obligation to tell the Inspector of Taxes.

You will be sent a **notice of coding**, a statement showing how your code is calculated. If you disagree with it don't be afraid of writing back and asking for it to be changed.

Every so often you may receive a **tax return**. The form is relatively simple to complete. Basically it is just a record of all your income. You must complete and return the form.

If you leave a job for any reason, your employer will issue you with a **P45**. It's important to give this form to your new employer as it shows your tax code.

If you think that your employer might be deducting PAYE but not passing it on to the Inland Revenue, you should contact the Inspector of Taxes immediately.

Step four: Itemized pay statements

When you receive your pay packet or salary notification you should receive a detailed written statement. This must show your gross pay and your take-home pay together with reasons and amounts for all other deductions such as season ticket or other loans, sick pay, unpaid holiday, etc.

Once again, if you don't receive an itemized pay statement bear in mind that you have very little job security when you begin new employment←.

Why haven't I got redundancy pay?

'I've been working at a local factory on the production line for the last year. Six of us have now been laid off. All my mates got redundancy pay but I didn't get anything like as much as them. The foreman said I wasn't entitled to any redundancy money. I don't understand why — I wasn't sacked and I didn't leave out of choice.'

The law lays down minimum amounts of redundancy money payable to a worker. These are calculated according to your length of service with the company up to a maximum amount. However, this is only a minimum and your employer may have agreed to pay more.

As you've been with your current employer for less than two years these rules don't apply. You have no right to statutory (what the law lays down) redundancy pay. This doesn't stop your employer making you an extra payment because you've been made redundant. Your wage slip will tell you whether any such payment has been made.

Regardless of whether your employer made you a special payment you should still check that in your last pay packet you received:

- All outstanding pay owed to you.
- A proportion of your holiday entitlement if you have not already taken it.

> *Example*
> In your first year you are entitled to twelve days' paid holi-
> day leave but you are made redundant after ten months. If
> you have only taken three days' holiday so far, your final pay
> packet should include a further seven days' pay (a total of
> ten days' holiday for the ten months you have worked). If
> on the other hand you had already taken your full twelve
> days' holiday, your employer would be entitled to deduct
> two days' pay from your last pay packet.

In addition you should have already worked out your period of
notice (as detailed in your contract). If you were asked to leave immediately instead of working out your final notice your employer
should have included 'pay in lieu of notice' in your last pay packet.

> *Example*
> Your employer agrees in your contract to give you one week's
> notice but one Friday he tells you you've been laid off and
> not to come in the following Monday. Your last pay packet
> should therefore include an extra week's wages for the week
> you should have worked as notice.

You should also make sure that you have been given your P45
.

It's also worth finding out whether your employer will give you
a reference for future jobs.

Dismissal

If you are dismissed by your employer, with or without notice and
you believe that the dismissal wasn't justified or that proper
disciplinary procedures weren't followed you can make a complaint to an industrial tribunal of **unfair dismissal**.

This only applies if you have worked for the same employer con-
tinuously for two years for at least 16 hours per week. Part-time
workers need to have worked a minimum of 8 hours per week for
at least five years to qualify.

Any employee, regardless of their hours, can complain of unfair dismissal if it relates to trade union membership or activity.

If you have worked for less than two years for the same employer you may be able to claim wrongful dismissal (p.209).

Example

Michael Faith has been working full time as a window dresser for a large department store for eight years. One Tuesday afternoon, his boss calls him in and tells him that he's no longer satisfied with his work and fires him.

Now Michael knows that his work hasn't been up to scratch recently — his wife's been really ill and his mind wasn't on the job. However, he could still take his case to an Industrial Tribunal, not only because he thinks the dismissal wasn't justified but also because his former employers didn't follow any disciplinary procedures, giving Michael the chance to 'pull his socks up'.

If you are forced to resign because your employer has broken the terms of your contract or they have shown intentions of doing so, then you can complain about another form of dismissal known as **constructive dismissal**.

Example

Lorna Miller has worked as a packer for a chain of food distributors for the last three years. She's just been informed that her hours have been changed. Instead of working a steady 8 am–4 pm, she's now expected to work shifts including a regular stint through the night and also at weekends.

Lorna's a single mum and the new hours mean she wouldn't be able to continue doing her job. Lorna could take a case of constructive dismissal to the Industrial Tribunal.

Either way, dismissal cases are rarely cut and dried. Constructive dismissal cases in particular tend not to be very straightforward. What might initially appear as constructive dismissal might actually be redundancy or might involve allegations of race or sex discrimination (p.220-3). You should always seek advice.

My job's been changed!

'For the last ten years I've been employed full time as a barman in a nightclub in a big London hotel. A new manager was appointed recently and there's been a bit of a shake up in staff, in fact a lot have left. Yesterday I was summoned into my boss's office and told that in addition to my regular bar duties I would also be responsible for cleaning the bar areas in the nightclub. I'm really angry about this because the work is menial and physically more demanding. I'd never take on a job as a barman if it involved cleaning duties.

'When I complained to the boss he said I could either accept the new position or I could leave. I really don't want to do this job, but I'm fifty and I don't see much alternative. Is there anything I can do?'

Basically, once you've been with a company for more than two years, you cannot simply be told to accept a change in your working conditions or go. If you are put in a position where you have to leave because the nature of your job or the conditions and terms of your employment have considerably changed you can take a claim of **constructive dismissal** to an Industrial Tribunal. You would be well advised to get some professional advice (p.237).

Step one: Make a note of what has happened

It's very important to keep a note of any conversations or letters you have had about your change of job. Write down the date and time the discussion took place, where and with whom and what you talked about.

Step two: Think through your options

Even if you go to an Industrial Tribunal and your complaint of constructive dismissal is upheld there is only a limited amount of financial compensation you can be awarded (p.233). If you think that you can get another job within a few months the money the Industrial Tribunal could award might be useful to tide you over until you find another position.

Consider whether there are any other options open to you at work which might be worth negotiating for. For example, could you work in a different bar in another part of the hotel?

Before you make up your mind, talk it through with your family or perhaps some trusted colleagues. Look through the job vacancies to see what's available.

Finally, find out whether the hotel management operates a grievance procedure — the personnel department will be able to tell you. You could also talk to your trade union representative. If you find you are getting nowhere, then consider the following.

Step three: Talk to ACAS
ACAS (p.201) will not only be able to advise you about your basic legal rights, but if you decide you want to try and negotiate another job in the company they may be able to help you.

Step four: Write to your employer
If you decide that it might be worth trying to negotiate a different job then write to your boss. If nothing else the letter could serve as a warning of your intention to go to an Industrial Tribunal.

> Following our discussion on [date] I am writing to tell you that I am extremely concerned that you have arbitrarily decided to change the terms and conditions of my current job.
>
> I find it unacceptable that after ten years working as a barman in the 'High Spots' nightclub I will now be expected to carry out, in addition to my normal bar duties, menial cleaning work which I was not employed to do. This will involve working longer hours than stated in my contract as I cannot clean the bar areas until the nightclub has closed.
>
> However, I have enjoyed working in the hotel and would like to continue to do so in a position similar to my current job. I would like to discuss with you the possibility of taking on the job as barman in the 'Lobby Bar' where I understand there is a full complement of cleaning staff. Perhaps you could tell me when it would be convenient to meet to talk about this.
>
> I have to inform you that unless you offer me a satisfactory position which meets the terms and conditions of my current employment, you will force me to consider taking a complaint of Constructive Dismissal against you in the Industrial Tribunal.

If you do not have a written statement of your terms and conditions (p.208) don't worry. You can show what were the accepted terms and conditions by the fact that you always carried out certain duties on a regular basis and with the agreement of your employers.

There is a risk in writing this letter or indicating that you might go to an Industrial Tribunal. Your employer might think that it's cheaper in the long run to fire you and pay you some compensation and then find someone prepared to take on the two jobs.

Step five: You decide to quit your job

If your negotiations come to nothing and your boss hasn't yet fired you for refusing to work according to the new arrangements, *do not leave until you have sought further advice* from a solicitor or CAB or advice centre. As far as your employer is concerned, leave your options open. You have to make it absolutely clear at all times that you are not leaving of your own free will.

Only when you've talked over your case with a solicitor or advice worker, or you find that your employer goes ahead and fires you, should you go ahead with the Industrial Tribunal procedure (p.229). You may well find your employer will offer you some kind of settlement before the tribunal hearing.

I want my job back!

'At the beginning of the week I had a bit of an argument with my immediate boss. She asked me to do something and I was already up to my eyes so I told her I'd do it later. Anyway we got into something of a row and finally I told her in no uncertain terms where to go. The next thing I knew she dismissed me. I'm really sorry now, because although I think she provoked me, I liked the job and I need the experience. It was my first real job and I'd only been in it six months. Can she just sack me like that and is there anything I can do to get my job back?'

As you've been in your job for less than two years you really have very little legal standing. However, many reputable companies have a standard grievance procedure which they adhere to regardless of how long you've been in their employment. Unless you've done something criminal like thieve or assault a colleague or customer you're unlikely to be dismissed on the spot. See wrongful dismissal (p.209).

You have no guarantees of getting your job back, but it may be worth trying one of the following.

Option one: Write to your senior manager

You should write to the most appropriate senior manager. For all you know, your immediate boss may not have had the authority to dismiss you. Besides you might want to put your side of the case. If your work, time keeping and so on had been okay up to date, there's no reason why you shouldn't ask for a reference. The letter should be delivered without delay.

<u>Dismissal, Tuesday 9th June</u>

I am writing to you regarding my dismissal yesterday afternoon. I was extremely upset by the incident and would ask you to reinstate me.

I had been working with my line manager, Ms Higgins, completing some stock taking. I was extremely busy and under a great deal of stress when Ms Higgins asked me to complete another task. I said rather abruptly that I would do it later. She took offence to my reply and we got into a somewhat heated discussion. Unfortunately I was rather rude to her and she dismissed me.

I am very sorry about my behaviour and am more than ready to apologize to Ms Higgins. I enjoyed my job with your company and value the work experience. All my reports to date have been excellent.

I would be very grateful if you would overlook the incident and give me back my position.

I look forward to hearing from you shortly.

Option two: See your personnel manager

Go immediately to the personnel manager and explain what has happened. If your boss should have followed a standard grievance procedure, the personnel department will tell you. They may decide to intervene on your behalf in any case.

Option three: Say it with flowers

If you really want your job back and there seems no other way out of the mess, try flowers, a bottle, or chocolates and an apology. It might work, where all else has failed!

If they refuse to take you back, make sure you get your P45 (p.210) and that your final pay packet is correct (p.211).

I'm a working mum-to-be — What are my rights?

'I've been working in the accounts department of my company for the last six years. I'm now pregnant and my baby is due in four months' time. I really enjoy my job and I want to return to work after the baby's born. However, when I spoke to my boss about this she said that, as much as she'd like to have me back, she couldn't guarantee that my job would still

be there. She said that the company, which employs about sixteen people, is simply too small for her to keep the post open. Is she actually right?'

Employed women who are pregnant have three main rights guaranteed by law:

- The right not to be unreasonably refused time off for antenatal care and to be paid when permitted that time off.
- The right to complain of unfair dismissal because of pregnancy.
- The right to return to her employer after having the baby.

However, these rights, particularly the last two, are not automatic for all women. A women's entitlement will depend largely on the amount of time she has been working for her employer.

Your boss is wrong — she must keep your job open for you. Any company which employs more than five people is required to uphold the right to return to work by any pregnant employee who is entitled to do so.

As you will have been employed by the company for at least two years by the time you're twenty-nine weeks pregnant, and providing you don't resign before this time, you will automatically qualify. Even so, you need to take certain steps to ensure that you maintain this right.

Basically, you are entitled to a maximum of eleven weeks off before the child is born and twenty-nine weeks off work after your child is born. You should also check your entitlement to Statutory Maternity Pay which comes under the Social Security Act 1986. These are minimum amounts of time and money laid down by law; individual employers may agree to give employees greater benefits.

Step one: Inform your employer of your intention to return to work

At least *twenty-one days* before you intend to begin your maternity absence you should write to your employer.

> This is to let you know that I am leaving work to have a baby. My expected week of confinement is [date]. I intend to return to work after the baby is born.

Your employer may ask you to produce a certificate of the expected week of confinement signed by your doctor or midwife.

Step two: Your employer writes to you during your maternity leave

Your employer has the right to send you a written request asking you to confirm, in writing, that you intend to return to work. She cannot request this confirmation until at least forty-nine days after the date you gave her as the week of confinement.

You should reply to this letter within *fourteen days* of receiving it. If you don't, you may lose your right to return.

Thank you for your letter of [date].
This is to let you know that I still intend to return to work.

Step three: You confirm the date you expect to return to work

At least *twenty-one days* before the date you intend to return you must write to your employer with that date. It is up to you to decide the exact date you go back to work, as long as it is within the twenty-nine week deadline. It is possible to extend the time by an extra four weeks if, for example, you are ill and can produce a medical certificate.

This is to let you know that I will be coming back to work on [date].

Step four: Returning to work

The point of the right to return is that you are entitled to be employed on terms and conditions which are no less favourable than when you left to start your maternity leave. In addition, you are entitled to benefit from any other improvements such as increased pay or holidays that have happened during your absence.

Step five: Taking it further

If at any time your employer refuses to give you the right to return, or puts you in a position where you have to resign prior to taking maternity leave you should consider taking your case to an Industrial Tribunal (p.229). But remember that strict time limits apply, so don't delay in making your application.

If you return to work and find that you have been made redundant or that your job has changed dramatically (and unfavourably) on your return, you might be able to claim unfair dismissal (p.212-13) at an Industrial Tribunal.

Race discrimination

The Race Relations Act 1976 deals with discrimination on **racial grounds**, that is, discriminating against a person because of their colour, race, nationality or ethnic or national origins.

It defines discrimination in three main ways:

- Direct discrimination which means treating a person on racial grounds **less favourably** than others are or would be treated in the same circumstances.
- Indirect discrimination which means applying a requirement or condition which, whether intentionally or not, adversely affects a particular racial group considerably more than others and cannot be justified on non-racial grounds.
- Discrimination by means of victimization which means treating a person less favourably than others are or would be treated in the same circumstances because that person has made a complaint or allegation about discrimination or has become involved in such proceedings.

Facing up to race discrimination

'I work for a computer firm as a salesman. Last month I applied for a promotion to Regional Sales Manager. Three of us went for the new job and one of my colleagues got it.

'I think I was the best qualified for the post — I've been in the job longest and I've done all the relevant training. All my appraisals so far have been excellent. The only thing I can think of is that I was turned down because I'm Asian.

'We've got a new Divisional Manager who's responsible for making this appointment and he's made some very odd comments to me. There's been nothing blatantly racist, just a couple of snide remarks. However, one of my colleagues who's a good friend, told me that he overheard this particular manager talking to someone in the pub and evidently he said, ''I'm not seeing one of these foreigners as my Regional Manager.''

'I like my job and I want to succeed, but this whole incident has really upset me. I'm so angry that this man can treat me in this way. Is there anything I can do?'

You will need to decide whether you want to make a formal complaint against your employer. But you will also need to weigh up the possible outcomes of such action and, more to the point, if you take your case to an Industrial Tribunal and are successful. What are the general attitudes of the people you work with? Do you have the option to work for someone other than the manager you believe discriminated against you? Are you prepared to rethink your long-term career plans?

Don't be put off challenging discrimination — just be well prepared. It can be a long, painful and very personal process, so try and get as much support as possible from your family, friends and colleagues.

If you do take the case to an Industrial Tribunal you will be dealing with a legal procedure so try and be as objective as you can. You will also need to ensure that your friend is prepared to act as a witness. He, of course, would also be protected by the Act's provisions.

Step one: Write to your employer

Before you do this you may want to discuss your case with a race relations specialist. This could be a trade union representative or lawyer. Or contact the COMMISSION FOR RACIAL EQUALITY (CRE) (p.23) who will give you free advice.

The CRE will provide you with a special questionnaire which basically asks the person against whom you are alleging discrimination to give their version of the story. You should send this questionnaire with a short covering letter to the person concerned, the Divisional Manager. You will probably also want to send a copy of the letter and the questionnaire to the Managing Director of the company.

I am enclosing a standard questionnaire from the Commission for Racial Equality in which you will see that I have alleged that you discriminated against me under the terms of the Race Relations Act 1976, in my recent application for the post of Regional Sales Manager.

I look forward to receiving your answers to the points I have raised within the next fourteen days.

c.c.[MD's name]

The manager concerned doesn't have to reply but failure to do so or to give a complete answer may be taken into account at an Industrial Tribunal should the matter get that far.

If you decide to make an application straight to an Industrial Tribunal, you can still put these questions to your manager but you must do so within *twenty-one days* of making the application.

Step two: Approach ACAS

If you get no reply or are not satisfied with the response you get you can contact ACAS (p.201) to see if they can settle the matter by conciliation. You may decide that you don't want to pursue this stage — but do discuss the matter with them or the CRE ← before making up your mind.

Step three: Make an application to an Industrial Tribunal

To find out how you should make an application to an Industrial Tribunal see p.229. However, here are some points which relate directly to cases of alleged racial discrimination.

You will be complaining about direct discrimination ← . Therefore you'll need evidence to prove that you were treated less favourably than the other candidates for the post *and* that the reason for this was because you are of Asian origin.

At the hearing you or your representative will be expected to explain how you were treated and why you consider this to be discriminatory. You will need as much documentary evidence as you can collect. Some of the information should have appeared on the questionnaire you sent your manager. You should seek answers to the following kinds of questions:

- What are the reasons for you having been turned down for the promotion?
- What are the qualifications and racial origin of the person who was appointed?
- What are the qualifications and racial origins of the other applicants who were turned down?
- What were the qualifications and racial origins of other people who have been appointed to similar posts?

You will need statements from any colleagues who can support your allegations. They must also be prepared to attend the hearing.

Step four: Dealing with racism at work

Unfortunately, racism still rears its ugly head daily in the workplace and elsewhere. Frequently, people make racist remarks without realizing that they have caused offence. In fact, in many instances, they are quite horrified when it's pointed out to them that what they have said is offensive and they usually brush it off, saying that they didn't really mean it. It's important to confront racism when it happens.

A typical exchange is shown in the example — the nationality or race are hardly relevant.

Example

Person A: I've just had to deal with that Paki/Jew/Irishman in the next office. I don't like dealing with those kind of people — they can't speak English properly, they ought to go back to their own country.

Person B: I'm Pakistani/Jewish/Irish and I find your remarks very offensive. Please do not say such things again.

Person A: Oh, you know I wasn't talking about you. I mean, you're not like the rest of them. Don't take it so personally.

Person B: As I'm a Pakistani/Jew/Irish, I do take your comments personally. I found what you said very offensive, so please don't make such statements again.

Much racism is based on ignorance. You can't hope to change attitudes overnight but you can challenge ignorance.

Sex discrimination

The process for challenging sex discrimination is very similar. The organization that will be able to give you help and advice is the EQUAL OPPORTUNITIES COMMISSION who may even take up your case on your behalf.

Sexual harassment

'I'm currently working for the Customer Relations Manager of a large chain of stores. I've been with the company for three years and enjoy the job. There are plenty of opportunities to go on to "greater things".

'However, one thing is making my life really miserable — my new boss. He's forever coming up to me and putting his arm round me. If he wants to discuss a document he insists on sitting on some sofas we have in the office rather than at a desk and moves close enough to make sure our legs or

knees are touching. I've tried moving away but he just moves over too. He keeps cornering me and sometimes I get really scared.

'*I've got a review coming up — which he's responsible for — and he's now suggesting that we "go somewhere quiet for dinner so that we can discuss my future". I've got a pretty shrewd idea what he has in mind and I don't want to go along with it. I do want to get ahead but what can I do about my boss without jeopardizing my career prospects?*'

Sexual harassment is one of the hidden work problems. The harasser usually has seniority (and therefore power) over his or her victim who is frequently too frightened of the possible consequences to complain. It affects people's work, their health and can endanger career and job prospects.

Most victims of sexual harassment are women. Age or position does not matter.

Sexual harassment may involve:

- Unnecessary and persistent touching or other unwanted physical contact.
- Verbal abuse, suggestive remarks or jokes.
- Pestering for sexual favours.
- Compromising invitations.
- Pin-ups or other offensive displays.
- Sexual assault and rape.

If you suffer from sexual harassment you may be able to take legal action. There is no specific law against sexual harassment at work but cases can be taken to an industrial tribunal under the Sex Discrimination Act and the Employment Protection (Consolidation) Act 1978. Employers have a duty to protect their employees from sexual harassment.

It won't necessarily be easy complaining about sexual harassment. You may find yourself up against a seeming 'conspiracy' where people either deny your claims or say that it's happened before but there really is nothing they can do about the way a senior manager behaves. Do persevere. If eventually you have to rethink your career plans and move to another company, ensure that if you're entitled to any compensation, you claim it.

Step one: Decide what you want to do

You have a number of options open to you. You will need to think how best to approach the problem.

You could:

- Confront your boss — verbally or in writing.
- Talk to your personnel department or senior management.
- Contact your local union representative or women's officer if you have one.

In addition you might want to get support from your local women's group or from a special advice organization such as WOMEN AGAINST SEXUAL HARASSMENT (WASH).

As a last resort you may consider taking your case to an Industrial Tribunal or seeking other legal redress→.

Whatever you do, try and talk over the situation with sympathetic members of your family, friends or colleagues. Talk to other women in your office — you might find that you are not the only person being harassed.

Step two: Collect the evidence
Whatever you decide to do, you will need to collect evidence about the way you've been harassed. This could include:

- A diary of events — dates, times, places.
- Details or tape recordings of conversations.
- Letters or memos.
- Witnesses. Try and tell someone else what has happened.
- Also keep a note of your reactions to these various incidents and how they have affected you, e.g. if you've had to visit your doctor.

Keep this information in a safe place. Don't leave it lying around the office or in a diary that might get lost.

Step three: You decide to confront your boss
You may want to try to talk to him about the situation first before you put anything in writing ☺.

You might want to run through and add to this scenario as appropriate. Consider also, whether you could ask for someone else to be present at your review.

YOU: I want to discuss the format of my forthcoming review with you. I know you mentioned that we could talk about the review over dinner one evening but I would prefer to discuss the matter during working hours. Perhaps you could suggest a time one morning or afternoon that would be convenient.

YOUR BOSS: Oh, come on Janine, (puts his arm round you), don't be such a spoil-sport. You know it would be much more fun to discuss things over a quiet dinner for two instead of in this stuffy office with the phone going all the time.

YOU: (Removing his arm) Please don't put your arm around me. I don't like it and I find it totally unnecessary. I know you think that it'll be more fun to discuss the review over dinner but I prefer to deal with working matters such as my review during the working day. If you are concerned about the telephone ringing perhaps you could ask the switchboard to hold your calls for the duration of our meeting.

YOUR BOSS: (Moving closer) Janine, what's got into you all of a sudden? Remember I am the boss and bosses usually have the final word.

YOU: I am very well aware that you are my manager. That is why I am concerned about maintaining a proper professional relationship. Perhaps I was wrong about not saying anything before but I'd like to set the record straight. I really do object to you persistently physically touching me. Would you please not do it any more. And once again, I would like my review to be held in the office during normal working hours. When would be convenient?

Confronting your boss face to face will probably have one of three results:

- He will apologize and agree to your requests.
- He will ignore you or his behaviour will get worse.
- He will challenge you to take your complaints further.

If you find yourself in either of the last two situations and you want to continue talking the matter over with him, you might add:

'I have asked you to stop putting your arm around me or physically touching me in any other way. I have also requested that we discuss my review during normal working hours. If you persist in any unnecessary physical contact or insist that we discuss my review over dinner I shall be forced to take the matter up with the personnel department/a more senior manager. You are sexually harassing me. If necessary I will take advice on taking the matter further.'

Step four: Making a formal complaint in writing to your boss

If you don't want to confront your boss in person or you feel that that hasn't worked, you can make a formal complaint in writing.

> I am writing to complain formally about your behaviour towards me.
>
> Despite the fact that I have made it clear to you that I do not wish you to persistently touch me and make other unnecessary physical contact you continue to do so.
>
> Furthermore, I want my review to be conducted in the office during normal office hours and not 'somewhere quiet over dinner' as you suggested. In addition, given the nature of my complaint, I wish [name of colleague] to be present during the review.
>
> If you do not stop sexually harassing me, I will have no alternative but to instigate formal grievance proceedings against you/seek legal advice with a view to taking the matter further.

You might want to copy the letter in confidence either to your personnel officer or to another more senior manager.

Step five: Making a formal complaint to the personnel department

You might want to discuss the matter informally with your personnel officer who may feel able to deal with it without formal proceedings. However, this shouldn't put you off making a formal complaint in writing.

> I am writing to make a formal complaint of sexual harassment against Mr Greg Ego.
>
> Since I started working with Mr Ego, last autumn, I have been very upset by his behaviour towards me which is beginning to affect my work.
>
> Mr Ego persistently touches me and makes other unnecessary physical contact. For example, he insists that we go over documents sitting on the office sofas and always makes sure his legs are touching mine. I have tried to move away but he simply moves too. I feel extremely uncomfortable in such a situation.

As you are no doubt aware, my annual review is coming up shortly. Mr Ego has suggested to me that we go 'somewhere quiet for dinner' to discuss my progress. In view of his behaviour towards me in the office I am naturally very concerned about such a suggestion.

I discussed the matter with him on last Wednesday, 6th October. I asked him to refrain from putting his arm round me and to stop any other physical pestering. I also requested that we should discuss my review in the office during normal working hours. Mr Ego turned down my requests and I found his manner very threatening and abusive.

I enjoy my job and my track record so far has been excellent. I look forward to continuing my career with the company and to progressing further with you. I am concerned that my current manager's behaviour will hamper my career with this company. Would you please take up my complaint with the appropriate managers.

Step six: Following a grievance procedure

Most established companies and organizations have formal grievance procedures. If they don't, they ought to and you should contact ACAS (p.201) to see if they can help you. You should have received a copy of the grievance and disciplinary procedure when you joined the company; the personnel officer will be able to advise you further.

You might also consider asking your union to take up the matter formally at this point.

If you do start a grievance procedure be very clear about what you want to happen; this might include getting the harasser to stop or moving to another department.

Step seven: Taking further action

If you feel that your company is not handling your case properly or you think that you have been so compromised that you can no longer go on working in the same place, seek specialist legal advice immediately, *before* you do anything drastic like resign.

You may well be able to take your case before an Industrial Tribunal. Alternatively, in some cases you could instigate criminal proceedings. However, you would be advised not to pursue this course of action without taking professional advice.

Many support groups such as WOMEN AGAINST SEXUAL HARASSMENT

(WASH) or RIGHTS OF WOMEN (ROW) offer free legal advice from sympathetic women lawyers. Your local CAB or advice centre will also be able to give you the names of specialist solicitors in your area (p.22).

What else?

Sexual harassment is not only confined to the work place. Other examples include:

- Landlords threatening and harassing tenants.
- Residents of hostels, B & B etc. harassing other residents or wardens or workers and vice versa.
- Students or staff harassing other students.
- Pupils harassing teachers.

If you find yourself in any of these situations follow a similar course of action to that suggested above: get support from other people or organizations; confront the harasser verbally or in writing; make a formal complaint if possible; take legal advice.

Step-by-step guide to making an application to an Industrial Tribunal

> **The Applicant** is the person making the complaint (the employee).
>
> **The Respondent** is the person against whom the complaint is made (the employer).
>
> **The Parties** refers to both the applicant and the respondent.

Step one: Act immediately!

Most applications to an Industrial Tribunal must be made within three months of the incident about which you are complaining taking place. But this is only a rough guide, so check the time limit that applies to your case and avoid getting caught out.

Step two: Fill in the application form

Once you are sure you have a case in law ← get a copy of the application form known as an **Originating Application** or **IT1**. There is an explanatory leaflet to go with it. The forms are available at job centres and unemployment benefit offices and at some advice centres.

You can always get help to complete the form from your trade union representative, CAB or advice centre. If you qualify you may also be able to get help from a solicitor under the Legal Advice and Assistance Scheme (p.242).

When the form is completed send it off immediately to the CENTRAL OFFICE OF INDUSTRIAL TRIBUNALS whose address will be on the front of the form. Remember to keep a copy of the form for your own information.

Step three: Registration of your application

Usually your application will be registered and acknowledged by the Central Office of Industrial Tribunals within a few days. If the Secretary of the Tribunals thinks that a tribunal will not be able to deal with your complaint then you will be notified.

Once your application has been registered a copy of it will be sent to the respondent. The respondent will be asked to complete a form known as a **Notice of Appearance** or **IT3**, stating whether he or she intends to contest the application and, if so, for what reasons. You will be sent a copy of the respondent's completed notice.

If the reasons given by the respondent are not clear to you, you can ask the respondent to provide **Further Particulars** (more information). If they refuse to do so you can apply to the tribunal to force them to do so.

Step four: ACAS is notified

Copies of your IT1 and the respondent's notice will be sent to ACAS (p.201) who will try and assist a settlement. However, this does not delay arrangements for a tribunal hearing and nothing said to the ACAS conciliation officer can be used as evidence at the hearing.

Step five: You receive a notice of hearing

This is the date the tribunal will hear your complaint. Usually you are contacted in advance and asked what day would be convenient for you. If you are given a day and time which you cannot make you must write to the tribunal office immediately, explaining your reasons and requesting an alternative day.

[applicant's name] vs [respondent's name/name of company]
to be heard on [date]

I am writing to ask you formally to postpone this case as [give
your reasons, these could include: witnesses not available; illness; you will be out of the country].

I would be most grateful if you will arrange a new date for the
hearing after [date] when [my witness will be available; I shall
be well enough to attend; I will be in this country].

Step six: Preliminary hearing

This only happens where there is some dispute over whether the
tribunal has the power to consider the complaint. The preliminary
hearing will deal solely with this question and won't go into
details of the case.

Step seven: Pre-hearing assessment

If either party or the tribunal decides that the applicant's or the
respondent's case has no substance and won't stand up at the
hearing, a pre-hearing assessment may be held. The tribunal can't
decide or dismiss the case at this point. But they may warn one or
other party that if they persist in a case which the tribunal considers to have no merit they may be liable for the costs (in
Scotland, the expenses) of the other person if they eventually lose
(p.202).

Step eight: Preparing for the hearing

If you take the time to prepare your case well you are more likely to
be successful. Obviously the exact information and documents
you will need will vary according to the nature of your complaint.
However, you should try to get together the following
information:

* Details about your employment: your contract; statement of
  terms and conditions; the date you started; salary (take a pay
  packet or wage slip); job title and duties; promotions; the
  organization of the company; fringe benefits; pension or
  superannuation schemes; any information relating to the search
  for a new job, if applicable, such as travelling and removal costs.
* The nature of your complaint. You will have already written
  down much of this information on your originating application

231

form (IT1). Make sure that there are no gaps — go over it again.

- The remedy you are seeking→. If you are claiming compensation then make a list of everything you are claiming for. You can include expenses incurred in looking for another job and in discrimination cases you can also claim compensation for abstract things such as general upset.
- Witnesses. Make a list of all the witnesses you want to call and the questions you want to ask them. Don't rely on inspiration on the day. You can apply to the tribunal for a **witness order** if your witness is unwilling to attend. But be aware that no witness is sometimes better than a reluctant witness forced to give evidence.
- If you want copies of documents which you think are relevant to your case and they are in the possession of someone else, for example your employer or a former employee, you can ask for them to be sent to you. If the respondent refuses to do so, you can apply to the tribunal to make an **order for discovery and inspection** which means that those documents must be made available for you to look at.

Step nine: The hearing

Tribunal hearings are almost always held in public, so go along to see what happens.

Before the hearing check:

- You have all your documents and other evidence.
- Your witnesses know where and when they are required.
- You know where you are going.
- You have an agreed time and place to meet your representative (if you have one).
- You leave in plenty of time!

The procedure at the tribunal hearing is intended to be orderly but informal and flexible. The tribunal clerk will explain the procedure before the case begins but if necessary the tribunal will give further guidance as the hearing progresses.

The applicant usually begins by giving the details of the complaint. The tribunal will tell you if the procedure is different in your case. If you are very nervous, imagine you are relating your story to a good friend. Start at the beginning and go through what happened stage by stage. The applicant then has the opportunity to call and question their witnesses as well as any witnesses called by the respondent. The respondent then presents their case following the same method.

Step ten: The decision

The tribunal will often announce its decision at the end of the hearing. The reasons for the decision are usually sent to you later. Always ask for **full written reasons** at the end of the hearing otherwise you may simply receive a summary of the reasons. If you do receive a summary, write and ask the tribunal to send you the full written reasons.

The tribunal has the power to award a number of **remedies**:

- It can make an order stating what the legal rights and wrongs of the case are.
- It can recommend steps to put the matter right.
- It can award compensation.

If a tribunal decides, for example, that you have been unfairly dismissed then it will first check with you whether you want to be reinstated and make sure this is practical from the employer's point of view before making an order.

If the tribunal makes an award of **compensation** this usually consists of a basic award and a compensatory award. The compensatory award is the amount the tribunal considers just for any loss you have suffered. The basic award is calculated according to your age, length of service and weekly pay.

If you do receive financial compensation, this might have an effect on any unemployment or other benefit you may intend to claim or have already claimed. So do check this out at the appropriate benefit office.

Step eleven: Appealing against the decision

There are two ways of getting a tribunal to reconsider its decision.

Firstly, you can ask for a **review** in which the tribunal looks carefully at its decision again. You can only request a review in certain circumstances, which include the following:

- A party did not receive notice of the hearing.
- New evidence has come to light.
- The decision was made in the absence of a party or someone else entitled to be heard.
- There was an error on the part of the tribunal staff.

If you want a review you must ask for one within *fourteen days* of receiving the tribunal's decision.

Secondly, you have a limited right of **appeal**. You can *only* appeal if you think that the tribunal applied the law wrongly to your case and not merely because you think their decision was wrong. When you receive a copy of the tribunal's decision you will also get information about how to make an appeal.

The appeal must be made in writing to the EMPLOYMENT APPEALS TRIBUNAL within *forty-two days* of the date that the tribunal's written decision was sent to you.

To make an appeal you will need the full written reasons ←. If you only received a summary version you have *twenty-one days* after the date they were sent to you to request full written reasons.

If, once you've got an award, you find that your employers don't pay up, seek legal advice because the award can be enforced.

Section three
Useful Tools

The legal profession

The legal profession is split into two camps, solicitors and barristers. Solicitors are governed by the Law Society and barristers by the Bar Council.

Your first legal port of call will invariably be a solicitor. You are unlikely to contact a barrister directly, as they tend to have more of a specialist consultant's role within the profession. If necessary your solicitor will find a barrister appropriate for your case.

Obviously the set-up in each law firm will depend upon the number of people employed and the type of work they undertake. A single solicitor practising on their own, an inner city practice specializing in legal aid work and a multi-partner city firm will all be very different.

However, in an average high street firm you will usually come across the following structure. At the bottom are Articled Clerks who, although they have probably passed all their law exams, will still not be fully qualified for two years; they work with more senior solicitors but may be assigned to your case if it is a minor matter. Then there are the main body of the firm's solicitors who will have a wide range of experience. You may also have a legal executive working on your case. Although not fully qualified lawyers, they do have some qualifications and many are very experienced. They usually undertake routine legal work. Finally, there are the firm's partners who, commensurate with their position, will charge you more for their services. The nature of your case will most often dictate the number and seniority of the lawyers assigned to it.

Finding the right kind of solicitor

Although solicitors are now allowed to advertise their services many of their clients come through personal recommendations.

- Ask your family, friends or neighbours if they have dealt with any solicitors and whether they were satisfied with them.
- Ask your employers whether they can recommend a local legal practice.
- Look for advertisements in local papers.
- Go through Yellow Pages.
- Visit your local library or advice centre who should have a list of solicitors in the area.
- Look at a copy of the *Regional Directory of Solicitors* published by the Law Society. The directory, which is kept by CABs, law centres, advice centres and libraries, will list not only names and addresses of practices in your area but give details of the kind of work they do, whether they offer **Fixed Fee Interviews**→or the **Legal Aid and Advice Scheme**→and if they speak any languages other than English.

How will I know if the solicitor is the right person to handle my case?

Well, you won't know for sure until the case is finally settled. But you can safeguard your interests. There are two important points to consider: does the solicitor regularly handle cases such as yours; do you get on with him or her?

Most high street solicitors handle a wide range of matters; however, in particular areas — for example, immigration or abuse cases — certain practices are especially renowned for their expertise or sympathetic approach. Your local CAB or advice centre may be able to point you in the direction of a particular law firm but the *Regional Directory of Solicitors*←will give you a good idea of who does what.

Just because your neighbour's solicitor was absolutely wonderful over the purchase of their new house does not necessarily mean they will be equally wonderful handling your divorce. You should always telephone or visit the law firm to make sure that they have the expertise to deal with your case and to find out which solicitor would be able to handle it.

Unless you have the opportunity to meet the solicitor socially (and that's not always a good indicator of professional expertise) or informally, your only option to check them out may be through a **Fixed Fee Interview** (p.245).

Although you can change solicitors if you are very unhappy

with the way they are dealing with you or your case (p.245) it is generally viewed as 'not a good thing' within the profession. If you want to get out, then get out right at the beginning. However, with a little tact, diplomacy and much assertive behaviour you can often get the most out of your legal beaver.

Getting the most out of your solicitor

Solicitors are expensive. If you use them as counsellors, sounding blocks, punch-balls or a shoulder to cry on then you will pay for the privilege. Be the professional client.

* When you telephone or visit to make the first appointment don't embark on a long saga to the receptionist, just tell them the nature of the problem and how quickly you need to see a solicitor. If you want to see a solicitor urgently, perhaps to get a violent partner out of your home, you'll need an appointment immediately, not in a week's time.
* Before you go for your first meeting with the solicitor collect together all the documents — letters, bills, diary dates of telephone calls, eye witness statements — whatever is relevant to your case. Photocopy them if you have access to a copier and put them into files.
* If you haven't already done so, sit down and make a list of everything that has happened to do with the case and set out the information in chronological order (the order in which events occurred). This will save an awful lot of time — and ultimately money — later. It will also help you to channel your thoughts and make it easier for you to communicate clearly with the solicitor. If you have a bad memory or need to check out the facts with someone else, it is vital that everything is committed to paper before your appointment.
* Be on time for your appointment. If for some good reason you cannot make the appointment, then telephone in advance. Even if the solicitor keeps you waiting (and it does happen) you have indicated the standards you expect.
* Establish how much the solicitor is going to charge you (p.241).
* Do not waffle during your meeting. Communicate the facts of the case clearly and succinctly, providing the relevant documents where necessary.
* Find out what the solicitor is going to do for you. If they take off on a flight of legal jargon (which is not uncommon), then ask

them to stop and explain it in plain, everyday language. They are acting on your behalf and you are paying for the service — you have every right to understand what they are doing.

- If your solicitor offers to write or telephone somebody about the case, establish when they expect to receive a reply and make a note of the date. Unfortunately, in many instances solicitors have to deal with large bureaucratic organizations or with solicitors 'on the other side' who may not consider a speedy reply in their client's best interests. It may be weeks rather than days before your solicitor contacts you again, so be patient. If you do think the delay is getting excessive, then chivvy them up.
- Avoid making unnecessary telephone calls or writing superfluous letters to your solicitor, they will all add to your final bill. If you do need to contact your solicitor then make a list of the points you want to raise before you telephone 📞 or write ✏.
- If you have an important piece of new information on your case, then tell your solicitor immediately, not least because you both might be made to look complete fools if you don't.

What happens if I don't think the solicitor is taking my case seriously?

There may be all sorts of reasons for you to feel that your solicitor is not working effectively: the solicitor may have misunderstood part of your instructions; they might be completely overworked and your case, because it doesn't have an immediate deadline, has gone to the bottom of the pile; your expectations of what your legal adviser can do for you are unrealistic.

If you think there's a problem you *must* talk it through with your solicitor immediately.

- Arrange to see your solicitor. If you have an appointment fixed, set aside time to discuss the way the case is being handled. You'll need to be assertive (p.30).
- Take the bull by the horns: 'I know that you are extremely busy and that this is a costly exercise. However, I want to raise a few points which are concerning me over the way I feel you are handling my case.'
- Be positive, highlight something that has gone well: 'I was very pleased that you agreed to take my case on. At our first meeting I appreciated the way you listened to me. I was also pleased that

you returned my calls immediately.'

- Be specific about what you think is wrong: 'I have since telephoned you a number of times about various matters which gave me a great deal of concern. I left messages with your secretary but you've never returned my calls. Furthermore I haven't received copies of your correspondence as you promised. I am concerned that my case is not receiving your full and prompt attention.'
- Be specific about what changes you want: 'This case is causing me a great deal of anxiety. I would like you to answer my calls within twenty-four hours or at least give me an indication of when we might speak. I would also like copies of all the letters you have sent to date and to receive copies of any future letters immediately they are posted.'

   The more specific you are about what you think is wrong and what you want done about it, the less likely you are to get into a time-consuming argument with your lawyer.

- Listen to the answers your solicitor gives. If you think that they are unreasonable, say so and reiterate your request. If there is some genuine reason for the communication breakdown, this conversation should help put things right.
- If you are still unhappy, you could consider changing your solicitor (p.245).

If you think that there is something seriously wrong with the way your case is being handled then you may want to complain to a higher authority (p.246).

Solicitors' charges

Before you instruct a solicitor and ask them to act for you, you must establish what their fees are likely to be. The Law Society requires solicitors to:

- Give you the best idea they can of the costs involved when you instruct them.
- Consider whether you are eligible for **Legal Aid and Assistance** ➝.
- Confirm in writing the fee agreed, what it covers and whether it includes VAT and disbursements (other costs the solicitor might incur on your behalf, e.g. stamp duty paid to the Inland Revenue or court fees).
- If no fee is agreed, then tell you how the fee will be calculated,

for example on an hourly rate, a percentage of the value of the transaction or some other agreed method.

• Confirm in writing any estimate. The final bill should not vary substantially from the estimate unless you have been informed in writing of any changes.
• Tell you at appropriate stages throughout the case, regardless of whether you are legally aided, what costs you may be liable for. For example, even if you win your case, you may not get all your legal costs met by 'the other side'.

Getting legal help at a police station or court

If you have been taken into a police station for questioning or you have been charged with committing an offence you are entitled to speak to a solicitor. Even if you refuse legal help to start with, you can change your mind at any time.

Ask the police to do one of the following:

• Contact your own solicitor or one you know of.
• Contact the Duty Solicitor, who is on call 24 hours a day, is independent and is not employed by the police.
• Give you a list of local solicitors who may be willing to help.

The services of the Duty Solicitor are free whilst you are at the police station.

If you find yourself at the Magistrates Court without legal representation, ask to see the Duty Solicitor who may be able not only to advise you about your court appearance but also to represent you in court. The first time you go to court you will not have to pay for the Duty Solicitor.

Financial help towards legal costs

If you need help from a solicitor or barrister but cannot afford to pay for it, you may qualify for help through the **Legal Aid and Advice Schemes**. **Legal Advice — The Green Form Scheme**, is for non-court work. **Civil Legal Aid** takes up where the Green Form Scheme stops and is for people involved in a court case. **Criminal Legal Aid** is available for people facing a charge for a criminal offence. The schemes are publicly funded and are administered by the Legal Aid Board with the exception of Criminal Legal Aid which is administered by the courts.

Free leaflets about the schemes should be available from your local CAB, advice centre, law centre or from the LEGAL AID BOARD HEAD OFFICE.

Legal advice under the 'Green Form Scheme'

What is it?

The Green Form Scheme is a means-tested scheme, so-called because your solicitor will need to complete a green form to establish whether you are eligible for help. If you qualify it will enable you to receive advice and assistance on any point of law. There is an upper limit on the cost of the work a solicitor can complete under the scheme, but the scheme may be extended so that the solicitor can do more work for you.

How do I know if I'm eligible?

Your solicitor or advice centre will be able to tell you whether you qualify. Basically the calculation is done according to your *disposable* income and capital.

They work out how much you have left after you have deducted your tax and outgoings. If the sum you have left falls below the amount specified by the scheme then you are entitled to help on a sliding scale. You may not have to pay anything at all.

If you are in any doubt about your eligibility for the scheme, it's always worth doing the calculation. People with quite substantial gross incomes but with hefty outgoings can still qualify.

Civil Legal Aid

Civil Legal Aid is means tested in much the same way as the Green Form Scheme, the only difference being that the financial limits vary. Legal Aid cannot affect the amount of work a solicitor undertakes on your behalf; it is simply a way of helping you to pay the fees of legal professionals. You should get exactly the same service as if you were paying the full costs privately.

If I qualify financially will I automatically get help?

The answer is no. Not only do you need to meet the financial requirements but your case will need to justify public money being spent on it.

You will not get help if the assessment officer decides that your case is of no public interest or stands every chance of failing before it even gets to court.

It is often wise to let your solicitor complete the form for you, particularly if the costs involved are likely to be high or the case complex.

If you are granted Legal Aid and you gain or regain money or property or win compensation as a result of a successful case you may have to repay all or some of your solicitor's costs. This is known as the **statutory charge**. Ask your solicitor what, if anything, you will have to pay if you win your case.

Criminal Legal Aid

You can apply for Criminal Legal Aid if:

- You have been charged with a criminal offence or are about to be sentenced or dealt with for committing a criminal offence.
- You wish to appeal against a Magistrates Court, Crown Court, or Court of Appeal decision.

Criminal Legal Aid must be granted if:

- You are committed for trial charged with murder.
- You have already been remanded in custody, you have had no legal representation and you may be held in custody again.
- You are found guilty and the court intends to send you to prison and you have had no legal representation.

If none of the above applies to you then the court will decide your case on its own merit and will only grant Legal Aid if they think it will be 'in the interests of justice'. Criminal Legal Aid is not normally granted for driving offences unless you may lose your job if convicted or if you have a suspended sentence for a similar offence.

What does the court consider when deciding whether to grant Criminal Legal Aid?

The court will look at a number of facts including: the complexity of the case, e.g. if it involves mistaken identity; whether it raises an important point of law; if the defendant would have difficulty in understanding the proceedings or conducting their case because of language difficulties or mental incapacity.

If you are unhappy with the amount of Legal Aid you have been granted, you can always ask the court to reconsider their decision.

The Fixed Fee Interview

This is quite different from the Legal Aid and Advice Schemes. The Fixed Fee Interview means that you get a half-an-hour interview with a solicitor for a flat fee, currently £5.

The advantages are:

- You get an idea of whether your case is worth pursuing.
- You have an opportunity to meet the solicitor on a working basis.

The disadvantage is:

- It may well take much longer than half an hour to explain and assess your case.

Words of caution:

- Prepare carefully and thoroughly for the interview ←.
- Be absolutely certain that the solicitor understands that you have come to consult them under the Fixed Fee Interview. You don't want any nasty surprise bills!

Changing solicitors

On the whole the legal profession is not keen on clients changing their advisers simply because it can be quite difficult to take up the case where the previous solicitor left off. However, if you are unhappy with the way your case is being dealt with:

- Find a new solicitor who will *agree* to take on your case. Make sure you inform him or her that you have previously instructed another solicitor.
- Write to your first solicitor stating that you have decided to withdraw your instructions from them.
- Ask your first solicitor to forward all your case papers to your new solicitor. They may not be prepared to do that until you have settled all their outstanding fees!

It may be that you just 'didn't get on' with your first solicitor. However, if this is not so, you may need to consider whether he or she was guilty of professional misconduct or negligence →.

If you were granted Legal Aid and you wish to change solicitors you will need to check this with the LEGAL AID BOARD first.

245

What to do if things go wrong

If problems do arise with solicitors the majority of them are complaints about **professional misconduct**. The LAW SOCIETY considers professional misconduct to include:

- Persistent delay in answering your letters or enquiries — or failing to answer them at all.
- Delay in dealing with your case.
- Failing to keep proper accounts of money held on your behalf.
- Acting for others involved in the same case as you, where your interests conflict.
- Overcharging.
- Dishonesty.
- Failing to hand over your papers if you have asked for them and don't owe your solicitor any money.
- 'Shoddy work'. This means work which is substandard and which may have caused you distress or inconvenience. However, if you think that the solicitor has been **negligent** and has made a major mistake for which you should receive **compensation**, read on →.

Overcharging

If you consider that your bill is too high, discuss the matter with your solicitor. If you are still not satisfied you can have your bill examined.

If the work was **non-contentious** (didn't involve you going to court) insist that your solicitor applies to the Law Society for a **Remuneration Certificate**.

A panel of solicitors appointed by the Law Society examine details of the work undertaken together with your comments. They will then issue a remuneration certificate stating whether they thought the bill was fair and, if it wasn't, by how much it should be reduced. The panel has no authority to increase the bill and their services are free.

If the work was **contentious** then it is up to the courts to assess the bill and decide whether it is fair. This is known as having the bill **taxed**. You should ask either your solicitor or the Law Society to explain the current procedures.

If you want to challenge your bill you must act immediately as strict time limits are enforced.

Professional misconduct

If you think that your solicitor is guilty of professional misconduct speak first to the most senior partner in the law firm you have been dealing with. If you cannot resolve the problem that way then you will need to complain to the SOLICITORS COMPLAINTS BUREAU, a separate organization set up by the Law Society to investigate complaints against solicitors.

Write to the Bureau with details of the following: ⌀

- The name and address of the law firm and the name of the solicitor handling your case.
- What kind of matter your solicitor was dealing with.
- Your complaint.
- Whether you object to the Bureau sending a copy of your letter to your solicitor.

Do not send any documents at this stage. If necessary the Bureau will write and ask you for further information.

If the Bureau decides that there has been a breach of the rules of professional conduct by your solicitor they will either deal with the solicitor themselves or refer the matter to the **Solicitors Disciplinary Tribunal** who will, if appropriate, strike the solicitor off the **Roll of Solicitors**, suspend them from practice or fine them. Neither the Bureau nor the Tribunal can order your solicitor to pay you compensation →.

Negligence

If you think that your solicitor has made a major mistake which has cost you money or caused some other loss, then you may be entitled to claim **compensation**.

You have a number of options open to you, although they are not necessarily exclusive.

- Find another solicitor to take on your case against the first solicitor.
- If you encounter difficulty in finding a willing solicitor then ask the Solicitors Complaints Bureau to put you in touch with the **Negligence Panel Scheme**. This is a panel of senior solicitors in your area who will give you free advice about your negligence case.
- You could take advantage of the **Law Society's Arbitration Scheme**. This means you avoid the expense and complications of a court case.

- You could take your case to court. Most negligence cases are settled 'out of court'.

Complaints against barristers

If you have a complaint about the way a barrister has handled your case, you should first register an official complaint with the barrister's **Head of Chambers** (the most senior barrister at that office or **chambers**) at the same address.

If you get no satisfaction, you can write to the BAR COUNCIL. You will need to give details of:

- The name of the barrister and their professional address.
- The name and address of the solicitor who employed the barrister.
- A detailed statement of your complaint including details of any court proceedings if appropriate.

The Bar Council has limited powers. They can reprimand their members and in extreme cases suspend or disbar barristers. However, even if your complaint is upheld they cannot offer you any compensation. It can be extremely difficult to take legal action against a barrister for negligence.

The legal system — Going to court

Most of this book is about how to avoid or settle disputes yourself without having to resort to legal action through the courts.

However, there may be times when you've tried everything you can to try and resolve a problem and yet you still find yourself up against a brick wall. Don't despair, you haven't reached the end of the line.

Going to court needn't be so complex that you cannot handle it yourself nor so costly that it becomes prohibitive.

In the past many people did not sue in courts because they were frightened of heavy legal costs and were often reluctant to do battle on their own with little or no formal legal expertise.

Now the system has been simplified so that people can bring small claims in the County court without the help of a solicitor.

The County court

The County court is a local court which decides private disputes about relatively small amounts of money, usually £5,000 or less. It is where most **civil** (as opposed to criminal) cases are heard.

There are about 300 County courts in England and Wales. You can find your local one by looking in the telephone directory under 'Courts'.

What kind of claims can the County court hear?
Almost any claim, providing it is for not more than £5,000.
Claims can include:

- Payment of debts due for goods sold or money lent.
- Claims against suppliers of defective goods or suppliers who fail to deliver goods ordered.

- Compensation for faulty workmanship or failure to do work that was agreed.
- Disputes between landlords and tenants.
- Claims for damages caused by negligence, e.g. damage to your car caused by a careless driver.
- Claims for wages or salary owing or payable in lieu of notice.

What exactly is the small claims procedure?

The **small claims procedure** is for anyone suing for less than £500. The aim is to keep the financial risks to a minimum by not allowing costs for the services of a solicitor. It is also intended to be far more informal than the traditional court system and therefore accessible to the lay person.

Basically, if your claim is for £500 or less you will not be awarded costs to cover your solicitor's fees even if you win your case. In the same way if your opponent decides to employ a solicitor, they do so out of their own pocket. If you lose the case, you won't be liable for their solicitor's fees.

The small claims procedure relies largely on an informal, and therefore — in theory — less intimidating system of arbitration to settle disputed claims. The arbitrator is usually the registrar of the court who hears the case in private without getting all dressed up in a wig and gown. If your opponent does not dispute your claim you may never even have to go to court.

Costs are kept to a minimum but you will have to pay a court fee and also a series of other minor charges for summonses, etc. ➡. Exactly how much will depend on the amount you are claiming and the details of the case.

The court staff are usually very willing to guide you through the maze of forms and help you complete them correctly. They obviously cannot help you decide whether your case is worth pursuing.

Think before you sue

There are three points you need to consider carefully before taking your claim to the County court.

- Have you tried every other possible way of resolving your conflict? If you're not sure, then read the first section of this book and any other relevant chapters.

- Are you sure you have a watertight case? This does not mean you should talk yourself out of pursuing what you think is rightfully yours. But if you do have any nagging doubts, talk them through with someone who can give a more objective opinion.
- Even if you win are you sure you will get your money? No matter how clear-cut your case, if you're suing someone for money, consider whether they can actually pay up if you win. It may simply not be worth your time and expense to try and sue someone who doesn't have a penny to their name.

If you've decided to go ahead and sue and your claim is for less than £500, read on. If your claim is for more than £500, still read this section.

Step-by-step guide to making a small claim in the County court

> **The Action** refers to the proceedings of the claim.
> **The Plaintiff** is the person who brings the action.
> **The Defendant** is the person against whom the action is brought.
> The plaintiff and the defendant are both known as **The Parties** to the action.

Step one: Write a final letter to your opponent
You may have already done this; if not, send one off. It may well save you the bother of going to court. Often the threat of legal action is enough to make someone pay up.

I have not yet received a reply to my letter of [date] concerning . . . .
   Unless I receive a cheque for . . ./a replacement . . ./you return my . . . within seven days, I will issue proceedings against you in the County court without further notice.

Step two: Find out about the defendant
If you are sure they are worth suing and can pay up if you win, find out their exact name and address. This is important: if you on-

ly have half an address it may be impossible to serve the summons (p.254).

If the defendant is a **private individual** check their details in the telephone directory or visit your local library or town hall who may be able to help.

If you're dealing with a **public limited company** it will have the words 'Public Limited Company' or 'plc' after its name. A **private limited company** will usually have the words 'Limited' or 'Ltd' after its name. In each of these cases the summons has to be delivered or sent to the company's 'registered office' which may not be the same address as the one you've been dealing with. The address of the 'registered office' might appear on the letterhead or invoice. If not, you will need to visit the COMPANIES REGISTRATION OFFICE in London or write to the Companies Registration Office in Cardiff.

If your defendant is a small firm without either 'plc' or 'Ltd' after its name it's likely to be a one-person business or a partnership. If you've only been dealing with one partner, it is still better to sue the partnership — **the firm** as a whole. If that partner can't pay, the others might be able to.

Example

Tony Brown and George Harris carry on business as 'B & H Electricians'. Tony Brown has failed to complete some wiring for you for which you've already paid him. You would claim against 'B & H Electricians (a firm)'.

Step three: Choose the right court

You can choose to have the case heard in either of the following:

- The court in the area in which the defendant lives or has a registered office.
- The court in the area in which the incident took place.

It is possible to ask for a transfer to another court if, for example, you are disabled and cannot travel easily.

You can get all the necessary documents and help from your local County court even if they are not in the right area to deal with your case.

Particulars of Claim

(A) IN THE . . . COUNTY COURT   (B) CASE NO: . . .

BETWEEN (C) ...... PLAINTIFF

     and

    (D) ...... DEFENDANT

(E) [Paragraph 1: give details of the purchase, loan agreement, repair, etc.]
Example
(1) On 14th July 2001 the Plaintiff purchased for the sum of £350 a sofabed from the Defendant's shop at Nightmare Beds, 3 Valium Way, Stupor-under-Line.
(F) [Paragraph 2: give the facts of the case.]
(2) After using the sofabed for three weeks the base collapsed. The Plaintiff wrote to the Manager of the shop on 14th August and again on 4th September requesting that he replace the sofabed or return the Plaintiff's money. He has refused to do so.
(G) [Paragraph 3: give details of the amount you are claiming.]
(3) The Plaintiff claims £350.

Step four: Write out your 'particulars of claim'

You can get a special form from the court or you can use a blank piece of paper.

Notes
- It is usual to write in the third person, i.e. 'The plaintiff told the defendant' rather than 'I told him'.
- Number your paragraphs for easy future reference.
- A — See 'Choose the right court'←.
- B — Leave this blank. You will be given a **case number** by the court. Always use the case number if you need to contact the court about your claim, otherwise they won't be able to find it.
- C and D — See p.251.
- E — Always include the date, type of goods, model number, size, colour, where they were bought, price, or place and date of

accident, car registration numbers, etc., according to your case.
- F — Try and be brief. You don't need to go into great depth, just give the most important points.
- G — If your claim involves compensation for personal injury do seek the advice of a solicitor (p.237) first. You can also claim for any interest you may have lost.
- You will need at least two other copies of the completed form together with any other evidence — receipts, invoices, letters, etc. One copy is for the court, one or more copies for the defendant(s) and one copy for yourself.

Step five: Taking out the summons

The summons is the document that the defendant receives from the court telling them about your claim and what they need to do (p.260).

Along with the particulars of claim ← you will need to complete a form known as a **request** in order that the court can prepare the summons. This is obtainable from the court. It looks a daunting form but once you have completed the particulars of claim, it shouldn't be too hard.

The form is in two parts: the first asks information about the plaintiff, the second about the defendant. Some of the questions ask about your role as the plaintiff. For example, if you are suing:

- In a **representative capacity**, e.g. as the executor for a deceased person.
- As a **next friend**, e.g. on behalf of a minor (someone under 18 years old).
- As an **assignee**, which means that someone else who had the right to sue originally has transferred that right to you. For example, a shop-keeper who sells the right to sue to a debt collector. The debt collector is the 'assignee'.

You will also need to complete three other items of information (see Steps six and seven).

Step six: A default summons or a fixed date summons

A court official may ask you which one you want. If you show them your particulars of claim they will be able to advise you. If you are claiming a particular sum of money it is likely you will issue a **default summons**.

This means that if the defendant makes no defence within fourteen days of receiving the summons you can ask the court for a **judgement** (an order for the defendant to pay the money to you) (p.259).

If you are claiming any other remedy such as your goods back or repossession of land you will ask for a **fixed date summons**.

Step seven: Do you want to go to arbitration?

If your claim is for less than £500 the action will automatically be referred to arbitration, if the defendant puts up a defence. An **arbitration** is a more informal hearing with the registrar or 'arbitrator' acting like an umpire.

If your claim is for more than £500 and you would like it dealt with by arbitration rather than in open court you should say so on both the particulars of claim and the 'request'. The judge may, however, decide otherwise.

Step eight: Find out the court fee

The court fee will be a percentage (currently about 10 per cent) of the amount you are claiming. But there is an upper limit so don't be put off if your claim is for more than about £350. This is known as the **plaint fee**.

You may also have other costs, for example if you decide to let the court issue the summons on your behalf→.

You ought to include these costs in your particulars of claim and the 'request'.

Step nine: Give or post the information to the court

You will need to make sure that the court has:

- Sufficient copies of the particulars of claim.
- The completed 'request' form.
- The plaint fee.
- A self-addressed envelope so that the court can send you a plaint note, your case number and a receipt.

Send all these documents to the Chief Clerk at the court which is issuing the summons. Cheques or crossed postal orders should be made payable to: The Paymaster General.

Step ten: Serving the summons

You have a number of choices:

- You can deliver the summons personally yourself.
- You can have it posted.
- The court bailiff can deliver it for you.

It's probably worth the small charge to have the court bailiff post or deliver it for you. The court will send you a form stating when the summons was posted or the date it was served.

Step eleven: The defendant's response to the summons
You will get one of five responses:

- The defendant sees you really mean business and pays up straight away.
- The defendant, whilst not admitting **liability** (agreeing that he or she is responsible), offers to settle out of court.
- The defendent ignores the summons.
- The defendant disputes your claim and files a defence.
- The defendant disputes your claim and files a **counterclaim** (they think you owe them something). This is particularly true of car accidents where neither side can decide who is to blame.

Step twelve: The defendant offers to settle
Usually the amount offered is less than your original claim but you can sometimes negotiate a higher figure. You must make a decision whether to accept this offer. Consider whether it's worth settling for slightly less but avoiding court procedures. Whatever you do, bear in mind two points!

- Make sure that you put on any letter negotiating a settlement, the words 'Without Prejudice'. This means that the contents cannot be referred to if and when a trial takes place.
- If you do accept a settlement make sure that the money has actually been paid into court before you write formally to the court to let them know that you're not going ahead with your case.

Step thirteen: The defendant doesn't respond
In which case, after fourteen days and providing you opted for a default summons←, you are automatically entitled to have **judgement entered** (made).

To enter judgement you have to fill in a very simple form and produce a copy of your plaint note←. As long as you provide a stamped addressed envelope, all this can be done by post.

If you are claiming damages which need to be assessed by the registrar or judge you will have to make an appointment to see them.

You can ask for the money to be paid: immediately; within a limited time, say a month (which may be to your advantage); or by instalments. Resist the latter if you can but you may have no option. It is possible that the defendant will refuse to pay the instalments you suggest usually because they say they can't afford that much each week. Ultimately it's up to the court to decide what is appropriate.

Step fourteen: The defendant files a defence

This means you will have to go to court. If a defence is made, go through your case again to make sure you are still certain that it's absolutely watertight *especially* if your claim is over £500 (p.259).

Don't be put off if a defence is made. They may ask you for more information about your claim. They are probably just trying to intimidate you. Answer the best you can.

Whether you opted for a default summons or a fixed date summons you will need to go to a **Preliminary Hearing** or a **Pre-Trial Review**.

Step fifteen: The Preliminary Hearing or Pre-Trial Review

This is much less formal than you might expect a court hearing to be. The aim of the hearing or review is to see if the matter can be resolved there and then without taking it further to final arbitration or trial.

If the parties involved cannot reach a satisfactory conclusion then the registrar will fix a date for the hearing, agree on the number of witnesses and so on. Make sure you turn up at this preliminary stage otherwise you might find that the judgement has gone against you by default or the action has been struck out.

If you cannot attend on the date fixed for this hearing then write and say so immediately and ask for it to be put off.

Take all the relevant documents — letters, receipts, invoices, etc. with you. This will help the registrar to decide your case. It will not do to say you've left them at home — so don't.

Step sixteen: Attending a hearing

Before you go
• Make sure you have all your evidence prepared. It is not enough simply to turn up in court, convinced that you are in the right and expect everyone else to believe you. You need to have evidence to support your claim.
• Work out in advance what you want to say and rehearse it. You're not Rumpole of the Bailey — don't rely on inspiration!
• You will have the defendant's side of the story. Consider seriously what their arguments might be and prepare your replies to counter them.
• Make sure your witnesses are prepared to give evidence. If necessary they can be compelled by the court to do so. Check this in advance and take action if necessary. If you need the evidence of expert witnesses make sure you have it in writing and that they have agreed to turn up in court and you have settled on their fee.
• Put the date of the hearing in your diary and check your witnesses have done the same.
• Find out exactly where the court house is. It may not be in the same building as the court office. If you need to ask directions make it clear that you want the County court and *not* the magistrates court.
• Make arrangements for time off work or for children or pets to be looked after — you could be waiting in court all day. Ask someone to go with you for moral support. It can be a great help if you feel nervous.
• Familiarize yourself with court proceedings. Courts are open to the public so go and listen to another case.

Aim to get there early!

At the court house
You will find noticeboards with lists of the cases to be heard telling you which court you will be in. There is usually a special 'arbitration list'.

Give your name to the court usher who normally wears a gown or if you have problems ask the clerk of the court where you should sit.

Step seventeen: Giving evidence
At an **arbitration** you will usually give evidence sitting at a table in-

stead of standing at a witness box. Even though the arbitrator will have your file in front of them you will still be asked to tell everyone about your claim.

- Start at the beginning and go through events as they happened. Imagine you are relating the story to a friend.
- Don't get overexcited and don't exaggerate. Get rid of any righteous indignation *before* you enter the hearing!
- If you are very nervous, the arbitrator will usually help you by asking questions. Concentrate carefully on what you are asked.
- The arbitrator will ask the witnesses and the defendant to speak and will usually question them. You will also be asked if there are any questions you want to put. If you are not asked and there is something you want to know, then say so.

A **trial** is much more formal and you will have to give evidence on oath standing in a witness box.

When telling your story avoid saying things like, 'So, Mr Smith told me that the defendant was going to . . .'. This is known as 'hearsay' and is generally not allowed as Mr Smith may not be in court to be questioned about what happened. Instead you can say, 'As a result of what Mr Smith told me, I did . . .'.

You will also have the opportunity to cross-examine the defendant and vice versa. Because cross-examination is a very complex skill (whatever it may look like on TV) most judges and registrars avoid formal cross-examinations where there are no professional lawyers present.

Step eighteen: Awards and judgments

Where the case has been heard by arbitration the registrar's decision is called an **award**. In a trial it is referred to as a **judgment**.

Usually you will get an immediate decision but if the case is very complex the arbitrator may send you the decision by post or you might be asked to attend court again for a judgment.

Step nineteen: Claiming costs and expenses

If you win your action you can ask the court to order the defendant to pay your expenses in addition to the judgment debt. These include:

- Court fees.
- Witness expenses.

- Out of pocket expenses, for example for photographs, travelling costs, search fees, etc.

Claims over £500 — A caution about costs

If you are suing for or defending a case involving more than £500 but less than £5000 and you lose, you could face solicitors' costs (for the defendant) of more than £1000 if the claim is near the maximum limit.

This means that you could end up paying:

- The cost of the judgment debt.
- The defendant's solicitor's fees.
- Any other court fees or expenses not included in the above.
- Your solicitor's fees.
- Your expenses.

Unless you agree with the defendant to exclude solicitors' costs you will need to weigh up very carefully the merits of your case. Costs are awarded on a sliding scale, with claims over £3000 attracting the highest amount for costs.

For substantial claims over £500 it is worth consulting a solicitor to establish whether you have a case in law. You can do this under the Fixed Fee Interview scheme (p.245). It's always worth checking as well if you are eligible for Legal Aid (p.242).

If you want to question any part of the defendant's solicitor's bill then you can ask to have the bill **taxed** (p.246) (asking the court to decide if the bill is reasonable).

Getting a summons — Step-by-step guide to what to do

Summonses rarely come as a complete shock. You will usually have received some kind of correspondence from the plaintiff or their solicitor. When the summons does arrive, *do not* ignore it. It won't go away but left alone the situation will get worse.

Step one: The summons arrives
You will usually receive three documents:

- The summons.

- The particulars of claim form (p.253).
- A **form of admission, defence and counterclaim**.

Read the particulars of claim form first to see what the action is about. You may be able to decide whether you want to defend the action.

Then look at the summons to see how much the plaintiff is claiming. The summons will also tell you what date to appear in court (fixed date summons (p.254)) or state that judgment will go against you unless you pay the amount of the claim and costs *into the court* within fourteen days (default summons (p.254)).

If the amount of the claim is substantial then consider seeking professional legal advice or visit your local CAB.

Step two: You decide you owe the money and pay up

If you do owe the money then complete the admissions section of the form of admission, defence and counterclaim and *pay up within fourteen days into the court and not to the plaintiff*.

If you leave it any longer you may be liable for additional court costs and you will have your name registered on the list of County court judgments, which won't do a lot for your credit rating (p.55).

If you agree that you owe the money but can't afford to pay it all in one go you can ask the court to let you pay it by instalments. The admissions section will ask about your financial situation. You can make an offer for the repayments.

If the offer is not accepted the registrar will ask you to attend a **Disposal Hearing** when they will assess your financial commitments and give an order for payment. Take along evidence of your pay or benefit and let them know whether you are paying any other court orders.

Step three: You decide to file a defence

Before you do this consider carefully:

- Do you have good reason to dispute the claim or is your defence simply that you don't want to pay?
- Do you feel that the plaintiff is morally in the wrong even though they are entitled legally to claim?
- Were you disappointed that the product or service did not meet your expectations even though there is nothing legally wrong?

If the answer to any of these is yes, go back to Step two.

If you are satisfied that you have a valid defence, complete the defence section of the form of admission, defence and counter-claim.

It is not enough simply to deny the claim. You will need to answer each of the plaintiff's allegations which appear on the particulars of claim form. If your version of events is very different you must state what happened.

Go back to the section on Particulars of Claim (p.252) for information on what you need to include.

Step four: You decide to file a counterclaim

This is particularly true of road accidents where neither party is sure who was at fault.

> *Example*
> You receive a summons asking you to pay £350 towards the cost of repair of the plaintiff's car. You may decide that he caused the damage to your car instead of the other way around. You therefore file a counterclaim for £430, the cost of repairing your car.

However, your counterclaim need not be related to the claim.

You will need to fill in the counterclaim section of the form of admission, defence and counterclaim. Refer back to the section on Particulars of Claim to see how a claim should be made (p.252).

Step five: You think you are only partly responsible for the claim

If you think that you do owe some of the money claimed, you can pay that amount and leave the court to decide about the rest.

Since you ought to take every precaution against incurring large legal costs if you lose the case ←, it's worth seeing whether you can admit enough of the claim to bring the balance below £500 or below £3000.

You can either admit to certain parts of the bill (see Example 1) or pay a percentage of the bill (Example 2).

Example 1
A builder sues you for £650 for unpaid work. You might
decide to pay him the £170 he is claiming for concreting your
conservatory foundations and dispute the rest of the bill as
you don't think he has done the work he promised. You will
then ensure you are not liable for any of their legal costs since
the claim is now for less than £500.

Example 2
A car drove into the central reservation because you stopped
suddenly when your tyre blew. You may decide that you
were partly to blame for the accident but not wholly — the
other driver shouldn't have been driving so fast or so close.
You could choose to pay 10 per cent of the claim. Do this immediately along with 10 per cent of the appropriate costs.
Court officials will tell you how much this should be.

If the plaintiff accepts your payment then the matter is at an end
and you only have to pay their costs up to the date when you made
your payment.

The plaintiff may decide that they have a good chance of getting
all the money owed if they go to court. Normally if the plaintiff
fails to get judgment for more than the sum you offered, then you
do not have to pay their costs incurred after the date of your
payment.

However, you should be aware of winning hollow victories➤.

Step six: Claiming money from another person or 'third party'

Sometimes a defendant is sued for money that really should have
been paid by another person.

Example
Maria Green and Carol Short agree to share a flat but the
tenancy is only taken out in Maria's name. If the landlord sues
them for unpaid rent, Maria will receive the summons but she
will want Carol to contribute. If the two friends can't agree
this amicably, Maria may well decide to ask the court to make
Carol a party to the action.

Court officials will tell you how to do this.

Step seven: Attending a Pre-Trial Review or Trial
Refer back to previous section for this (p.257).

What happens if a judgment is given against me without my knowlege?
This might happen for three reasons:

- You never received the summons.
- You received the summons but you weren't able to do anything about it in the time available.
- You couldn't attend the pre-trial review or trial.

If you find yourself in this situation go to the court office immediately. The judgment can be set aside by the court.

If the registrar finds that the summons wasn't properly served and as a result you had no knowledge of the proceedings, then you are entitled to have the judgment set aside as of right.

If you failed to file a defence or turn up at court for any other reason it is up to the judge to decide whether or not to set aside the judgment.

If you're defending be wary of expensive 'victories'
If you have a substantial claim you must watch out for getting landed with substantial costs. This can happen even if you 'win' your defence.

Example

Jackie Kray had her car repaired at a local garage, Wreck Repairs. When she was given a bill for £800 she disputed it and refused to pay up. Wreck Repairs finally issued a summons against Jackie.

She considered the particulars of claim and the summons and decided she was only responsible for paying two-thirds of it. Consequently she paid £600 into court and filed a defence.

Having notified Wreck Garages of her decision it was up to them to decide whether to accept what Jackie had paid and end the matter or to go to court in the hope of recovering the full amount. They chose to do the latter.

The judge (who would not have been told about Jackie's offer) decided Jackie was right and agreed she should only pay £600.

Now although Jackie considered she had 'won' the action by limiting her liability, she hadn't thought about the costs involved. In legal terms Wreck Repairs won the action. They had recovered £600 and were awarded costs on scale 2 (p.260) which amounted to £400. Jackie therefore was faced with paying a total of £1000.

If Jackie had admitted the whole claim in the beginning the legal costs would probably have been under £100. In this case the total amount she would have had to pay out would have been less than £900.

The moral of the story given in the example is: weigh up the costs before you start or defend court actions. What's more important to you — to win a moral victory or to keep cash in your pocket?

Going to court — General points

This chapter has dealt only with civil matters — issuing and receiving summonses in the County court. Most other court cases are terribly complicated and should not be tackled by a lay person.

If you receive any kind of summons, don't ignore it. If you don't understand it get professional advice immediately.

Litigation (legal disputes) can be extremely costly. If you think that you've good reason to take out an action against someone else, perhaps because you think they've slandered or libelled your name, it might cost you in the region of £1000 just to establish that it's not worth pursuing the case.

If you think that you are only one of a number of people who might want to take action against an individual or organization, then you might be able to work as a group. In some cases you might even get Legal Aid (p.242).

Campaigning and lobbying

There are times when a straightforward letter of complaint or a visit to your solicitor simply won't help you win your case.

Have you ever wanted to complain about:

- Your street used as a rush-hour rat run?
- A dangerous footpath outside your child's school?
- Dog mess fouling the footpaths and parks?
- The closure of a local swimming pool or other amenity?
- The lack of play space or crèches in your area?

If you want to win your case, or at the very least make an impression on the powers-that-be, you will need to know the nuts and bolts of campaigning.

Six golden rules of campaigning

- Do your homework:
  - (a) Is a campaign really necessary?
  - (b) Is this the only way to win your cause?
- Be positive. Keep faith. Don't let anyone put you off.
- Campaigning is only for people who like hard work.
- Keep things in perspective. Don't become a fanatic.
- Involve everyone affected by the problem but keep your fire power for the enemy. Don't waste it on your supporters.
- Do it well. Just because you are not a professional, it doesn't mean you should campaign like an amateur.

And by the way — *make it fun*!

Good campaigns are not self-igniting. They do not start spontaneously with packed public meetings and political fireworks. They need meticulous planning.

Can I go it alone?

A one-man or one-woman campaign can work but it is likely to be more effective and to succeed more quickly the greater the number of people involved. A really good campaign takes a lot of resources and stamina — usually more than one person can give.

Before you start trying to involve others you must be very clear about your objectives.

What exactly is it that you want to achieve?

Where do I start?

Once you've got your objectives clear in your own mind you can begin to convince others to join you.

Form a *small* committee. You don't need to call it a committee if you think that will put people off. You could just invite them round for coffee.

Find three or four like-minded people — personal friends, neighbours, other parents, colleagues, representatives of organizations who might be supportive — whoever is appropriate.

These people are vital to you. You need them to actually do some work — so make sure they can spare the time! If you can, ask people who have some experience of campaigning or who know the local community or local council well.

Find people who have skills — who can type, deliver leaflets. Outgoing, friendly people are important to your campaign team.

What should we think about first?

Your small committee will need to consider:

- Your aims and objectives:
  (a) Are you all agreed on what you are setting out to achieve?
  (b) Are you all agreed on the solution to the problem?
- Whether you have all the right background information and facts and figures.
- Your campaign strategy→.
- Your resources — financial and human.

Whatever you discuss make sure it's not just all hot air. Before you all go home, decide who is going to do what and by when, and fix a date for your next meeting.

Plan a campaign strategy

- Decide who or what your target is. You will need to establish who can make the final decision about your case. For many campaigns in the community this will be the local authority.
- Decide who or what is most likely to influence your target.
- Decide whether it's best to fight a public campaign that everyone knows about or whether you should choose a few key people to work from 'inside'→.
- Decide whether to go for a big splash campaign or a long haul — chipping away at your target bit by bit.
- Think about who is most likely to support you.
- Consider the strengths and weaknesses of your case. Face up to the fact that you will be criticized — do you know the answers?
- Think about which aspects of your campaign are most likely to appeal:
  (a) to your target, and
  (b) to your potential supporters.

Plan a campaign programme

- Find out whether there are any time limits or other deadlines that are important to your case. You don't want to shut the stable door after the horse has bolted!
- Find out when your target is actually available. For example, if you are campaigning against a local council decision you don't want to plan a major event when the elected councillors are all on their summer holidays!
- Be logical. Be realistic. Don't try and run before you can walk. Build up your supporters first before you begin planning major publicity events.
- Be prepared! Document all the relevant evidence. Check and double check your facts. If you need more information then find it out *now*.

Build up your supporters

Once you've identified your potential supporters decide what it is you want them to do:

- Simply indicate their support at this stage.
- Tell you about skills or time they can offer the campaign.

- Ask them to attend a meeting or event➔.
- Ask them to carry out some activity, e.g. letter writing➔.

Let them know about your campaign:

- Use the 'grapevine'.
- Knock on doors and talk face to face.
- Telephone supporters.
- Visit other groups or organizations.
- Put a leaflet through doors.
- Display posters in libraries, shops and community centres.

Campaigning tactics

When it comes to campaign tactics the list is almost endless. However there are four basic elements, one or more of which will form the cornerstone of your campaign strategy: the **media**; **big public events**; **ongoing activities**; **lobbying**.

The media

Very few campaigns can survive without the support of their local papers, radio and television stations. Just think — it's the quickest, cheapest way to get to the most people.

Make a list of all your local papers, their addresses, telephone and fax numbers. Find out the name of the editor and any other journalist who might be useful. Don't forget the 'free' newspapers. Check when they 'go to press', i.e. the latest you can get your story in.

Make a list of your local radio and television stations. Watch or listen to the programmes and find out which ones might cover your campaign (usually early morning and evening current affairs and news programmes). Get the name of the producer.

Ring up the journalist or producer and tell them about your campaign or special event. Ask them if they can 'cover' the story, i.e. send a reporter. *Don't* waste their time but *do* remember that they need good campaign stories to make their papers or programmes. You could be doing each other a favour!

Write a press release to send to all the papers and programmes.

- Put the name of your campaign, a contact name, address and telephone number at the top of the paper.
- Date it.

- Keep it brief — one side only.
- Type it, double spaced.
- Include the five 'W's — Who, What, Why, Where and When.

Stoppitt Campaign
(Stop Parking in Treadwell Terrace)

Campaign Co-ordinator: Chris Charisma
12 Treadwell Close, Potterton Village. Tel: 95073

Press Release
6th June 2001

LOCAL RESIDENTS TO STAGE MASS
DEMONSTRATION AGAINST LORRY PARKING
MENACE

Over three hundred angry Potterton residents are expected to attend a demonstration outside the town hall this Tuesday, 14th June at 2 pm to protest against lorries parking in Treadwell Terrace.

Residents formed the STOPPITT Campaign two months ago, when local schoolgirl, Lisa James, 7, was seriously hurt after running out between two parked lorries.

Chris Charisma, who is leading the campaign to get the lorries banned from Treadwell Terrace says, 'Local people are fed up with juggernauts lining our streets. They're a complete menace. The road has become a death-trap. We want the council to ban them now.'

For more information contact: Chris Charisma on 95073 or Bill Malohney on 67102 (after 6 pm).

If you can get a radio or television interview *do* send someone who knows the whole story and is articulate. Tell them to brief the journalist properly before they begin. If you get really daft questions just ignore them and tell the audience what you think they ought to know about your campaign.

Big public events
These are excellent for attracting new support, making your 'target' sit up and for gaining the attention of the media ←. If you

can make the event visually exciting you are more likely to get a photo in your paper or local TV coverage.

Every big public event should be planned as if it were a campaign in itself.

Golden rules for any big public event:

- DO have a set of clear objectives.
- DO be meticulous in your organization.
- DO put one person in overall charge.
- DO be realistic — remember your resources and the weather!
- DON'T leave things to chance. Chance is never there when you need him — or her!

There are two main kinds of big public activities — **meetings** and **events**.

Meetings

- Choose an appropriate venue — somewhere central and accessible for people who may have difficulty with steps, etc., such as the elderly, disabled, young children *especially* if they are the focus of your campaign.
- Select a good chairman or chairwoman and brief them well. Choose someone who sounds authoritative (not bossy!) but who won't spend the entire time giving their opinions — that's not their role.
- Ask two or three good speakers and tell them precisely how long they are expected to speak for and what you want them to speak on.
- Decide in advance whether to have questions 'from the floor', i.e. from the audience, and make time for them.
- Advertise the meeting well.
- Start on time.

Events

Think in terms of marches, demonstrations, protest gatherings, presentations of petitions, concerts, sports activities, 'set pieces', and then get creative with costumes, colour and gimmicks. Remember the suffragettes chained to railings, CND 'die ins', prisoners of conscience in striped pyjamas in cages outside the House of Commons.

Be realistic about what you can undertake successfully!

- Make sure it's legal and non-violent. You don't want people arrested.

- Get permission where necessary, e.g. from the police if you want to hold a march or demonstration.
- Be somewhere visible.
- Be disciplined.
- If you are outside have contingency plans in case it rains.
- Involve 'influential' people.

Ongoing activities

These form the backbone of many campaigns. The important thing is to be consistent. If you start a letter-writing campaign, a petition, a series of meetings, then keep them going. Here are some ideas.

- **Letter writing**. This could be to the press or perhaps a particular person or organization. It's always worth preparing a short briefing paper for prospective letter writers, stating the basic facts about the campaign and the name and address of the person to whom letters should be sent. You could always give them a draft copy of the kind of letter you want them to write.
- **Petitions**. This of course gives you a great opportunity to plan a big publicity event to present the petitions when you have enough signatures. Do make sure that each petition paper clearly states what the signatories are committing themselves to!
- Hold a **regular stall** in your local high street or community centre. Have relevant literature ready and perhaps a petition if it's appropriate. If you want to raise money for your campaign you might be able to sell things. Do check whether you need permission to set up a stall. Often a friendly shopkeeper can be helpful.

Lobbying

Lobbying is when a group of people or a pressure group try and persuade someone, perhaps an MP or local councillor, to favour their particular interests.

You might decide that your campaign is best fought from the inside. You could find someone influential and ask them to have 'a quiet word' with your target person or organization. Basically that's just a form of lobbying.

Alternatively could decide to lobby more publicly.

- Write letters.
- Send a briefing paper outlining your case together with any evidence to your target or to people who might support your case.

- Organize a delegation. Make sure that you arrange an appointment in advance with the person you want to lobby and tell them what you want to discuss.

  Get together no more than five people, all of whom understand your case fully and ask one to act as spokesperson. Take along with you any additional written material or evidence. If you can, ask someone 'influential', perhaps your MP, to come with you if you think it would help.

Getting on with your fellow campaigners

Many good campaigns fail simply because the people who should be working together fall out. Very silly, really!

- *Do* keep everyone informed about what is going on — otherwise they'll suspect a plot.
- *Do* remember that your fellow campaigners are voluntary helpers, not your employees. You cannot sack them if you don't like the way they do things.
- *Do* explain things properly — people can't be expected to carry things out if they don't understand what they are doing and why.
- *Don't* overburden people — a young mum with three kids probably has her hands quite full already!
- *Don't* gossip. **Keep your fire power for the enemy!**

Keep the campaign going

- Review your campaign strategy ← and campaign plan ← regularly.
- Celebrate your successes and give praise where praise is due.
- Keep recruiting new support.
- Involve new people and tap them for fresh ideas.
- Don't give up.

Other campaign ideas

- If you are concerned generally about your local area, join or set up a **Residents'** or **Tenants' Association**. Most have a nominal annual fee and many may only meet very occasionally.
- If you are worried about security in your neighbourhood set up

a **Neighbourhood Watch Scheme** — your local police will give you information on how to go about it.
- Find out what your local political parties are up to. You may be interested in joining in their campaigns in your area.

Extra notes for people living in Scotland and Northern Ireland

Looking after your money

Scotland

Debt cases are usually dealt with by the Sheriff Court. Debts of less than £1000 are dealt with through the Summary Cause Procedure and those over £1000 through the Ordinary Cause Procedure.

Buying goods

Northern Ireland

In Northern Ireland, the Trading Standards Branch of the Department of Economic Development corresponds to Trading Standards Departments.

Services — Getting things done

Scotland

The Supply of Goods and Services Act 1982 does not apply in Scotland; however, Scots common law gives broadly similar rights. In Scotland, the Sheriff Court is the equivalent of the County court.

Home sweet home

There are differences in many aspects of law relating to property matters in both Scotland and Northern Ireland. In particular the procedure for buying property in Scotland is considerably different. You should always seek the advice of a local lawyer or an advice agency.

Family matters

There are differences in many aspects of law relating to family matters in both Scotland and Northern Ireland. In many cases equivalent rights and remedies exist. You should always seek the advice of a local lawyer or an advice agency.

Scotland
Family Practitioner Committees do not exist in Scotland. Complaints should be addressed to the administrator of the Primary Care Division of the Area Health Board. Local Health Councils are the equivalent of Community Health Councils.

Northern Ireland
Neither Family Practitioner Committees nor Community Health Councils exist in Northern Ireland. Complaints should be addressed to the Central Services Agency, who may be willing to give general advice about complaints.

All in a day's work

Scotland
The Sheriff Court is more or less equivalent to the County Court.

Northern Ireland
- The Employment Protection (Consolidation) Act 1978 does not apply in Northern Ireland; however, the Industrial Relations (Northern Ireland) Order 1976, as amended in 1982, gives many of the same rights.
- The Race Relations Act 1976 applies only to a *very* limited extent in Northern Ireland, and it may be difficult to pursue complaints relating to racial discrimination.
- ACAS does not operate in Northern Ireland; the equivalent organization is the LABOUR RELATIONS AGENCY.

The legal profession

Scotland
- Scotland has a separate Law Society and a separate Legal Aid Board from those in England and Wales.
- The 'Pink Form' Scheme is the Scots equivalent of the Green Form Scheme.
- In Scotland, the Sheriff Court and the High Court have similar roles to the magistrates court, the Crown Court and the Court of Appeal.
- The Law Society of Scotland does not arbitrate on fees. If you

are not satisfied with the fee your solicitor has charged, you may ask the Auditor of Court (an independent official) to review or **tax** it. You will usually have to pay for this service, which covers both contentious and non-contentious matters.

- There is no separate complaints bureau in Scotland from the Law Society of Scotland. Complaints about the professional conduct of Scottish solicitors should be sent to the Law Society of Scotland. If your complaint cannot be easily resolved, it will be considered by the Complaints Committee. This committee can recommend that the complaint be referred to the Scottish Solicitors Disciplinary Tribunal which has powers in extreme cases to strike the solicitor off the Roll of Solicitors.
- The Law Society of Scotland will not deal with allegations of negligence. They do maintain a list of 'troubleshooters' which is similar to the negligence panel.
- In Scotland, **advocates** are the equivalent of barristers. In Scotland, advocates do not practise from chambers, and there is no Bar Council. Complaints about the professional conduct of an advocate should be made to the Dean of the Faculty of Advocates, who is the head of the Scottish Bar.

Northern Ireland

- Northern Ireland has a separate Law Society and a separate Legal Aid Board from those in England and Wales.
- Complaints about solicitors' fees can be sent to the Law Society of Northern Ireland. Alternatively, the procedure for taxing fees can be obtained from a local County court office..
- There is no separate complaints bureau in Northern Ireland from the Law Society of Northern Ireland. Complaints about the professional conduct of Northern Irish solicitors should be sent to the Law Society of Northern Ireland.
- The Law Society of Northern Ireland will not deal with allegations of negligence. If you have difficulties in finding a solicitor who is prepared to take on a case of negligence against another solicitor, the Law Society of Northern Ireland will help in finding a senior solicitor to advise you.
- In Northern Ireland, barristers do not practise from chambers. Complaints about the professional conduct of a barrister should be made to the Bar Council of Northern Ireland at the ROYAL COURTS OF JUSTICE, Belfast.

The legal system — Going to court

Scotland
The legal terms used and the procedures adopted in Scotland are somewhat different from those in England.

- There is no equivalent yet in Scotland of the Small Claims procedure. Claims of up to £1000 are dealt with in the Sheriff Court under the Summary Cause Procedure. The appropriate forms and an explanatory booklet can be obtained from the Sheriff's Clerk's Office at the Sheriff Court. The court staff will explain the procedure to you, but obviously cannot advise on the merits of your case. Under the Summary Cause Procedure, the expenses of the winner (including solicitor's costs) usually have to be met by the loser. Legal aid may be available.
- Details of Scottish companies are kept at the Companies Registration Office, Edinburgh.

Northern Ireland
- The Small Claims procedure is available in Northern Ireland for claims up to a maximum of £300.
- Details of Northern Irish companies are kept at the Companies Registration Office, Belfast.

Section four

How to Get More Help and Information

Useful addresses

How to use this section

Many of the organizations listed below are mentioned in the preceding sections of the book. Others have been included to provide an additional source of information and advice.

An asterisk (*) after the name of the organization indicates that additional local or regional offices can be found by looking in your telephone directory.

Organizations do change addresses. If you find a number is unobtainable or the telephone is answered by another organization or business, *don't give up*. Ask the new occupants if they have a forwarding address or a telephone number for the people you are seeking, or telephone Directory Enquiries.

If you can't trace a particular organization, try and contact a similar organization and ask them for the address and telephone number. Alternatively, see if your library, CAB or one of the general advice agencies listed below can supply the number.

This list is by no means complete and there are numerous other groups, trade associations and regulatory bodies that might be able to help you. The organizations given below will be able to put you in touch with other bodies concerned with the same issue. In the case of professional bodies or trade associations they may be able to give you details of other organizations which have a different membership list.

If you're unsure whether a particular organization can help you, do contact them — you've nothing to lose. If they can't help, they'll no doubt recommend someone who can.

If you feel uncomfortable asking for information over the telephone or you're concerned about writing a letter, look back over Section One of this book (p.32, 36).

General advice agencies

NATIONAL ASSOCIATION OF
CITIZENS ADVICE BUREAUX*
115 Pentonville Road
London N1 9LZ
071 833 2181

SCOTTISH ASSOCIATION OF
CITIZENS ADVICE BUREAUX*
26 George Square
Edinburgh EH8 9LD
031 667 0156/7/8

NORTHERN IRELAND
ASSOCIATION OF CITIZENS
ADVICE BUREAUX*
New Forge Lane
Belfast BT9 5NW
Northern Ireland
0232 681117/8/9

General consumer bodies

CONSUMERS ASSOCIATION
(publishers of *Which?*)
2 Marylebone Road
London NW1 4DX
071 486 5544

NATIONAL CONSUMER
COUNCIL
20 Grosvenor Gardens
London SW1W ODH
071 730 3469

SCOTTISH CONSUMER
COUNCIL
314 St Vincents Street
Glasgow G3 8XW
041 2265261

WELSH CONSUMERS
COUNCIL
Castle Buildings
Womanby Street
Cardiff CF1 2BN
0222 396056

NORTHERN IRELAND
CONSUMERS COUNCIL
Elizabeth House
116 Holywood Road
Belfast BT4 1NY
0232 672488

OFFICE OF FAIR TRADING
Director General of Fair Trading
Field House
15–25 Bream's Buildings
London EC4A 1PR
071 242 2858

TRADING STANDARDS
DEPARTMENT*
You should also look in the
telephone directory under
'Consumer Protection
Department' or ask at your local
council offices.

General information on voluntary organizations

NATIONAL COUNCIL FOR
VOLUNTARY
ORGANIZATIONS
26 Bedford Square
London WC1B 3HU
071 636 4066

Advertising

ADVERTISING STANDARDS
AUTHORITY
Brook House
Torrington Place
London WC1E 7HN
071 580 5555

Anti-discrimination

COMMISSION FOR RACIAL
EQUALITY*
Elliot House
Allington Street
London SW1 5EH
071 828 7022

EQUAL OPPORTUNITIES
COMMISSION
Overseas House
Quay Street
Manchester M3 3HN
061 833 9244

EQUAL OPPORTUNITIES
COMMISSION (SCOTLAND)
249 West George Street
Glasgow G2 4QE
041 226 4591

EQUAL OPPORTUNITIES
COMMISSION (WALES)
Caerwys House
Windsor Place
Cardiff CF1 1LB
0222 43552

NATIONAL COUNCIL FOR
CIVIL LIBERTIES
21 Tabard Street
London SE1 4LA
071 403 3888

Business

COMPANIES REGISTRATION
OFFICE (ENGLAND AND
WALES)
Companies House
Crown Way
Maindy
Cardiff CF4 3UZ
0222 388588

COMPANIES REGISTRATION
OFFICE (Personal Callers Only)
Companies House
55 City Road
London EC1Y 1BB
071 253 9393

COMPANIES REGISTRATION
OFFICE (SCOTLAND)
102 George Street
Edinburgh EH2
031 225 5774

COMPANIES REGISTRATION
OFFICE (NORTHERN IRELAND)
43–47 Chichester Street
Belfast BT1 4RJ
0232 234121

Disability

There are numerous organizations catering for the needs of people with different disabilities. The following organizations should be able to point you in the right direction.

DIAL — DISABLEMENT
INFORMATION AND ADVICE
LINE*
Victoria House
117 High Street
Clay Cross
Chesterfield
Derbyshire S45 9DZ
0246 250055

DISABILITY ALLIANCE
25 Denmark Street
London WC2H 8NJ
071 240 0806

RADAR — ROYAL
ASSOCIATION FOR DISABILITY
REHABILITATION
25 Mortimer Street
London W1N 8AB
071 637 5400

See also National Council for Voluntary Organizations above.

Drugs and addictions

Illegal drugs
STANDING CONFERENCE ON
DRUG ABUSE (SCODA)
1–4 Hatton Place
Hatton Garden
London EC1N 8ND
071 430 2341

Will put you in touch with services in your area for people with drug problems.

NARCOTICS ANONYMOUS
POB 417
London SW10 0RS
071 351 6794

Alcohol

ALCOHOLICS ANONYMOUS*
POB 1
Stonebow House
Stonebow
York Y01 2NJ
0904 644126/7/8/9

AL ANON
61 Great Dover Street
London SE1 4YF
071 403 0888
Provides information and support
for relatives and friends of
alcoholics. Will give information
of local groups.

Smoking

ACTION ON SMOKING AND
HEALTH (ASH)
5–11 Mortimer Street
London W1N 7RH
071 637 9843

Tranquillizers

TRANX
25a Masons Avenue
Harrow
Middlesex HA3 5AH
081 863 9716

Employment

ADVISORY, CONCILIATION
AND ARBITRATION SERVICE
(ACAS)*
27 Wilton Street
London SW1X 7AZ
071 210 3000

ACAS (SCOTLAND)
Franborough House
123–157 Bothwell Street
Glasgow G2 7JR
041 204 2677

ACAS (WALES)
Phase 1
Ty Glas Road
Llanishen
Cardiff CF4 5PH
0222 762636

LABOUR RELATIONS AGENCY
(NORTHERN IRELAND)
Windsor House
9–15 Bedford Street
Belfast BT2 7NU
0232 321442

CENTRAL OFFICE OF
INDUSTRIAL TRIBUNALS
93 Ebury Bridge Road
London SW1 8RE
071 730 9161

CENTRAL OFFICE OF
INDUSTRIAL TRIBUNALS
(NORTHERN IRELAND)
2nd Floor, Bedford House
16/22 Bedford Street
Belfast BT2 7NR
0232 227666

EMPLOYMENT APPEALS
TRIBUNAL
4 St James Square
London SW1Y 4JU
071 214 3367

Trade Units

For details of individual unions contact:

TRADES UNION CONGRESS (TUC)
23–28 Great Russell Street
London WC1B 3LS
071 636 4030

Everyday goods

Electrical goods

ASSOCIATION OF
MANUFACTURERS OF
DOMESTIC APPLIANCES
(AMDEA)
Leicester House
Leicester Street
London WC2H 7BN
071 437 0678
Deals with complaints about members.

BRITISH ELECTROTECHNICAL
APPROVALS BOARD
Mark House
9–11 Queens Road
Hersham
Walton on Thames
Surrey KT12 5NA
0932 244401

BRITISH STANDARDS
INSTITUTE (BSI)
Linford Wood
Milton Keynes MK14 6LE
0908 221166

RADIO, ELECTRICAL AND
TELEVISION RETAILERS
ASSOCIATION (RETRA)
RETRA House
St John's Terrace
1 Ampthill Street
Bedford MK42 9EY
0234 269110
Deals with complaints about members.

Furniture

NATIONAL ASSOCIATION OF
RETAIL FURNISHERS
17–21 George Street
Croydon
Surrey CR9 1TQ
081 680 8444

Shoes

FOOTWEAR DISTRIBUTORS
FEDERATION
Commonwealth House
1–19 New Oxford Street
London WC1 1PA
071 404 0955

SOCIETY OF MASTER SHOE
REPAIRERS
St Crispin's House
Station Road
Desborough
Northants NN14 2SA
0536 760374
These organizations will take up complaints against their members and may be able to give you general advice.

Everyday services

British Telecom
OFFICE OF
TELECOMMUNICATIONS
(OFTEL)
Atlantic House
Holborn Viaduct
London EC1N 2H9
071 353 4020

ADVISORY COMMITTEE ON
TELECOMMUNICATIONS*
Look in your local telephone
directory for the number of a
committee in your area or contact
OFTEL above.

Coal
DOMESTIC COAL
CONSUMERS' COUNCIL
Gaverelle House
2 Bunhill Row
London EC1Y 8LL
071 638 8914

Electricity
OFFICE OF ELECTRICITY
REGULATION (OFFER)*

Gas
GAS CONSUMERS COUNCIL*
Look in your local telephone
directory for a council in your
area or ask at your local gas
showroom.

OFFGAS (OFFICE OF GAS
SUPPLY)
Southside
105 Victoria Street
London SW1E 6QT
071 828 0898

Post Office
POST OFFICE USERS'
NATIONAL COUNCIL (POUNC)
Waterloo Bridge House
Waterloo Road
London SE1 8UA
071 928 9458

POUNC (SCOTLAND)
43 Jeffrey Street
Edinburgh EH1 1DN
031 244 5576

POUNC (WALES)
Caradog House (1st Floor)
St Andrew's Place
Cardiff CF1 3BE
0222 374028

POUNC (NORTHERN IRELAND)
Chamber of Commerce
22 Great Victoria Street
Belfast BT2 7PU
0232 244113

Family

Children and young people

CHILDLINE (for children in trouble or danger)
0800 1111 Free

NATIONAL SOCIETY FOR THE PREVENTION OF CRUELTY TO CHILDREN*
67 Saffron Hill
London EC1N 8RS
071 242 1626
London 24-hour response: 071 404 4447

BRITISH YOUTH COUNCIL
57 Charlton Street
London NW1 1HU
071 387 7559
An umbrella organization for young people's clubs and societies throughout the country.

NATIONAL ASSOCIATION OF YOUNG PEOPLE'S COUNSELLING AND ADVISORY SERVICES (NAYPCAS)
17–23 Albion Street
Leicester LE1 6GD
0533 558763
They will put you in touch with a local youth counselling service.

Relationships
RELATE (FORMERLY THE MARRIAGE GUIDANCE COUNCIL)*

Lone parents
NATIONAL COUNCIL FOR ONE PARENT FAMILIES
255 Kentish Town Road
London NW5 2LX
071 267 1361

GINGERBREAD ASSOCIATION FOR ONE PARENT FAMILIES
35 Wellington Street
London WC2 7BN
071 323 1413

Parenthood
NATIONAL CHILDBIRTH TRUST
Alexander House
Oldham Terrace
London W3 6NH
081 992 8637

NATIONAL STEPFAMILY ASSOCIATION
162 Tenison Road
Cambridge CB1 2DP
0223 460312

Childcare
NATIONAL CHILDMINDERS ASSOCIATION
8 Masons Hill
Bromley BR2 9EY
081 464 6164

(Au pairs)
HOME OFFICE
Lunar House
Wellesley Road
Croydon
081 760 1666

Carers
NATIONAL ASSOCIATION OF CARERS
21–23 New Road
Chatham
Kent ME4 4OJ
0634 813981

Older people

AGE CONCERN (ENGLAND)*
Bernard Sunley House
Pitcairn Road
Mitcham
Surrey
081 640 5431

HELP THE AGED*
St James Walk
London EC1R 0BE
071 253 0253

Funerals and the bereaved

NATIONAL ASSOCIATION OF
FUNERAL DIRECTORS
618 Warwick Road
Solihull
West Midlands B91 1AA
021 711 1343

NATIONAL ASSOCIATION OF
MASTER MASONS
Crown Buildings
High Street
Aylesbury
Bucks HP20 15L
0296 434750

CRUSE (THE NATIONAL
ORGANIZATION FOR THE
WIDOWED AND THEIR
CHILDREN)
126 Sheen Road
Richmond
Surrey TW9 1UR
081 940 4818

See also Age Concern and Help
The Aged above.

Finance

BRITISH INSURANCE AND
INVESTMENT BROKERS
ASSOCIATION (BIIBA)
BIIBA House
Bevis Marks
London EC3 7NT
071 623 9043

INSTITUTE OF CHARTERED
ACCOUNTANTS IN ENGLAND
AND WALES
Chartered Accountant's Hall
Moorgate Place
London EC2P 2BJ
071 628 7060

INSTITUTE OF CHARTERED
ACCOUNTANTS OF
SCOTLAND
27 Queen Street
Edinburgh EH2 1LA
031 225 5676

INSTITUTE OF CHARTERED
ACCOUNTANTS OF IRELAND
(ULSTER BRANCH)
11 Donegal Square South
Belfast BT1 5JE
0232 321600

CHARTERED ASSOCIATION OF
CERTIFIED ACCOUNTANTS
29 Lincoln's Inn Fields
London WC2A 3EE
071 242 6855

CHARTERED INSTITUTE OF
PUBLIC FINANCE AND
ACCOUNTANCY
3 Robert Street
Londons WC2N 6BH
071 895 8823

INSTITUTE OF PUBLIC LOSS
ASSESSORS
14 Red Lion Street
Chesham
Bucks HP5 1HB
0494 782342

Banking institutions
BANKING OMBUDSMAN
Citadel House
Fetter Lane
London EC4A 1BR
071 583 1395

BANKING INFORMATION
SERVICE
10 Lombard Street
London EC3V 9AP
071 626 8486

BUILDING SOCIETIES
OMBUDSMAN
35 Grosvenor Gardens
London SW1X 7AW
071 931 0044

THE BUILDING SOCIETIES
ASSOCIATION
3 Savile Row
London W1X 1AF
071 437 0655

Credit
CONSUMER CREDIT PUBLIC
REGISTER
Government Building
Bromyard Avenue
London W3 7BB
081 743 5566 ext. 3086

CONSUMER CREDIT TRADE
ASSOCIATION
159 Great Portland Street
London W1N 5FD
071 636 7564

HIRE PURCHASE
INFORMATION PLC
Enquiries to:
Customer Services
POB 61
Dolphin House
New Street
Salisbury
Wilts SP1 2TD
0722 413434

Credit Unions
ASSOCIATION OF BRITISH
CREDIT UNIONS
48 Maddox Street
London W1 9BB
071 491 1832

Friendly Societies
REGISTRY OF FRIENDLY
SOCIETIES
15–17 Great Marlborough Street
London W1V 2AX
071 437 9992

Financial advice
FINANCIAL INTERMEDIARIES,
MANAGERS AND BROKERS
REGULATORY ASSOCIATION
(FIMBRA)
22 Great Tower Street
London EC3
071 929 2711

LIFE ASSURANCE AND UNIT
TRUST REGULATORY
ASSOCIATION (LAUTRO)
Centre Point
New Oxford Street
London WC1
071 379 0444

See also section on **Insurance**.

Pawnbrokers

NATIONAL PAWNBROKERS
ASSOCIATION
1 Bell Yard
London WC2A 2JP
071 242 1114

Health and medical services

COMMUNITY HEALTH
COUNCIL*
See your local telephone directory
for a list of CHCs in your area.

FAMILY PRACTITIONER
COMMITTEE*
See your local telephone directory
for a list of FPCs in your area.

CENTRAL SERVICES AGENCY
25 Adelaide Street
Belfast BT2 8FH
0232 324431

GENERAL MEDICAL COUNCIL
44 Hallam Street
London W1N 6AE
071 580 7642

GENERAL DENTAL COUNCIL
37 Wimpole Street
London W1M 8DQ
071 486 2171

ASSOCIATION OF
OPTOMETRISTS
233 Blackfriars Road
London SE1 8NW
071 261 9661

BRITISH COLLEGE OF
OPTHALMIC OPTICIANS
10 Knaresborough Place
London SW5 0TG
071 373 7765

GENERAL OPTICAL COUNCIL
41 Harley Street
London W1N 2DJ
071 580 3898

INSTITUTE FOR
COMPLEMENTARY MEDICINE
21 Portland Place
London W1N 3AF
071 636 9543
Keeps a directory of registered
therapists practising a wide range
of complementary medicine.

HEALTH SERVICE
OMBUDSMAN (ENGLAND)
Church House
Great Smith Street
London SW1P 3BW
071 276 3000

HEALTH SERVICE
OMBUDSMAN (SCOTLAND)
11 Melville Cresent
Edinburgh
031 225 7465

HEALTH SERVICE
OMBUDSMAN (WALES)
4th Floor
Pearl Assurance House
Greyfriars Road
Cardiff CF1 3AG
0222 394621

PATIENTS ASSOCIATION
18 Victoria Square
London E2
081 981 5676

PATIENTS ASSOCIATION
(SCOTLAND)
13 Pinewood Avenue
Lenzie
Glasgow G6
041 776 4583

ACTION FOR THE VICTIMS OF
MEDICAL ACCIDENTS
1 London Road
London SE23
081 291 2793

Homes, building and moving

Architects
ROYAL INSTITUTE OF BRITISH
ARCHITECTS
66 Portland Place
London W1N 4AD
071 580 5533

Estate agents
National Association of Estate
Agents
Arbon House
21 Jury Street
Warwick CV34 4EH
0926 496800

Surveyors
ROYAL INSTITUTE OF
CHARTERED SURVEYORS
12 Great George Street
London SW1P 3AD
071 222 7000

Removers
BRITISH ASSOCIATION OF
REMOVERS
3 Churchill Court
58 Station Road
North Harrow
Middlesex HA2 7SA
081 861 3331

Builders
BUILDING EMPLOYERS
CONFEDERATION
82 New Cavendish Street
London W1M 9FG
071 580 5588
Will put you in touch with a wide
range of trade associations in the
building industry.

SCOTTISH BUILDING
EMPLOYERS FEDERATION
13 Woodside Cresent
Glasgow G3 7UP
041 332 7144

FEDERATION OF MASTER
BUILDERS
14–15 Great James Street
London WC1N 3DT
071 242 7583/7

GUILD OF MASTERS
CRAFTSMEN
106 High Street
Lewes
East Sussex BN7 1YE
0273 478449

Central heating and plumbing

HEATING AND VENTILATING
CONTRACTORS ASSOCIATION
(HVCA)
34 Palace Court
London W2 4JG
071 229 2488

INSTITUTE OF PLUMBING
64 Station Lane
Hornchurch
Essex RM12 6NB
04024 72791

NATIONAL ASSOCIATION OF
PLUMBING, HEATING AND
MECHANICAL SERVICES
CONTRACTORS
6 Gate Street
London WC2A 3HX
071 405 2678

SCOTTISH AND NORTHERN
IRELAND PLUMBING
EMPLOYERS FEDERATION
2 Walker Street
Edinburgh EH3 7LB
031 225 2255

Decorating

BRITISH DECORATORS
ASSOCIATION*
6 Haywra Street
Harrogate
North Yorks HG1 5BL
0423 567292

Double glazing

GLASS AND GLAZING
FEDERATION
44–48 Borough High Street
London SE1 1XB
071 403 7177

Electrical contractors

ELECTRICAL CONTRACTORS
ASSOCIATION
34 Palace Court
London W2 4NF
071 229 1266

ELECTRICAL CONTRACTORS
ASSOCIATION OF SCOTLAND
23 Heriot Row
Edinburgh EH3 6EW
031 225 7221

NATIONAL INSPECTION
COUNCIL FOR ELECTRICAL
INSTALLATION
CONTRACTING
Vintage House
36–37 Albert Embankment
London SE1 7UJ
071 582 7746

Gas installation

CONFEDERATION FOR THE
REGISTRATION OF GAS
INSTALLERS (CORGI)*
St Martin's House
140 Tottenham Court Road
London W1P 9LN
071 387 9185

Insurance

ASSOCIATION OF BRITISH
INSURERS
Aldermary House
Queen Street
London EC4
071 248 4477

INSURANCE BROKERS
REGISTRATION COUNCIL
15 St Helens Place
London EC3A 6DS
071 588 4387

INSURANCE OMBUDSMAN
BUREAU
31 Southampton Row
London WC1
071 242 8613

PERSONAL INSURANCE AR-
BITRATION SERVICE
Chartered Institute of Arbitrators
International Arbitration Centre
75 Cannon Street
London EC4N 5BH
071 236 8761

See also BIIBA under **Finance**.

Launderettes and dry cleaning

ASSOCIATION OF BRITISH
LAUNDRY, CLEANING AND
RENTAL SERVICES (ABLC)
7 Churchill Court
58 Station Road
North Harrow
Middlesex HA2 7SA
081 863 7755

NATIONAL ASSOCIATION FOR
THE LAUNDERETTE INDUSTRY
South Lodge
79 Glen Ryre Road
Basset
Southampton
Hampshire
0703 766328

Legal System

THE LAW SOCIETY (FOR
ENGLAND & WALES)
133 Chancery Lane
London WC2A 1PL
071 242 1222

THE LAW SOCIETY (FOR
SCOTLAND)
26–27 Drumsheugh Gardens
Edinburgh EH3 7YR
031 226 7411

THE LAW SOCIETY (FOR NOR-
THERN IRELAND)
Law Society House
90–106 Victoria Street
Belfast BT1 3JZ
0232 231614

ROYAL COURTS OF JUSTICE
Chichester Street
Belfast BT1 3JZ
0232 235111

SOLICITORS COMPLAINTS
BUREAU
Portland House
Stag Place
London SW1E 5BL
071 834 2288

THE BAR COUNCIL
11 South Square
Grays Inn
London WC1R 5EL
071 242 0082

DEAN OF FACULTY OF
ADVOCATES
Advocates Library
Parliament House
Edinburgh EH1 1RF
031 226 5071

THE LEGAL AID BOARD (Head
Office)*
Newspaper House
8–16 Great New Street
London EC4A 3BN
071 353 7411

THE LEGAL AID BOARD
(SCOTLAND)
44 Drumsheugh Gardens
Edinburgh EH3 7FW
031 226 7061

LEGAL AID (NORTHERN
IRELAND)
The Law Society
Bedford House
16–22 Bedford Street
Belfast BT2 7FL
0232 246441

CHILDREN'S LEGAL CENTRE
20 Compton Terrace
London N1 2UN
071 359 6251

COURT OF PROTECTION
Stewart House
24 Kingsway
London WC2B 6JX
071 405 4300

POLICE COMPLAINTS BOARD
10 Great George Street
London SW1
071 273 6450

RIGHTS OF WOMEN (ROW)
52–54 Featherstone Street
London EC1
071 251 6577

Mail order

MAIL ORDER PROTECTION
SCHEME (MOPS)
16 Tooks Court
London EC4A 1LB
071 405 6806
Deals with newspaper mail order.

MAIL ORDER TRADERS
ASSOCIATION OF GREAT
BRITAIN
25 Castle Street
Liverpool L2 4TD
051 227 4181
Deals with catalogue mail order.

MAIL ORDER PUBLISHERS'
AUTHORITY
1 New Burlington Street
London W1X 1FD
01 437 0706
Members are firms which publish
books, magazines or records sold
by post.

Motor vehicles

DRIVER AND VEHICLE LICENS-
ING CENTRE (DVLC)
Swansea SA99 1BN

SOCIETY OF MOTOR
MANUFACTURERS AND
TRADERS
Forbes House
Halkin Street
London SW1X 7DS
071 235 7000
For complaints about new cars.

MOTOR AGENTS
ASSOCIATION
National Conciliation Service
73 Park Street
Bristol BS1 5PS
0272 293232
For complaints about member
dealers.

SCOTTISH MOTOR TRADE
ASSOCIATION
3 Palmerston Place
Edinburgh EH12 5AQ
031 225 3643
For complaints about member
dealers.

VEHICLE BUILDERS AND
REPAIRERS ASSOCIATION
Belmont House
102 Finkle Lane
Leeds LS27 7TW
0532 538333

MOTOR CYCLE ASSOCIATION
Starley House
Eaton Road
Coventry CV1 2FH
0203 227427
For all complaints about new bikes.

MOTORCYCLE RETAILERS
ASSOCIATION
201 Great Portland Street
London W1N 6AB
071 580 9122
For complaints about member
dealers.

NATIONAL MOTORCYCLE
STAR RIDER TRAINING
SCHEME
Federation House
2309–11 Coventry Road
Sheldon
Birmingham B26 3PB
021 742 4296

BRITISH MOTORCYCLISTS
FEDERATION RIDER TRAINING
SCHEME
POB 2
Uckfield
East Sussex TN22 3ND
082571 2896

RoSPA MOTORCYCLE TRAIN-
ING SCHEME
Cannon House
The Priory
Queensway
Birmingham B4 6BS
021 233 2461 ext 216

Parliament, local government and political parties

HOUSES OF PARLIAMENT
London SW1A 1AA
071 219 3000

LOCAL GOVERNMENT OMBUDSMAN
21 Queen Anne's Gate
London SW1H 9BU
071 222 5622

29 Castlegate
York YO1 1RN
0904 30151

CONSERVATIVE PARTY
32 Smith Square
London SW1P 3HH
071 222 9000

FRIENDS OF THE EARTH
26 Underwood Street
London N1 7JQ
071 490 1555

GREEN PARTY
10 Station Parade
Balham High Road
London SW12
071 673 0045

LABOUR PARTY
150 Walworth Road
London SE17 1JT
071 703 0833

LIBERAL DEMOCRATS
4 Cowley Street
London SW1T 3NB
071 222 7999

Immigration

JOINT COUNCIL FOR THE WELFARE OF IMMIGRANTS
115 Old Street
London EC1V 9JR
071 251 8706

UNITED KINGDOM IMMIGRANTS ADVISORY SERVICE
7th Floor
Brettenham House
Savoy Street
Strand
London WC2E 7LR
071 240 5176

Religious organizations

COUNCIL OF CHURCHES FOR BRITAIN AND IRELAND
35 Lower Marsh
London SE1 7RL
071 620 4444

GENERAL SYNOD OF THE CHURCH OF ENGLAND
Church House
London SE1P 3NZ
071 222 9011

BRITISH HUMANIST
ASSOCIATION
13 Prince of Wales Terrace
London W8
071 937 1341

THE BOARD OF DEPUTIES OF
BRITISH JEWS
Woburn House
Upper Woburn Place
London WC1
071 387 3952
071 387 4044 (Central Enquiry
Desk)

UNION OF MUSLIM
ORGANIZATIONS
109 Campden Hill Road
London W8 7TL
071 221 6608
071 229 0538 (ansaphone)

Travel and holidays

ASSOCIATION OF BRITISH
TRAVEL AGENTS (ABTA)
55–57 Newman Street
London W1P 4AH
071 637 2444

NATIONAL CARAVAN
COUNCIL
Catherine House
Victoria Road
Aldershot
Hants GU11 1SS
0252 318251

TIMESHARE DEVELOPERS
ASSOCIATION
23 Buckingham Gate
London SW1E 6LB
071 821 8845

AIR TRANSPORT USERS
COMMITTEE
103 Kingsway
London WC2B 6SX
071 242 3882

LONDON REGIONAL
PASSENGERS COMMITTEE
Golden Cross House
8 Duncannon Street
London WC2N 4JF
071 839 1898/9

TRANSPORT USERS
CONSULTATIVE COMMITTEE*
You can find the address of your
local committee by looking in your
telephone directory or asking at
your nearest railway station.

Women's organizations

NATIONAL ALLIANCE OF
WOMEN'S ORGANIZATIONS
122 Whitechapel High Street
London E1 7PT
071 247 7052
An umbrella organization for
many women's groups, especially
the smaller ones.

NATIONAL COUNCIL OF
WOMEN
36 Danbury Street
London N1 8JU
071 354 2395
Will provide information about a
range of affiliated organizations
throughout the country. Also has
individual branches.

See also Rights of Women (ROW)
under **Legal System**.

The following have branches and
groups throughout the country:

NATIONAL WOMEN'S
REGISTER
245 Warwick Road
Solihull
West Midlands B92 7AH
021 706 1106

TOWNSWOMEN'S GUILD
Chamber of Commerce House
75 Harborne Road
Edgbaston
Birmingham B15 3DA
021 455 6868

NATIONAL FEDERATION OF
WOMEN'S INSTITUTES
39 Eccleston Street
London SW1W 9NT
071 730 7212

Women in danger

WOMEN AGAINST SEXUAL
HARASSMENT (WASH)
242 Pentonville Road
London N1 9UN
071 833 0222

The following organizations will
provide a temporary refuge for
women and their children suffering mental and physical harassment:

NATIONAL WOMEN'S AID
FEDERATION
POB 391
Bristol BS99 7WS
0272 428368

LONDON WOMEN'S AID
52 Featherstone Street
London EC1Y 8RY
071 251 6537

SCOTTISH WOMEN'S AID
Ainslie House
11 St Colme Street
Edinburgh EH5 6AG
031 225 8011

WELSH WOMEN'S AID
38–48 Crwys Road
Cardiff CF2 4NN
0222 390874

Index